KU-660-888

THE
WORK AND WORDS
OF JESUS

A. M. HUNTER
B.D., PH.D.(GLASGOW), D.PHIL.(OXON)
Professor of Biblical Criticism, Aberdeen University

S C M PRESS LTD
56 Bloomsbury Street, London W C 1

First published June 1950
Reprinted March 1951
Reprinted February 1954
Reprinted February 1956

Printed in Great Britain by The Camelot Press Ltd.,
London and Southampton

PREFACE

This book was written, not *mihi et Musis*, but to serve a practical purpose. Whatever be the reasons, our New Testament scholars nowadays are not writing 'Lives' of Christ; and when I looked around for a short one, embodying the results of recent scholarship, to put into the hands of my divinity students, I found none suited to my purpose. This is a very modest attempt to supply the want. It tries to use seriously the four sources which Streeter and others have found to underlie the Synoptic Gospels. And since there are many who vaguely know about Q, M and L, but have small idea what these sources contain, I have printed an English text of them at the end. This follows the R.V., and so do my quotations in the 'Life' except where, for special reasons, I have made my own translation.

The book makes no claim to originality, except perhaps in a few points of detail. My debt to the writings of C. H. Dodd, T. W. Manson and Vincent Taylor (to name only my principal creditors) will be plain to the knowledgeable reader on nearly every page.

For valued help in proof-reading and index-making my grateful thanks are due to my wife and to my colleague, the Reverend A. Allan McArthur, B.D., Chaplain to the University of Aberdeen.

A. M. HUNTER

KING'S COLLEGE,
ABERDEEN UNIVERSITY
1950

CONTENTS

INTRODUCTION

Everything in the Christian Faith goes back ultimately to the story of Jesus recorded in the little books we call the Gospels. As all true Christian morality is based on the ethic of Jesus, so all sound Christian doctrine must be built on the person and work of Christ as they are presented to us in the Gospels. 'Councils and creeds,' said Moberly in *Lux Mundi*,[1] 'cannot go behind, but must wholly rest upon the history of our Lord Jesus Christ.' And a modern theologian, Dr. W. M. Horton, has declared: 'Theologians must base their teaching about Jesus the Christ (at least primarily) upon the most faithful portrait of our Lord that objective Biblical scholarship can paint; and if they do not like the looks of that portrait, they must not retouch it, lest they be found guilty of trying to correct the Wisdom of God by the wisdom of man.'[2]

We shall begin with a brief account of 'the quest of the historical Jesus.'

Then we shall briefly discuss sources and chronology.

Then we shall paint the setting.

In 'Before the Ministry' we shall describe the Birth and Early Years, the Mission of the Baptist, the Baptism and Temptation of Jesus.

In the main section of the book we shall sketch the Ministry, in broad outline, up to the Transfiguration. There we shall turn aside to study the miracles of Jesus, His training of the Twelve, and His teaching about the kingdom, His own person, His death, and the future. Then, picking up the thread of the narrative again, we shall tell the story of the Last Journey and the Passion. The final chapter will deal with the Resurrection.

---

[1] p. 177.   [2] In the Foreword to J. W. Bowman's *The Intention of Jesus*.

PART ONE

I

THE QUEST OF THE HISTORICAL JESUS

Of all those who attempt the impossible—the writing of a Life of Christ—the saying is true, 'Others have laboured, and ye are entered into their labours.' Before we begin, then, let us look back briefly on the road which our innumerable predecessors have travelled.

We take the title of this chapter from the English translation of Albert Schweitzer's famous book *Von Reimarus zu Wrede* (1906), in which with a brilliant—and often pungent—pen he tells the story of German research into the Life of Jesus and ends with an account of his own views. Nothing similar will be attempted here. It will be enough if we trace the broad lines on which research has proceeded. It falls roughly into two periods: pre-critical and critical.

THE PRE-CRITICAL PERIOD

This period reaches down to the eighteenth century, and the 'Lives' which it produced are of two kinds.

First came the orthodox 'Lives' in which the story of Jesus follows the lines dictated by orthodox Christian belief. Earliest of these was Tatian's *Diatessaron*, a harmony of the Gospels produced about A.D. 170 by 'scissors-and-paste' methods and long used by the Syriac-speaking Church. It was to have many successors. In this type of Life the four Gospels are ranked equally as historical authorities. This method survived into the nineteenth century, and is exemplified in that volume which adorned many Victorian bookshelves, Dean Farrar's popular and picturesque *Life of Christ* (1874).

Second, there were the 'rationalist' Lives. The flowering time of Rationalism was the eighteenth century, and its fruitage English Deism and the German 'enlightenment.' When the writers of this time and temper set themselves to write a Life, they generally cut and carved the Gospels to suit their own presuppositions. As their name implies, they had no compunction about rationalising the miracles of Jesus, and their general

9

tendency was to see in Him 'the admirable revealer of true virtue which is coincident with right reason.' Perhaps the best of these writers was the German Paulus.

THE CRITICAL PERIOD

The nineteenth century saw the beginning of a critical approach to the problems of the Gospels and the Life of Christ. Of all the many Lives produced in it the two most famous were those by Strauss (1835) and Renan (1863). Strauss's two-volumed work was very radical. No one before him had so thoroughly set about dissolving the Gospel history into myth and legend. Such was the storm of controversy loosed by his book that when he wrote a second Life, he was glad to recant many of his opinions. Renan's *Life of Jesus*, written in Syria, which ran into twenty-three editions in the author's lifetime, caused an even bigger furore and drew down on itself the thunders of orthodox churchmen. 'Whoever wore a cassock and could wield a pen,' says Schweitzer sardonically, 'charged against Renan, the bishops leading the van.'[1] But Renan's picture of Jesus as 'the amiable carpenter' who later turned apocalyptist, was not really a scientific Life; it was a work of art, and owed its wide circulation to its charm of style. 'M. Renan,' commented one reviewer, 'thinks too much of beauty, and not enough of the truth.'[2]

Most of the many Lives written in the nineteenth century, can be labelled either conservative or liberal.

Writers of the conservative type tended to use the Fourth Gospel equally with the Synoptics. They did not ignore criticism, for as early as 1840 scholars had argued for the priority of Mark, and all through the century they were slowly groping their way to that fundamental solution of the Synoptic Problem which we now know as 'The Two Document Theory.' Rather, they still set a high historical value on the Fourth Gospel as the work, in one sense or another, of the Apostle John. William Sanday's *Outlines of the Life of Christ*, first contributed as an article to Hastings' *Dictionary of the Bible* in 1899 and later printed separately, is an admirable example.

The best-known Lives written in the second half of the nineteenth century were of the type known as liberal. Convinced that Mark was the earliest Gospel, the liberals took it as their basis and, for the most part, dismissed the Fourth Gospel as unhistorical. Adjudging the apocalyptic elements in the Gospels to be husk rather than kernel, they spiritualised them or

---

[1] *The Quest of the Historical Jesus*, 188. [2] Goguel, *The Life of Jesus*, 51.

eliminated them altogether. If there were gaps in Mark's narrative, they filled them in with the aid of a speculative psychology. For them, the core of the Gospel was the Fatherhood of God (with its corollary of the brotherhood of man) and the law of love, as we find them taught in the Sermon on the Mount and in such parables as the Good Samaritan and the Prodigal Son. They had no difficulty about rationalising the harder miracles to suit the current view that 'miracles do not happen.' For them, the Life of Jesus was one that 'never overstepped the limits of the purely human,' and His death was the supreme martyrdom. In short, Jesus was the greatest religious teacher of mankind, the supreme prophet, the first true believer in God the Father, or whatever phrase was preferred, and no effort was spared to make Him attractive and acceptable to modern man. Harnack's famous lectures *What is Christianity?*, though not a 'Life,' exemplify such liberalism at its best.

The main charge to be levelled against these liberal 'Lives'— and it is a grave one—is that they give us a lay figure quite incapable of accounting for the rest of the New Testament. At their worst, the liberals 'scaled down the imperial mind of Christ . . . to the level of a well-meaning Sunday School teacher.'[1] The liberal Jesus is not nearly big enough to explain Christianity. 'Why any man should have troubled to crucify the Christ of liberal Protestantism,' said William Temple with some asperity, 'has always been a mystery.'[2]

THE LIFE OF JESUS IN THE TWENTIETH CENTURY

In the first year of the new century there appeared in Germany two books, one by Wrede[3] and the other by Schweitzer,[4] which showed, in different ways, the *impasse* which liberal scholars had reached. Wrede's book dealt a blow at one of the liberals' basic assumptions—that in Mark we have a plain, straightforward chronological account of Jesus' ministry. Schweitzer's book raised afresh the problem of the eschatological sayings in the Gospels (e.g. Mt. x. 23; Mk. i. 15, ix. 1, xiv. 62), a problem which the liberals had burked.

Three main trends are discernible in twentieth-century investigation.

[1] F. R. Barry, *The Relevance of Christianity*, 98.

[2] *Readings in St. John's Gospel*, xxiv.   [3] *Das Messiasgeheimnis in den Evangelien.*

[4] *Das Messianitäts—und Leidensgeheimnis* (Eng. tr., 1925, *The Mystery of the Kingdom of God*).

(a) The Method of Comparative Religion

Renouncing the attempt to write a Life, scholars now began to study the New Testament in the light of contemporary religions, Jewish and Gentile. All manner of sources—the rabbinical literature, the Greek mystery religions, the Hermetic writings, Iranian eschatology, etc.—were ransacked for materials to illustrate the religious ideas of the New Testament. These scholars then proceeded to draw conclusions—some of them outrunning the evidence—about the religion of the New Testament. The broad result was to make Jesus the decisive factor in the religious syncretism which they supposed early Christianity to be. He became 'a splendid column of spray set up by the collision of East and West.'[1] The finest example of this kind of approach to the New Testament was Bousset's *Kyrios Christos* (1916), a book which never achieved the honour of an English translation.

(b) The Reaction against Rationalisation

The second trend was the reaction against rationalisation, which brought with it a revived interest in the numinous and eschatological elements in the Gospels. Here the two great names are those of Otto and Schweitzer.

Rudolf Otto wrote two books which have powerfully influenced the theological thought of his time. The first, written in 1917 and translated into English with the title, *The Idea of the Holy*, was a timely reminder that the essence of religion lies not in knowledge or in good conduct but in awe. It impelled men to re-examine the non-rational elements in religion: it focused attention afresh on the eschatology of the Gospels. With this last element Otto's second great book *Reichgottes und Menschensohn* (1934), rendered into English as *The Kingdom of God and the Son of Man* (2nd ed., 1942), was specially concerned.

The renewed interest in eschatology did not begin with Otto. It was Johannes Weiss who pioneered the way which Schweitzer's *Quest* made known to English readers. Weiss and Schweitzer both urged that the master-key to the understanding of the Life of Jesus was 'consistent eschatology.' The crucial terms in the Gospels (they said) are the Kingdom of God and the Son of man, and both are to be interpreted eschatologically. Inevitably, Schweitzer made his new key fit many locks it was never meant to fit. Thus, when he found the ethical teaching of Jesus a grave difficulty for his theory, he dismissed it as 'an ethic of the interval'—a code of emergency regulations valid only for the brief time till God should catastrophically end the existing

[1] P. T. Forsyth, *The Person and Place of Jesus Christ*, 42.

order and bring in the new one. Convinced that Jesus expected the end of the world in the near future, he turned a Nelson eye to those many well-attested sayings which proclaim the Kingdom to be present in Jesus and His mission. And having destroyed the liberal portrait of Jesus, he set about painting a new one in terms of his own eschatology—a portrait which satisfies no one but himself and reminds us, as Streeter said, 'of the Superman of Nietzsche wearing Galilean robes.'[1] Nevertheless, his excesses should not blind us to the great services he rendered scholarship. Two things he did. He compelled scholars to face squarely the problems of eschatology and to produce better solutions of them than he had done. And, second, he put the Life of Jesus in its true setting:

'The whole story moves in an atmosphere of wonder, fringed, as it were, with a numinous corona, whose flames leap up in immeasurable splendour into spaces which we cannot chart. We cannot tear it out of that setting. Apart from it there is no story to tell. And it is the triumph of the eschatologists to have recovered that atmosphere.'[2]

(c) Form Criticism

The year 1919 saw the rise in Germany of a new sort of Gospel criticism. It bore the forbidding name of *Formgeschichte* (English: 'Form Criticism'). Its chief exponents were Rudolf Bultmann and Martin Dibelius. Form Criticism is the investigation of the oral tradition about Jesus which has received literary shape in the Gospels. Our earliest Gospel sources (the Form Critics argued) cannot take us back farther than, at most A.D. 50. Thus, there is a gap of some twenty years between the events themselves and the first written record of them. Can we not get back, behind these sources, into 'the twilight period' and study the oral tradition about Jesus as it was actually taking shape? Can we not learn something about the *form* of the stories and sayings in the Gospels before they were committed to writing? What were they like? What interests led to their formation and preservation?

The Form Critics laid down certain guiding principles and aims, as for example, (1) that all the Gospel stories and sayings, except the Passion Story, existed originally as isolated units or *pericopae*; (2) that these can be arranged in classes according to their form: pronouncement-stories, miracle-stories, legends and so on; (3) that we can remove editorial embellishments and lay bare the *pericopē* as it existed in the oral period; and (4) that we must try to discover the *Sitz im Leben*, or 'life-setting,' of these

[1] *Foundations*, 77.   [2] F. R. Barry, *The Relevance of Christianity*, 98.

narratives and sayings. (Thus, many of the stories about Jesus may originally have been illustrations in early Christian sermons.)

The aims and intentions of the new critics were laudable; but, thus far, the new criticism has not fulfilled the high hopes with which it was launched. If it has emphasised the importance of 'the twilight period,' it has really not told us much about Jesus that we did not know already. The truth is that the new method leaves far too large a field for subjective speculation, and has been vitiated by an excessive scepticism. Reading the Form Critics, we get the impression that when the Gospel tradition was taking shape, all the eye-witnesses of our Lord's ministry were either dead or in hiding. Far too much is ascribed to the creation of the Early Church; far too little to the creative genius of the Church's Founder. But for a sane appraisal of the new science and its limitations we must refer the student to Vincent Taylor's *Formation of the Gospel Tradition.*

What is the truth about Jesus Christ? We have hurriedly sketched the story of the Quest, and perhaps the chief impression left on the reader's mind is the astonishing variety of the portraits of Jesus which our learned men have given us. Thus, to choose only a few, in the last century we have had Renan's 'Amiable Carpenter,' Tolstoi's 'Spiritual Anarchist,' Schweitzer's 'Imminent Cataclysmist,' Klausner's 'Unorthodox Rabbi,' and Otto's 'Charismatic Evangelist.'

Yet this immense making of books about Jesus has not been wholly profitless and jejune. If it has showed the amazing ingenuity of the human mind, it has also showed the perennial fascination of the story of Jesus. If it has pained orthodox Christians, it has added enormously to our understanding of the life and times of Jesus. Nor is this all; for it seems to many of us that this long labour of the scholars is now promising to bear rich fruit. The problems are not all solved, but many of them are; and the scholarship of the last two or three decades, by its patient research on many aspects of Christ's Life and Teaching, has gradually been accumulating materials for a worthier and truer portrait, a portrait indeed much nearer to that conception of Jesus Christ, at once human and divine, which has been the nerve of all truly vital Christianity down nineteen centuries.

II
SOURCES AND CHRONOLOGY

1   THE SOURCES

What are our sources of information about Jesus? Apart from the New Testament, they amount to no more than a few references in the *Talmud* and Josephus and a sentence or two in three Latin writers.

Non-Christian Sources

The allusions to Jesus in the *Talmud* are mostly late, slanderous and worthless. The sum of what they say is that Jesus practised sorcery, ridiculed the wise men, led the people astray and was hanged on the eve of the Passover. His disciples, five in number, cured sick people in their Master's name. What these references do prove is that there is no reason to doubt the existence of Jesus, as a few cranks still do. Men, as a rule, do not vehemently slander myths.

Two passages in the *Antiquities* (A.D. 93) of Josephus, the Jewish historian, mention Jesus. One, which is probably genuine, records the stoning of 'James, the brother of Jesus who was called the Christ.' The other runs: 'Jesus, a wise man, if indeed we should call Him a man, for He was a doer of miracles and a master of men who receive the truth with joy . . . He was the Christ.' Can we believe this of Josephus? It is hard to believe that a Jew could have written thus of Jesus. The passage suggests a Christian hand.

The three Latin writers are Pliny, Tacitus and Suetonius. Pliny, governor of Bithynia, writing to his Emperor Trajan about A.D. 112, reports that the Christians there are wont 'on a fixed day to assemble before daylight and sing by turns a hymn to Christ as a god.' Tacitus, in his *Annals* (*c.* A.D. 115), relates how the great fire in Rome was blamed on the Christians, and proceeds: 'Christ from whom they derive their name, was put to death in the reign of Tiberius by the procurator Pontius Pilate.' Finally, Suetonius, a contemporary of Tacitus, records that the Emperor Claudius 'banished the Jews from Rome when they made a constant rioting at the instigation of Chrestus.' Chrestus is probably a corruption of Christus. Evidently Suetonius thought that Jesus was physically present in Rome at that time.

Such is our information from non-Christian sources. A single page would hold it all. Its smallness is surprising till we remember that what we now see to be the most pregnant fact in all history must have struck contemporary pagans as simply another Oriental superstition.

Christian Sources

This means, for all practical purposes, the New Testament. For the *Agrapha*, or uncanonical sayings of Jesus, scattered about in the early Fathers, and the *Logia* of Jesus dug up in Egypt (in 1897 and 1903), even if all proved genuine, would not add much to our knowledge. As for the apocryphal gospels, it is just possible that they contain the slenderest tithe of history, but it is irretrievably smothered beneath legend and fantasy.[1]

In the New Testament our earliest source is St. Paul (A.D. 50–60). For various reasons, Paul does not tell us all he knows about Jesus. But passages like 1 Cor. vii. 10, xi. 23ff., and xv. 3ff. show that he knew the main facts about His life and teaching. Later in date are the references in Hebrews (e.g. v. 7–9 and xiii. 12). Nor must we forget the apostolic speeches in Acts, especially Acts x. 34–43. The value of these is enhanced if, as scholars increasingly admit, they preserve early Jerusalem tradition.

But our main sources are the Gospels, and we must say a brief word about their trustworthiness.

Admittedly, the Gospels are not simple objective history—if ever such a thing was written. They are interpreted history— religious documents written (to borrow Paul's phrase) 'from faith to faith.' What we find in them is 'facts plus faith.' Yet none but the sceptic denies that they are good sources of history. 'It is of no use,' said John Stuart Mill, no biased critic, 'to say that Christ as exhibited in the Gospels is not historical, and that we do not know how much of what is admirable has been super-added by the tradition of His followers. Who among His disciples, or among their proselytes, was capable of inventing the sayings ascribed to Jesus, or of imagining the life and character revealed in the Gospels?'

This is not to say that everything in them is history, or that

[1] The student who is interested should read M. R. James, *The Apocryphal New Testament*. 'Apocryphal' here means not 'fictitious,' but 'uncanonical.' In the first two or three Christian centuries many such gospels were in circulation, and some were very popular. Three of the best known are *The Gospel of the Nazarenes*, *The Gospel of the Ebionites* and *The Gospel of Peter*. Written either to gratify popular curiosity about the birth and boyhood of Jesus or to subserve some heretical doctrine, they are for the most part legendary.

all are of equal value. In this respect, Mark stands first and Matthew (among the Synoptics) last. But literary analysis discovers four sources underlying the first three Gospels, and if we are to proceed scientifically, we must appraise them.

First comes Mark, a source of great value. Its date is early (A.D. 65–70), and, as reflecting the witness of Peter, it has high authority.

Q is the sayings-source behind Matthew and Luke. Its date is thought to be about 50, and all admit that it is a first-rate source.

L (the symbol for the matter peculiar to Luke) is probably the fruit of Luke's personal enquiry in Palestine round about A.D. 57–59. There can be no doubt that Luke is a competent historian, and his special matter must be judged second only to Mark and Q, our primary sources.

M (the matter peculiar to Matthew) is the least valuable of our sources. It consists of two sorts of material: (a) narratives and (b) teaching. Most scholars admit that the narratives found only in Matthew are of small historical value. On the other hand, the teaching material, while it is sometimes vitiated by what looks like an anti-Pauline bias, is important; and if we must use it with care, we cannot ignore it.

The biggest question remains: How far can we use St. John as a historical source?

In the Fourth Gospel history and interpretation are inextricably interwoven. Since the Evangelist's aim is to express spiritual truth through historical fact, he handles the historical tradition about Jesus with sovereign freedom. Consequently, while most of us feel (with Calvin) that 'this Gospel is the key which opens the door to the understanding of the other three,' we cannot use it in precisely the same way as we use the Synoptics. Consider, for example, the words of Jesus in the Fourth Gospel. There is no doubt that many utterances of Jesus in St. John are 'inspired airs composed on the basis of original themes'—true expansions of genuine words of Jesus. But since they are cast in 'the Johannine idiom,' we cannot be so sure of finding in them the actual words of Jesus as in the first three Gospels. Jn. xiv. 25f. perhaps best explains what underlies the Johannine record: (a) the words of Jesus—'These things have I spoken unto you, while yet abiding with you'; (b) the illuminated memory of the disciples—'He shall bring to your remembrance all that I have said unto you'; and (c) the interpreting Spirit—'He shall teach you all things.' To say all this is not to aver that the Fourth Gospel is devoid of historical value—far from it. 'It is no longer possible to say,'

B

writes a distinguished modern scholar,[1] ' "If the Fourth Gospel contradicts the Synoptics, so much the worse for the Fourth Gospel." ' Indeed, in certain points (e.g. the record of Jesus' visits to Jerusalem, a detail like Jn. vi. 15, and the dating of the Crucifixion) most scholars agree that John preserves a better tradition than the Synoptists. Therefore, while we cannot reckon the Fourth Gospel among our main sources, we cannot ignore it; nay, we shall have to give particular heed to its notes of place and time which, to say the least, are peculiarly like truth.

2   CHRONOLOGY

The evangelists, who were not interested in chronology, have left us few data. Yet in an age which loves to probe the historical truth of things, there are certain questions which demand the best answers we can give them:

When was Jesus born?

How long did His ministry last?

In what year was He crucified?

The Date of the Birth

According to Mt. ii. 1, Jesus was born 'in Bethlehem of Judaea in the days of Herod the king.' Herod died in 4 B.C. Jesus must therefore have been born at least five years before the year which we call *Annus Domini*. According to Lk. ii. 1, Jesus was born during a census carried out in Syria by the Roman legate Quirinius. Now, the only census conducted by Quirinius of which we certainly know took place in A.D. 6. It appears as if Luke had got the legate's name wrong.[2] Yet we need not question his assertion that Jesus' birth coincided with the taking of a census. Tertullian records the taking of such a census in Judaea while Saturninus, the penultimate predecessor of Quirinius, was legate, i.e. between 9 and 6 B.C. If this was the Nativity census, a date about 6 B.C. would suit the evidence of Matthew and Luke.

The Length of the Ministry

Here we may exclude Matthew who takes no interest in chronology and Luke who gives little help. (Lk. iv. 19, being a quotation

---

[1] T. W. Manson in *The Bulletin of the John Rylands Library*, May, 1947.

[2] Unless, following the idiom of Jn. i. 15, 30, we translate Lk. ii. 1, 'This enrolment took place *before* Quirinius was governor of Syria.' Sir William Ramsay thought that Quirinius held office *twice* in Syria, on the former occasion being associated with Saturninus.

from Isa. lxi, provides no solid basis for the theory of a one-year ministry.)

Mark implies a ministry of at least two years. Thus, Mk. ii. 23 describes a time when the corn was ripe—April or May. When in Mk. vi. 39 we learn that the Feeding of the Multitude occurred when the grass was 'green,' we infer that a year has elapsed. The events recorded in Mk. vi. 45–x. 52, which include much journeying, imply the passage of another year between the Feeding and the fatal Passover (Mk. xiv. 1).

John mentions three Passovers (ii. 13, vi. 4 and xii. 1). In other words, he represents Christ's ministry as lasting more than two years—roughly the same length as Mark suggests. Incidentally, the earlier visits to Jerusalem recorded only by John receive indirect confirmation in the Synoptic Gospels.

We therefore conclude that Jesus' ministry must have lasted over two years and was located in Judaea as well as Galilee.

The Date of the Crucifixion

The day of the Crucifixion was Friday. But while Mark suggests that the Friday was 15 Nisan (the first month of the Jewish year), John implies that it was 14 Nisan. According to John, Jesus died at the time of 'preparation' while the Passover lambs were being slaughtered. The Synoptists, on the other hand, apparently identify the Last Supper with the Passover. To decide between Mark and John is difficult, but most scholars prefer the clear and consistent testimony of John.

Our problem then is to determine in which year 14 Nisan, the day of the full moon, fell on a Friday. Since the Crucifixion occurred while Pilate was governor and Caiaphas the reigning high priest, the possible years are A.D. 27–33. Now astronomical considerations dealing with the visibility of the moon[1] suggest that the only two probable years are A.D. 30 and 33. The latter seems too late, if, as is likely, Paul's conversion should fall about 33. And since 30 fits nearly all the requirements set forth by C. H. Turner in his famous article (Hastings' *Dictionary of the Bible*, Vol. I) besides being free from the astronomical objections to 29 (the year preferred by Turner), we prefer it to 33.

The three Passovers of the ministry will then be A.D. 28, 29 and 30.

[1] See J. K. S. Fotheringham's article in the *Journal of Theological Studies*, xxxv (1934).

III
THE BACKGROUND

I   GEOGRAPHY

Palestine, deriving its name from 'Philistia' and situated at the
western end of the Fertile Crescent, is about the size of Wales.
It is bounded on the west by the Mediterranean; on the east
by the Jordan; on the north by the Lebanon and Hermon; and
on the south by the hills of Judaea, which slope away into the
Negeb and desert. Its length—'from Dan to Beersheba'—is
roughly one hundred and fifty miles, its average breadth barely
fifty. It is a mountainous land, and he who would understand
it must often 'lift up his eyes unto the hills'. It is a land with
surprising climatic contrasts, from the temperate airs of Jerusalem to the tropical heats of Jericho, only fifteen miles away.
It is a colourful land—a land whose most famous features are
the blue lake of Galilee, the vivid green of the Jordan valley,
and the gleaming snows of Hermon.

The geography of Palestine is best explained in terms of four
great parallel bands running north and south. The outermost
is the Coastal Plain, a strip of low-lying land along the shores
of the Mediterranean, forming a highway from Egypt along
which have marched many conquerors. The second band is
the central range of limestone hills, running, like a great back-
bone, through Galilee, Samaria and Judaea. The third band is
the deep cleft of the Jordan valley where the river, after rising
at Hermon's base, winds its serpentine way down through
Lake Huleh and the Lake of Galilee to end in the deep-dug
grave of the Dead Sea. The fourth band is the Highlands of
Transjordan—a barricade of hills east of Jordan running from
north to south.

Galilee

Galilee is the garden of Palestine, well watered and fertile. In
our Lord's day it was thickly populated and had many good roads.
'Judaea,' it has been said,[1] 'is on the road to Nowhere; Galilee
is covered with roads to Everywhere.' Of these the chief was the
great highway which ran between Damascus and the Mediterranean and crossed Lower Galilee, touching Capernaum where
once Levi sat at 'the receipt of custom' (Mk. ii. 14). In Christ's

[1] G. A. Smith, *The Historical Geography of the Holy Land*, 425.

day, Galilee was very open to Greek influences. 'Galilee of the Gentiles' contained many people who had non-Jewish blood in their veins. The Galileans were a hardy and gallant race, 'inured,' as Josephus says, 'to war from their infancy'; and from Galilee sprang most of the leading Zealots. They were also a religious people, though the strict Jews of the south doubted their orthodoxy and despised their accent.

The Lake of Galilee is pear-shaped and measures thirteen miles in length and eight at its broadest: a sheet of lovely fresh water lying 685 ft. below sea-level, surrounded by low brown hills and notorious for sudden storms (Mk. iv. 37). In the time of Jesus it supported a large fishing industry, and its western shore was studded with sizeable towns. Of these Chorazin and Capernaum (the modern *Tell Hum*)[1] were scenes of Christ's ministry; but there is no evidence that He visited Tiberias, the Greek city farther south on the Lake shore which Herod Antipas had built as his capital.[2] If we travel north-east round the Lake past the place where the Jordan enters it, we reach Bethsaida Julias (Mk. vi. 45). Bethsaida, which means 'Fishermen's Town,' owes its second name to Philip, the tetrarch who rebuilt the town and named it after the daughter of Augustus. Near Bethsaida was the 'desert place' where Jesus fed the multitude.

Twenty-odd miles to the north, near the base of Hermon (9,100 ft.) are the ruins of Caesarea Philippi (Mk. viii. 27). It had been re-built by Philip and named 'Philip's Caesarea,' to distinguish it from Caesarea on the coast where the Roman governor had his residence.

Nazareth 'his own country' (Mk. vi. 1) lies high on a sharp slope of the Galilean hills a dozen miles south-west of the Lake, and commands from its northern hill-tops magnificent views of the whole country. Not so secluded or small a town as we commonly suppose, for from its hills the boy Jesus would look down on the great trade-routes carrying travellers and caravans from all parts of the civilised world.

Samaria, the Decapolis and Peraea

South of Galilee lies Samaria, a land of fat valleys diversified by hills, of which the two chief are Ebal and Gerizim: in area, a territory of twenty miles from north to south and thirty from

[1] The synagogue whose ruins are visible to-day at *Tell Hum* is probably to be dated around A.D. 200 and is doubtless a reconstruction of the one in which Christ taught. See Finegan, *Light From the Ancient Past*, 227f.

[2] Three miles north of Tiberias is Mejdel, the ancient Magdala from which hailed Mary Magdalene.

east to west. Its inhabitants were the descendants of Assyrian
colonists who had intermarried with the Jewish remnant left
behind after the fall of Samaria (721 B.C.). They claimed, as
they still claim, to be the true representatives of Israel. But 'the
Jews have no dealings with the Samaritans.' True then, it is
true still. So the Samaritans had set up a rival temple and
priesthood; their holy place was Mount Gerizim; their holy
book the Pentateuch, and their holy city not Samaria (which
was Greek), but Sichem (O.T. Shechem, modern *Nablus*).
Sychar in Samaria (Jn. iv. 5) was probably the village now
called *Askar*, five furlongs north-east of Jacob's well, which still
exists.

A Galilean pilgrim trekking south for the Passover would
normally cross the Jordan before reaching inhospitable Samaria,
and travel down the east bank of the river before recrossing it
at the ford near Jericho. On this eastern side he would touch
the fringe of the Decapolis (Mk. v. 20, vii. 31), a federation of
ten Greek cities, and then set foot in Peraea. If the men of the
Decapolis were Gentiles, the Peraeans were Jews. Though the
name never occurs in the Gospels, we know that Jesus passed
through 'the borders of Judaea and over Jordan' (Mk. x. 1),
i.e. through Peraea, on his last journey to Jerusalem.

Judaea

Judaea is a high table-land cleft by deep gullies running east
and west: altogether, a small territory fifty-five miles long by
thirty broad, in area about the size of Aberdeenshire. The
country was divided into five parts: the Coastal Plain, the
Shephelah (or Lowlands, near the coast), the Negeb (or South-
land), the Hill Country and the Wilderness. Only the last two
concern us here. The Hill Country is a rough, stony land cut
by deep ravines and rising 2,500 ft. to the bare plateau on which
Jerusalem stands. The Wilderness is the bleak, barren region
where the eastern Judaean mountains slope down 4,000 ft. to
the lowest region on the earth's surface, the Dead Sea (1,275 ft.
below sea-level). In this grim and houseless region, haunted
by wild beasts (Mk. i. 13), John the Baptist summoned Israel
to repentance, and Jesus was baptised and afterwards tempted.

The population of Judaea was purely Jewish. Crowning the
rocky plateau stood the grey city of Jerusalem with its splendid
Temple on Mount Zion. 'He who has not seen Jerusalem in
its beauty' said the rabbis proudly, 'has not seen a beautiful
great city in his whole life, and he who has not seen the building
of the Second Temple has not seen a handsome building in his

life.' Adjoining the Temple on its northern side was the Fortress Antonia, garrisoned by Roman auxiliary troops (five cohorts and an *ala* of cavalry) under a prefect or chiliarch. Due west of the Temple was the gilt palace built by King Herod, which now probably served as Pilate's *praetorium*, or official residence, while he was in Jerusalem (Mk. xv. 16). On the south and west the city-fortress was moated by the Valley of Hinnom (Gr. *Gehenna*)—a place of sinister name for the Jew—and on the east by the valley of the Brook Kidron (Jn. xviii. 1). Across this valley rose the bare ridge known as the Mount of Olives, where Jesus wept over the doomed city (Lk. xix. 37ff., L). Not far up its slopes was the olive-orchard known as the Garden of Gethsemane. The site of Golgotha, called in Latin 'Calvary,' is disputed. It stood 'outside the gate' (Heb. xiii. 12). 'Gordon's Calvary,' a skull-shaped eminence north of the *present* city wall, has its advocates. Tradition, going back to the fourth century, and gaining some support from recent research on the city walls,[1] places the site hard by the present Church of the Holy Sepulchre.

About two miles to the south-east lay Bethany, home of Martha and Mary (Jn. xi. 1). Six miles south of Jerusalem was Bethlehem, the city of David, where Jacob buried Rachel, Ruth gleaned in the harvest fields, and Jesus was born. Fifteen miles to the north-east stood Jericho, the abode of Zaccheus and, though now only a heap of ruins, a rich and prosperous city when Jesus passed through it.

Such is the geography of Palestine—an insignificant mountain terrain on the eastern shores of the Mediterranean, during most of its recorded history the pawn of world-empires, yet destined, under God, to be the cradle of a universal kingdom.

2 HISTORY

From geography we turn to history. Herods and Romans seem always to be somewhere in the background of the Gospel story; and we must have some knowledge of the rulers of Palestine in the time of Christ.

Let us, first, glance back at the story of the Jews after their return from the Exile. At the Battle of Issus (333 B.C.) Alexander of Macedon overthrew their Persian overlords, and after his death Palestine became a bone of contention between Egyptian Ptolemies and Syrian Seleucids. The Seleucids prevailed and spread Greek civilisation over the land. But the attempt of

---

[1] Finegan, *Light from the Ancient Past*, 239ff.

Antiochus Epiphanes to stamp out Judaism broke down before
the heroic resistance of the Maccabees. For eighty years thereafter (143–63 B.C.) the Jews enjoyed a precarious independence
under their priest-kings of the Hasmonean line. (All through this
period there was a long struggle for power between the Pharisees
and the Sadducees.) At length, in 63 B.C., the Roman Pompey
took Jerusalem, and the Jewish state became subject to Rome.

Troubled years followed until in 37 B.C. the Edomite Herod,
with Rome's help, made himself king. A Jew by religion, Herod
was a Greek by sympathy and a Roman by allegiance. The
Jews hated him from the beginning. 'He stole along to his throne
like a fox,' it has been picturesquely said, 'he ruled like a tiger,
and he died like a dog.' Yet for all his ruthless brutality he was
an able, energetic and adroit ruler. His passion was for building,
and with money extorted from the Jews by taxation, he gratified
it to the full. It was he who in 20 B.C. began the rebuilding of
the Temple. For the rest, he outwardly respected the Jews'
religion in Jerusalem, and elsewhere zealously promoted Greek
culture, to the disgust of the Jews whom he restrained by a
strong mercenary army. Before he died in 4 B.C., he arranged
with Rome that three of his sons should divide his dominions.
Archelaus obtained Judaea, Samaria and Idumaea; Antipas,
Galilee and Peraea; and Philip the north-east regions. Archelaus,
however, did not inherit his father's title of king: he was styled
ethnarch, and his brothers tetrarchs.

Like father, like son: in cruelty at least Archelaus was a true
son of his father, and the Jews cordially hated him. For ten
years Rome tolerated his misrule, but at last in A.D. 6 Augustus
deposed him, and set a Roman procurator in his stead.

The new régime pleased the Jews no better. Under the procurator the high priest and the Sanhedrin enjoyed the semblance
of autonomy, but no grave decision—such as the passing of the
death penalty—could be taken without the approval of the
procurator.[1] Of these procurators Pilate (A.D. 26–36) was the
fifth. In his contempt for the Jews he typified the baser sort of
Roman governor, and he had no scruple about spilling blood in
order to preserve the *Pax Romana* (Lk. xiii. 1, L). At last, the
cruel massacre of some Samaritans caused his deposition in
A.D. 36.

Meanwhile Antipas (4 B.C.–A.D. 39), the Herod who figures
most in the Gospels, ruled as tetrarch over Galilee and Peraea,
maintaining his position by means of an army of his own, in
which no doubt the centurion of Capernaum served. In his

[1] Cf. Jn. xviii. 31.

subtlety, love of women and craze for building, he too resembled
his father. Of his subtlety our Lord's 'that fox' is witness (Lk.
xiii. 32, L); to his love of women his liaison with Herodias bears
testimony; and of his passion for building Tiberias is the monu-
ment. An attempt to gain for himself the title of king ended in
his banishment to Gaul.

Philip (4 B.C.–A.D. 34), the tetrarch of the north-east country,
was the best of Herod's sons. His wife was Salome, daughter of
Herodias (Mk. vi. 22). He too was a builder, and Caesarea
Philippi and Bethsaida Julias were his monuments.

Altogether, these were troubled times with much bloodshed
and misery. The Jews groaned under the Roman yoke or that
of their satellites, the Herods. Jew did not understand Roman,
or Roman Jew. Two classes of men this suffering bred among
the Jews: on the one hand, fanatical seekers after freedom like
the Zealots; on the other, quietists like 'the meek in the land'
who fed their souls with apocalyptic hopes and dreamed of a
supernatural deliverance.

Politics cannot be separated from economics, and a word
must be said on the economic situation. Palestine was at this
time in a state of economic malaise, of which the root-cause was
the twofold taxation. When the Jews, tired of the Herods, invited
the Romans to take over the government, they got more than
they bargained for. Rome imposed a fresh burden of taxation
in the shape of a poll-tax, not to mention other land and cattle
dues. These taxes the Romans collected through their *publicani*,
though we must note that the tax-gatherers of the Gospels were
only the underlings of their Romans superiors—the small fry
of the bureaucracy. The whole system, being honeycombed
with graft, exasperated the Jews. When on top of all the taxes
'due to God' were piled these new taxes 'due to Caesar'—and
the double taxation must have exceeded 8s. in the £1—not
surprisingly there were riots and a smouldering unrest destined
one day to blaze out into open rebellion.

Another cause of unrest was increasing over-population causing
an acute food-shortage. And a third cause was the introduction
of slave-labour, which threw many smallholders out of business
and drove desperate men to brigandage.

In short, the economic system was out of joint, and there
seemed to be only one remedy—the expulsion of the Romans.
This was the avowed aim of the Zealots. 'No tribute to the
Romans!' was the battle-cry of Judas the Galilean (Acts v. 37).
As we study the Gospels, we ought to remember all this. Two
elements in the popular expectation of the Good Time Coming

were the abolition of the Roman taxes and the establishment of
an economic plenty. On the first issue Jesus was challenged to
give a ruling (Mk. xii. 14), and the second issue confronted Him
more than once.

3   RELIGION

In our Lord's time there were two main religious parties—the
Pharisees and the Sadducees. (We need not spend time on the
Essenes, a society of some four thousand ascetics living a com-
munal life near the Dead Sea. They never appear in the Gospel
pages, and the notion that Jesus or the Baptist had some connection with them is nowadays left to cranks or the writers of
historical romances.)

The people's party were the Pharisees. Their name means
'separated ones'—doubtless a reference to the higher standard
of ritual purity which they observed. They were 'the practising
Jews' and, as Josephus says, 'had the multitude on their side.'
To find their origins, we must go back to the *Hasidim*, or Pious,
who in Maccabaean times fought for the Law by the side of
Judas, but, with their object achieved, withdrew from the
campaign. Their religion was legalism. The Law, or Torah,
which for them included the mass of scribal comments on it
known as 'the tradition,' was 'the master light of all their seeing.'
They bound themselves to observe the Sabbath, tithing and
the rules of ceremonial purity. They believed in a future life
with post-mortem rewards and punishments, and in angels and
spirits. They cherished the hope of a Messiah. Josephus says that
they were modified determinists. 'All is foreseen,' said Rabbi
Akiba, 'but the right of choice is permitted.' For the rest, they
fasted twice a week (Lk. xviii. 12, L) and were active prosely-
tisers (Mt. xxiii. 15, M).

Most of the scribes, or professional teachers of the Law, were
Pharisees. (Note Mark's phrase: 'the scribes of the Pharisees.')
They supplied the Pharisees with their theology and ethics.
It was their accumulated lore that formed the tradition and
was later codified in the *Talmud*. Notoriously, many of them
were formalists and casuists (though we have no right to make
the automatic equation 'hypocrite'=Pharisee); but there were
great men among them, notably Hillel and Gamaliel. The
latter lives in history chiefly by reason of a brilliant pupil from
Tarsus who was to forsake 'the traditions of his fathers.' It was
Hillel who, on being invited by a Gentile enquirer to summarise
the Law while standing on one leg, replied memorably: 'That

which thou hatest, do not to thy neighbour. This is the whole Law. The rest is commentary. Go, study.'

On the left wing of this party stood the Zealots, for they were simply 'active and extremist Pharisees' (Klausner), fonder of the sword than the phylactery. Proclaiming God to be their only king, they believed that the deliverance of Israel from Rome lay in the power of their own right arms; and when at length the great revolt burst into flame, they fought with savage cruelty and superb heroism. One of the Twelve, Simon the Cananaean (Luke: 'the zealot'), may have been one of them—if the name is not, like Cephas, a reference to his character.

As the Pharisees were the people's party, so the Sadducees were the priestly party. They took their name from Zadok, the high priest under Solomon (1 Kings ii. 35). Most of them were wealthy aristocrats who found it possible to accept their Roman overlords. Such internal autonomy as the Romans allowed, the Sadducees exercised, and among their number in the time of Jesus were the reigning High Priest Caiaphas and his father-in-law, Annas (Jn. xviii. 13). Hellenists in cultural sympathies, they held it the best political wisdom to let sleeping dogs lie. In religion, they were conservatives. For them, the Five Books of the Law of Moses were alone truly canonical, and they rejected the tradition of the scribes as so much new theology. The doctrine of the resurrection (Mk. xii. 18 and Acts xxiii. 8) and the new lore of angels and spirits they repudiated. According to Josephus (a biased witness, however), they also rejected the doctrine of divine providence. In matters of practice, we gather that they were harsh administrators and that they were 'rather boorish in their behaviour.'

Besides Pharisees and Sadducees, the Gospels mention Herodians. The name means 'partisans of Herod.' We know little about them beyond the fact that they twice conspired with the Pharisees against Jesus (Mk. iii. 6 and xii. 13). Possbly they were not a party but simply a group of men who in those distressful times pinned their hopes on the Herodian family.

Besides these sects and parties, however, there must have been many who owned no formal allegiance to any party—'the quiet in the land,' humble, pious folk whose spiritual ideals find exquisite expression in the *Magnificat* and the *Nunc Dimittis*: people like Simeon and Anna who were well content to stand aloof from the hurly-burly of religion and politics and quietly to wait for the salvation of the Lord. If the motto of the Zealots might have been, 'God helps those who help themselves,' that of the quietists could be expressed as, 'In God's good time.'

In some such circles, 'the special seed-plot of Christianity' (as Sanday phrased it), our Lord and His forerunner must have been born.

What we have said will have suggested the religious background of the time. The keystone of Judaism was a noble monotheism—belief in one God transcendent, righteous, holy—but a national monotheism, for the only God was pre-eminently the God of the Jews. Between God and His People stood the Torah, God's revealed will for men, at once the law of the nation and the private law of the individual, in keeping of which there was great reward. To this, we saw, the Pharisees added 'the tradition'—a mixture of narrative and doctrine designed to amplify and elucidate the Torah. If in Jerusalem the Temple cult of ritual and sacrifice still flourished, elsewhere the synagogue, a sort of chapel-cum-school, was the rallying place of Judaism.

Thus far the religion of the Torah. But we err if we suppose that the religious aspiration of the times found entire satisfaction in the punctilious keeping of the Law. When the times are out of joint and a God-fearing people contrasts the ideal with the actual—the glorious future promised by God through seer and prophet with their present miseries—they inevitably seek comfort in apocalypses of one kind or another. They dream of a divine vindication and of a heaven-sent saviour. Thus did many of the Jews in our Lord's time. For the present, evil seemed in the ascendant, clouds and thick darkness were about God's throne and His people groaned under the alien yoke. But the living God was merely biding His time: yet a little while, and He would decisively manifest His rule in the world, the powers of evil would be vanquished, and the faithful gain salvation. That would be the coming of the Kingdom of God—the beginning of that new age which was part of God's reserved purpose. Some looked for God to interpose directly, without the help of any intermediary; but many expected the coming of God's great vicegerent, the Messiah, who should be the bearer of His Rule to the world. Many and various were the dream-pictures which they painted of the Kingdom and the Messiah. But, however variously they conceived of them, all save the Sadducees, who found their present lot tolerable, yearned for the decisive intervention of God. When that blessed day dawned, they would say, 'Lo, this is our God; we have waited for Him; we will be glad and rejoice in His salvation' (Isa. xxv. 9).

PART TWO

BEFORE THE MINISTRY

IV

BIRTH AND EARLY YEARS

I THE BIRTH

The birthplace of Jesus was Bethlehem (Mt. ii. 1; Lk. ii. 1–7).
According to Matthew and Luke, He was born of Mary, while
still a virgin, through the special action of the Holy Spirit (Mt.
i. 18–25; Lk. i. 34–35). Various attempts to shake the testimony
of these two passages have not succeeded. Thus, for example,
the attempt to prove Lk. i. 34f. an interpolation breaks down on
the distinctively Lucan diction of the passage and the almost
unbroken MSS. evidence. Beyond question both Matthew and
Luke teach the Virgin Birth.

This evidence, however, stands alone in the New Testament.
Neither Mark, nor John, nor Paul, nor Peter, nor the Writer
to the Hebrews has anything to say about the Virgin Birth.
What historical value are we to attach to the tradition?

Mt. i. 18–25 comes from M, not a very reliable Gospel stratum.
If it stood alone, we might dismiss the whole matter as pious
legend. But we have also to reckon with the Lucan account
which has two notable features. The first is the strongly Semitic
flavour of the Greek which suggests that these two opening
chapters of Luke are based on Aramaic originals. The second
feature is that the Lucan Nativity narratives are unmistakably
poetical in character. No one can read them without realising
that he is moving in the realm of art, not of scientific description.
This does not mean, however, that Luke's stories about the
birth of Jesus have no basis in fact. Bernard Shaw's *Saint Joan*
is a highly imaginative work of art; yet no one dreams of doubting
that Joan of Arc was a very real and remarkable person. It may
well be that the story of the Virgin Birth is of the same order—a
fact clothed in imaginative colouring—as it may be that the
substance of these two chapters, written by one who expressly
claims to have 'gone into the sources,' comes from the only
source that could make it trustworthy—Mary herself.

Some will judge the evidence sufficient for belief; others will
find it inadequate. Those who find it insufficient will soon discover ways of explaining the tradition away. Thus, some have
held that the LXX version of Isa. vii. 14, 'Behold, the *virgin*
shall conceive and bear a son,' is the origin of the tradition.
But no trace of a Messianic interpretation of this passage has
been found. Others regard the story as an importation from
pagan mythology (one remembers the old legend of Zeus and
Danaë); but the strongly Jewish colouring of the tradition is
decidedly against this. In a problem of this sort dogmatic considerations inevitably influence a man's verdict. Thus, if a man
is unimpressed by Jesus' own claim to a unique and unshared
place in the ways of God with men, he will doubtless reject the
Virgin Birth and see in it only an artificial wreath set on the
brow of the infant Jesus. In fairness, we must add that men
like Brunner reject the doctrine for dogmatic reasons, arguing
that if there was to be a true incarnation, Jesus must have been
born as other men are. But others, and perhaps a majority, will
feel that the tradition of the Virgin Birth is entirely congruous
with the whole picture of Christ in the New Testament. They
will see in the story a fitting preface to a life which was crowned
by resurrection from the dead. They will say: 'Jesus came from
God, all the apostles declare, in a sense in which no other came.
Does it not follow that, as two of our evangelists declare, He
came in a way in which no other came.'[1]

2   EARLY YEARS

Except for a few facts to be gleaned from the Gospels we know
little directly about the early years of Jesus. This is the sum of
it. He grew up in Nazareth as the son of Joseph and Mary;
besides sisters he had four brothers (Mk. vi. 3); He worked as a
carpenter, and at the age of twelve visited Jerusalem.

And yet from scattered hints in the Gospels we can picture
the Nazareth home and the sort of education He must have
received. If we visit Nazareth, we can still see the well where
Mary drew water. From the Nazareth hill-tops we can command
the magnificent prospects of Galilee and beyond on which the
youthful gaze of Jesus must have rested. Across the foot of those
hills ran a branch of the great trade route, and from the hill-top
Jesus must have seen all sorts and conditions of men posting
along the highways—imperial dignitaries, Midianite caravans,
princes with their retinues, the gleaming eagles of the Roman

[1] Denney, *Studies in Theology*, 64.

legionaries, and all 'the great ones of the Gentiles.' News of the wider world must have found its way to Nazareth—the scandals of the Herods, the latest decrees of the Procurator, and even rumours of Augustus in Rome. All this should remind us that it was in no place far from the dusty ways of men that Jesus grew up, but in surroundings where He must have felt the pressure and problems of the wider world.

Sayings in the Gospels enable us to picture the Nazareth home. We are to think of a clay-built, flat-roofed, one-roomed house whose owner when disturbed by a midnight caller does not need to rise in order to chat with a man outside the door (Lk. xi. 5f., L). The furniture is simple: the saucer-shaped lamp made of clay, the bed—a light, low frame on which a mat was stretched—the bushel, or meal-tub, which could be put over the lamp's smoking wick at bed-time. Something of what went on by day we can also guess: Mary His mother baking for the family's needs and hiding the leaven in three measures of meal— a process that was later to become a parable of God's Reign (Lk. xiii. 20f.=Mt. xiii. 33, Q). Not a rich house but one in which the finding of a lost shilling was matter for real rejoicing (Lk. xv. 8–10, L). And where if not in the Nazareth home did Jesus learn that 'an old coat' will not tolerate 'a new patch of unshrunk cloth'—a bit of domestic knowledge which was later to symbolise the incompatibility of the new order with the old (Mk. ii. 21)?

Other sayings help us to conjure up the sights and sounds around the Nazareth home: the streets and market-places where by day the children 'made believe' at weddings or at funerals (Lk. vii. 32=Mt. xi. 16f., Q) and where by night 'the outer darkness' reigned supreme. Doubtless Jesus' sayings about yokes (Mt. xi. 29, M) go back to days when He wrought at His trade, as the sight of a ploughman at his job suggested the firm, quiet 'holding to it' which was the quality demanded later of a true disciple (Lk. ix. 62, Q?).

We know little about His education except by inference. Yet three books must ever have been open before Him—the Bible (i.e. the Old Testament), Nature and Man. That He read well in all three, every page of the Gospels attests.

He must have received His early education at home and in the synagogue-school. Its staple would be the Law, the prophets and the tradition. The Gospels show His knowledge of His people's scriptures to have been profound. He does not handle scripture like a Scribe; with an unerring instinct He goes to its essential heart. And yet, though He handles it with sovereign freedom, it remains for Him the Word of God, and in great crises of His life like the Temptation and the Crucifixion His thought instinctively clothes itself in scriptural phrase. Certain books seem to have spoken to Him with peculiar power: Deuteronomy, Psalms, Daniel and Isaiah in whose Servant Songs (Isa. xlii. 1–4, xlix. 1–6, l. 4–9 and lii. 13–liii) He saw as in a mirror, when the time came, His own face. Whether His eyes ever lighted on extra-canonical books like Enoch or Ecclesiasticus, we cannot certainly say.

Much has been written about His mother-tongue. It is certain that Aramaic, the language of His prayers, was the tongue in which He preached and taught, and we are grateful to St. Mark for preserving a few of His actual words like *Talitha cumi*, *Ephphatha* and *Abba*. But He must have known something of the 'common Greek' which was the international language of the time and must have been frequently heard in 'Galilee of the Gentiles.' Probably also He could read Hebrew, for according to Lk. iv. 16ff., L, He read from a Hebrew roll in the synagogue at Nazareth.

Of His deep reading in 'the open volume' of Nature we have abundant evidence in the Gospels:

> He spoke of grass, and wind, and rain,
> And fig-trees, and fair weather,
> And made it His delight to bring
> Heaven and earth together.[1]

If we want evidence that our Lord was country-bred, we have only to study Q. 'There is,' writes Canon Crum,[2] 'as good internal evidence of the country origin of Q as any you will find in William Cobbett's *Rural Rides* or the poems of Robert Burns with their memories of boyhoods spent in Surrey or Ayrshire.'

'He knew what was in man,' says St. John of our Lord. Parable after parable attests His insight into human nature, showing that from His youth He must have walked with shrewd, discerning eyes amid the human scene. Doubtless it was during 'the hidden years' that He watched or met those characters who people His parables: the far-seeing rogue whom we call the Unjust Steward, the truculent, self-sufficient pagan whom we know as the Unjust Judge, that type of the crass materialist the Rich Fool, the self-righteous Pharisee who thanked God that he was not as other men—and many another drawn to the life

---

[1] T. T. Lynch.   [2] *The Original Jerusalem Gospel*, 62.

in a few deft, verbal strokes—a testimony to Jesus' knowledge of common men and common things.

But all this is indirect evidence. With one exception the canonical Gospels say nothing directly about the early years of Jesus. That exception is, of course, Luke's story of the Boy Jesus in the Temple (Lk. ii. 41–51)—a story which shows Jesus aware from His early years of a special filial relationship to God. The apocryphal Gospels, on the other hand, contain many stories of how the boy Jesus

> made him small fowl out of clay
> And blessed them till they flew away[1]

and the like; but they really add nothing to our sure knowledge of Jesus. It is enough to know that He 'increased in wisdom and stature, and in favour with God and man'; for it 'behoved Him in all things to be made like unto His brethren.'

> He has been our fellow, the morning of our days,
> Us He chose for housemates, and this way went.[2]

[1] H. Belloc.   [2] G. Meredith.

C

V

THE FORERUNNER, THE BAPTISM
AND THE TEMPTATION

The Forerunner (Mk. i. 1–8; Lk. iii. 7–9, 16–17=Mt. iii. 7–10,
11–12, Q; Lk. iii. 10–14, L)

'Even as it is written in Isaiah the prophet . . . John the baptiser
appeared in the wilderness, preaching a baptism of repentance
for the remission of sins' (Mk. i. 2–4). St. Mark begins his Gospel
with the mission of the Baptist. Our knowledge of this strange
figure is derived not only from the New Testament, but also
from the *Antiquities* of Josephus.

John, son of Zacharias and Elisabeth, was an ascetic, an
apocalyptist and a prophet. Especially the last: in him the
voice of prophecy silent for centuries rang out again like a
trumpet. 'In the fifteenth year of the reign of Tiberius Caesar,'
says Luke finely, 'the word of God came to John the son of
Zacharias in the wilderness' (iii. 1f., L). In dress he recalled
Elijah; in message and temper, Amos: a strong, blunt, fearless
man—'no shaking reed, no soft courtier,' as Jesus was to say of
him (Lk. vii. 24f.=Mt. xi. 7f., Q). The New Testament and
Josephus alike declare that his mission profoundly influenced his
contemporaries.

The burden of his message was 'the wrath to come' (Lk.
iii. 7–9=Mt. iii. 7–10, Q). The day of doom was at hand. In
that day God would judge men by His Messiah and winnow the
wheat from the chaff. 'I baptise you with water,' he said, 'but
he [the Messiah] will baptise you with fire.' Since in that day
racial privilege would count for nothing, John's summons was
'Repent.' This word should be interpreted in its *prophetic* sense.
It means not so much 'Change your mind,' or 'Be sorry for your
sins' as 'Return.' It denotes 'a turning of the mind and will,
in response to the prophetic voice, away from self and the world,
to God.'[1] It calls to decision for or against God's cause, as Elijah
had called for decision centuries before on Mount Carmel. In
short, John's message was: 'The Day of Judgment is about to
dawn. The Messiah is coming. Repent—or be damned.'[2]

[1] Bowman, *op. cit.*, 10.

[2] It is improbable that John predicted baptism with the Spirit. See T. W.
Manson, *The Sayings of Jesus*, 41, and Creed, *St. Luke*, 53. It is also unlikely
that, as Mt. iii. 2 asserts, John preached 'the kingdom of heaven.' See Burkitt,
Christian Beginnings, 15f., Streeter, *The Four Gospels*, 206, and Otto, *The Kingdom
of God and the Son of Man*, 69.

According to Luke (iii. 10–14, L), John also gave some sort of ethical teaching. To the multitudes he said, 'Share with your needy brethren'; to the tax-gatherers, 'Be honest in your exactions'; to the soldiers, 'Don't bully or blackmail.' Useful advice, it has been said, but not an epoch-making moral discovery. Clearly John's teaching was 'an ethic of the interval'—a makeshift morality till the day of doom should dawn.

If we ask what was the meaning of the baptism which John administered, Mark's answer is that it was 'for the remission of sins.' Probably the rite symbolised moral cleansing and initiation into a new community. Resembling Jewish proselyte baptism in some respects it seems to have differed from it in others—notably in its strong moral emphasis and its eschatological forward-look to the Day of Judgment.[1]

Christian tradition has always seen in John the forerunner and herald of Jesus; and rightly so, for in fact his mission did prepare the way for the ministry of the Mightier One. But did John ever recognise Jesus as the Messiah? The Fourth Evangelist (Jn. i. 29ff.) says so expressly; but if we follow our primary sources, Mark and Q, all we may say is that John seriously entertained the idea, but was deeply perplexed. The Messiah he had predicted was to come in the terrors of judgment—a fire-messiah—but Jesus had come in grace and mercy proclaiming 'good news.' Hence John's puzzled question from prison, 'Art thou he that should come?' and Jesus' reply, which said, in effect, 'I am, but not exactly the Messiah you expected' (Lk. vii. 18–23=Mt. xi. 2–6, Q).

Of John's importance there can be no doubt. There he stands 'in the beginning of the Gospel'; and twenty or more years later Paul can find some of his followers as far afield as Ephesus (Acts xix. 1–7). Above all, there is our Lord's own impressive testimony to him. By His acceptance of John's baptism and His later words about it (Mk. xi. 30) Jesus made it plain that He regarded John as 'a man sent from God.' He declared that he had fulfilled the role predicted for Elijah (Mk. ix. 13; cf. Mal. iv. 5f.). And He pronounced him 'more than a prophet,' the greatest indeed of men outside the Kingdom of God, the last representative of the Old Order ('the law and the prophets') which ends with the advent of the Kingdom and the Messiah.

[1] So far as it involved immersion in flowing water, and signified incorporation into some sort of community, John's rite resembled proselyte baptism. But in its moral emphasis, its eschatological forward-look, and the fact that John himself (and not the subject) did the actual baptising, it was different. Perhaps the last distinguishing point earned for John his name—'John the Baptiser.' See W. F. Flemington, *The New Testament Doctrine of Baptism*, 13-24.

'I tell you,' said Jesus, 'among those born of women none is greater than John; yet he who is least in the kingdom of God is greater than he' (Lk. vii. 24–28=Mt. xi. 7–11, Q and Lk. xvi. 16=Mt. xi. 12f., Q).

The Baptism of Jesus (Mk. i. 9–11; Lk. iii. 21–22=Mt. iii. 16–17, Q)

'And it came to pass in those days that Jesus came from Nazareth of Galilee, and was baptised of John in the Jordan. And straightway coming up out of the water, he saw the heavens rent asunder, and the Spirit as a dove descending upon him: and a voice came out of the heavens, Thou art my beloved Son, in thee I am well pleased' (Mk. i. 9–11).

Among the crowds who flocked to John's baptism came Jesus from Nazareth in Galilee. Why did One whom Christian tradition regarded as sinless undergo 'a baptism of repentance for the remission of sins?' Was he conscious of sin? Did he come, as Middleton Murry has said, 'as a sinner among a crowd of sinners?'[1] This is a very ancient difficulty to which Mt. iii. 14f. (M) attempts an answer. But the question is surely an academic one; for we have no reason to suppose that the question of His own sinlessness occupied Jesus' mind at the time. Jesus went down to Jordan because He discerned the hand of God in John's mission, and by His acceptance of John's baptism identified Himself with the people whom He came to save. If, as we shall see presently, He knew that He must tread the path marked out for the Servant of the Lord, it is not too much to say that Jesus in accepting John's baptism was deliberately 'numbering himself with the transgressors.' His act was 'an act of loving communion with us in our misery.'[2]

At His Baptism Jesus saw a vision and heard a voice. There can be little doubt that Mark is right in declaring that the vision and the voice came to Jesus alone. (Matthew and Luke imply that others heard and saw.) Jesus sees in vision the Spirit of God coming down upon Him like a dove, and from the rent vault of heaven hears the divine voice speaking to Him. Here the first point to seize is that the story (which must have been told by Jesus Himself to the disciples) is couched in symbolical terms. We are dealing with oriental poetry. The dove-like descent of the Spirit and the voice from the rent heavens are conventional Jewish images to express what is imperceptible to outward eye and ear. To literalise them is to miss the point. What is the meaning of the story of the Baptism? Clearly,

[1] The Life of Jesus, 22.

[2] Denney, The Christian Doctrine of Reconciliation, 252.

for Jesus, it was the occasion of (to put it at its lowest) an extraordinary spiritual experience; but what signify the descending
Spirit and the heavenly voice?

The descent of the Spirit means that from that time onwards
Jesus knew Himself to be 'the Anointed of the Spirit' (cf. Isa.
lxi. 1 and Lk. iv. 18, L), to be equipped with divine power;
for the Spirit, whatever else it connotes, always carries with it
the idea of power, and power in which God is active. (Cf. Acts
x. 38, 'God anointed him with the Holy Spirit and with power'—
a clear reference to the Baptism.) Thus only can we explain the
manifest note of authority and finality which informs His later
words and deeds.

What is the meaning of the heavenly voice? God speaks to
Jesus in the language of scripture, and most significant scripture
it is. 'Thou art my [beloved] Son' is the coronation formula of
the Messianic king of Israel (Ps. ii. 7); 'With thee I am well
pleased' is the ordination formula of Isaiah's Servant of the
Lord (Isa. xlii. 1). This remarkable combination cannot be
accidental. It was His own calling, His own destiny that Jesus
saw in the ideal king of Israel and the lowly servant of Isaiah.

'Son of God' was in Christ's time a Messianic title. (It is so,
for example, in 2 Esdras and in Mt. xvi. 16 and Mk. xiv. 61.)
We are entitled therefore to say that the story of the Baptism
implies a Messianic consciousness in Jesus. Yet that is probably
not the whole truth; for the spiritual basis of His own self-awareness from the age of twelve and right through His ministry, was
not primarily official, but filial: it was the awareness of being
the Son of God in an intimate and unshared sense—the sense
which moved the first Christians to speak of God as 'the Father
of our Lord Jesus Christ.' But when we have said all this, we
have not quite exhausted the meaning of the Baptism. Jesus
knows that He is the Messiah, but such a Messiah as no Jew
had hitherto envisaged, a Messiah who takes upon Him the form
of a Servant. But the lot of the Servant was more than service—
it was, as the final and greatest of the Servant Songs proclaimed,
a service that for 'the many's sake' must issue in shame and
death. May we not say that as the Messiah began His work
there must have fallen across His path the shadow of a cross?

The Temptation (Mk. i. 12f.; Lk. iv. 1–13=Mt. iv. 1–11, Q)

After the Baptism there follows, with psychological fitness, the
Temptation.

'The Spirit immediately drove him out into the wilderness.
And he was in the wilderness forty days, tempted by Satan;

and he was with the wild beasts; and the angels ministered to him' (Mk. i. 12f.). So Mark records the fact of the Temptation. It is to Q that we owe the full account of what befell Jesus in that bleak and barren land down near the Dead Sea.

How do we know anything about it? For 'forty days'—an oriental round number[1]—He was quite alone. Obviously, the story of the Temptation is a piece of spiritual autobiography told to the disciples by Jesus Himself—told (as Sanday says) with utter simplicity 'as a Jewish mother might have told it to a Jewish child.'[2] We may be sure that no later Christian would have invented such a story. It bears upon its face the authentic stamp of the supreme Master in parable.

The next point is that the story is poetry, not prose, and that to literalise it in terms of some dialectical passage-at-arms in a gloomy picture-book wilderness is to misunderstand it. The Temptation story describes inward experiences, not external events. It is the story of a searching spiritual struggle—a real, not a sham fight—told in the language of parable. (The point is superbly made in Dyce's well-known picture, 'The Temptation in the Wilderness.' All we see is a sombre rocky landscape, and in the foreground the figure of Jesus with clasped hands and an expression of intense thought upon His features.)

The Temptation story is intelligible only against the background of the Baptism. At His Baptism there had come to Jesus the assurance of His divine appointment as Messiah and of His endowment with extraordinary powers. Only if we remember this, can we make sense of the three temptations. For these are not the temptations of Jesus; they are the temptations of the Christ; the temptations not of a private person but of one called to be God's Messiah in the establishment of the Kingdom.

Jesus is the Messiah, but what kind of a Messiah? How is He to fulfil His high destiny as the bearer of God's Rule to men? What course of action is open to one whose Messiahship is to be construed not in terms of kingly triumph but of lowly service? With such problems Jesus wrestles in the wilderness, and the Evil One is ever nigh to suggest all sorts of wrong roads to the Kingdom.

We shall consider the Temptations in Matthew's order which, whether it preserves the original order of Q or not, provides the more striking climax.

'If thou art the Son of God, bid these desert stones become

---

[1] Cf. Exod. xxiv. 13, 18 (Moses in the mount of God) and 1 Kings xix. 8 (Elijah at Horeb).

[2] *The Life of Christ in Recent Research*, 110.

loaves.' The first temptation admits of two interpretations. The first finds the clue in Jesus' own acute physical hunger at the time. Around Him lie the flat desert stones, and He seems to hear the Tempter say: 'You are starving. Can you really be God's Messiah? Test it and see. If you really are the Messiah, you can use your supernatural powers to turn these stones into bread. So shall you confirm your conviction and preserve yourself for your high mission.' But for Jesus to do so would mean that He had already begun to doubt God. His mission was spiritual, and He must trust God to supply His physical needs.

The other interpretation finds the clue in the nature of the Kingdom. When contemporary apocalyptists pictured the Good Time Coming, they sometimes thought of it as an economic paradise in which there would be a miraculous abundance of material blessings—'a feast of fat things for Israel.' On this view, the Tempter says, 'If you are the Messiah, produce one of the signs of his coming—provide an economic plenty. Do that, and men will flock to you.' Jesus' reply seems to favour this view. 'Man shall not live by bread alone' (Dt. viii. 3). It was a real temptation. Jesus knew Himself what it was to be hungry and He had a deep sympathy for the poor in their economic as well as their spiritual need. Once later, He was moved by pity to feed a hungry multitude to find, according to Jn. vi. 15, that they wanted to make Him a king. Such was the kingdom they craved—a kingdom built on bread. But this was not God's Kingdom. It was a very temptation of the devil to suppose that God's Reign meant 'bread alone.'

In the second temptation Jesus stands, in imagination (cf. Ezek. viii. 3), on a pinnacle of the Temple in Jerusalem. Below, the multitudes clamour for a sign—some spectacular proof that He is the Messiah, some dazzling act that will blazon the truth of His claims across the sky. Why not fling Himself from the pinnacle, assured that God will supply a flight of angels for His Messiah's protection? This is the second temptation—to pander to the Jews' love of a sign. ('The Jews,' said Paul who knew them, 'ask for signs.') But Jesus repels it—refuses this demand for a sign, as He was later to refuse it in His ministry. 'Thou shalt not tempt the Lord thy God' (Dt. vi. 16). To accept the devil's suggestion would be to challenge God, not to trust Him. Besides, Jesus well knew that no transient impression made on men's senses would establish God's sovereignty in the spirit.

In the third temptation Jesus stands, in imaginative vision (this is the sense of Luke's 'in a moment of time'), on some lofty height commanding a prospect of 'all the kingdoms of the

world and their glory.' (This surely is an argument against
those who say that Jesus had no consciousness of a world-mission.
If this passage is evidence, 'nothing less than the world was to
be His parish.')[1] 'Here is dominion and authority,' says the
Tempter, 'such as even the great ones of the Gentiles might
envy. All shall be Yours—on one condition, that You do homage
to me. Lower Your standards, use the world and its methods,
and You cannot fail to succeed as Messiah.' So we may paraphrase Satan's words. Jesus repels the suggestion with horror.
Homage is due to God alone (Dt. vi. 13). No man, let alone one
who knows Himself to be God's Messiah, can serve both God and
the devil.

Thus, in travail of soul, Jesus fought His way through this
tangle of specious alternatives to a clear vision of His Messiahship. The first battle in the fight with the power of evil had
been won. But there were to be further battles. 'Christendom,'
says H. R. Mackintosh, 'speaks of the Temptation as if that
which followed His Baptism were an isolated fact. But the
pressure lasted to the end; and few things in the Gospels are
more subduing than the words in which Jesus gratefully acknow-
ledges the fidelity of those who had remained with Him throughout
His trials (Lk. xxii. 28f., L).'[2] Nevertheless, from the truth reached
in the wilderness He never afterwards swerved. The way He
chose was one of utter self-dedication and obedience to the
will of His Father: He would wait for the hour when the Father
chose, and as the Father chose, to make Him known as the
Messiah:

> The kingdom that I seek
> Is Thine; so let the way
> That leads to it be Thine.[3]

---

[1] C. J. Cadoux, *The Life of Jesus*, 51.
[2] *The Doctrine of the Person of Jesus Christ*, 12.   [3] Horatius Bonar.

PART THREE

THE MINISTRY

VI

SKETCH OF THE MINISTRY: (1)

Excluding the last journey to Jerusalem, we trace three periods, or stages, in Jesus' ministry:

> An early Judaean period.
> The Galilean ministry.
> The period of travel.

I   THE EARLY JUDAEAN PERIOD

If we had only Mark's Gospel, we should infer that Jesus' ministry was located in Galilee with one first and final visit to Jerusalem, and that the Galilean ministry began after John the Baptist was imprisoned.

The Fourth Gospel takes a different view. Here the scene shifts backwards and forwards between Galilee and Judaea during the first six chapters. (From chapter vii onwards the scene is laid wholly in Judaea and Jerusalem.) Moreover, St. John explicitly states that Jesus was active in Judaea and Jerusalem *before* the Baptist was imprisoned. 'For John was not yet cast into prison' (Jn. iii. 24).

There can be little question that St. John is to be trusted. That Jesus was active in the south before 'He came preaching in Galilee' after John the Baptist's arrest, is likely, for various reasons:

(1) Mark's statement 'Now after John was arrested, Jesus came into Galilee, preaching the Gospel of God' (Mk. i. 14) seems to hint at activity elsewhere before this.

(2) There is the express testimony of the Fourth Gospel already quoted.

(3) There are several hints in the Synoptic Gospels themselves which almost compel us to believe that Jesus had made an appeal to the people of Judaea and Jerusalem before He made the last journey south. Most important of these is the lament of Jesus: 'O Jerusalem, Jerusalem, *how often* would I have gathered thy children together . . . and ye would not!' (Lk.

41

xiii. 34=Mt. xxiii. 37, Q)—an utterance which suggests not one, but many appeals. Moreover, we have to remember that on the last journey to Jerusalem Jesus had friends there who could lend Him a colt and furnish Him with a guest-chamber. Further, the sudden call of the Galilean fishermen to be disciples is more intelligible if, as St. John says, they had had some previous knowledge of Jesus before 'they left all and followed Him.'

We conclude that St. John's testimony to an early Judaean ministry is to be accepted. Of its precise course and sequence of events we cannot say much. Since Mark has not seen fit to record it, we may even regard it as of a preliminary nature. But of its historicity we may be tolerably sure.

2   THE GALILEAN MINISTRY (Mk. i. 14–vi)

'Now after that John was put in prison . . .' Jesus' real work began after Herod Antipas had imprisoned the Baptist in the lonely fortress of Machaerus near the Dead Sea.

From now on we follow Mark's narrative, which we may summarise. After describing Jesus' appearance in Galilee and the call of some disciples, Mark relates a memorable Sabbath in Capernaum. There follows a group of stories—often called 'the Conflict Stories'—narrating how Jesus came into ever sharper conflict with the Jewish authorities (ii. 1–iii. 6), and how at last Pharisees and Herodians resolved to get rid of Him. Jesus now withdrew to the lake-side, and somewhere in the 'hill-country' chose twelve disciples. His work of healing continued, and He was charged with being in league with Satan (iii. 7–35). Mark now records three parables of the Kingdom followed by a series of 'mighty works' (iv. 1–v. 43). Then comes the mission and the return of the Twelve (the story of the Baptist's death being dovetailed between the two events). The Galilean ministry culminates in the feeding of the multitude, the voyage and the walking on the water (vi. 1–56). (Thereafter follow the period of travel and the last journey to Jerusalem.)

So Mark describes the march of events. Did they really happen in this order? We raise the question because the Form Critics have said that we cannot trust Mark's order of events. Mark (they say) likes to group his stories topically and 'the generalising summaries' with which he links them together are his own invention.

We need not hesitate to reject this view. If Mark groups some of his narratives topically, he does also give us a broad outline of how things developed—an outline we have reason to believe was derived from the tradition of the Church's *kerygma*[1] (see Acts x. 37–41). It reveals three distinct stages:

(*a*) Synagogue preaching in Capernaum and elsewhere.

(*b*) Teaching and healing by the Lakeside in the presence of crowds from all over Palestine.

(*c*) Retirement to the hill-country with a disciple-band who are sent out on a teaching and healing tour.

So the Galilean ministry developed, and we must now try to describe its main features.

'Jesus came into Galilee,' says Mark, 'preaching the gospel of God and saying, The time is fulfilled, and the kingdom of God is at hand; repent and believe in the gospel.' Familiarity with these words has dulled our ears to their wonder. What they mean is something like this: 'The time of which Isaiah spoke (Isa. lii. 7f.) is come true. The Reign of God is now a blessed reality. Turn[2] to God, and accept these good tidings.'

Such was Jesus' message. How did it differ from John's? John's was a 'burden' or 'doom' in the comminatory sense characteristic of the old prophets; Jesus' message was an *evangel*— the proclamation of good tidings, as in Second Isaiah. John declared that the *Dies Irae* was near; Jesus said, 'The Reign of God is here.' His Good News was that the Rule of God was no longer a shining hope on the far horizon but a glad reality, a blessed *fait accompli*. 'From the realm of the invisible beyond, the one far-off divine event had suddenly projected itself into history. What had formerly been pure eschatology was there before their eyes: the supernatural made visible. No longer were they dreaming of the kingdom age: they were living in it. It had arrived.'[3]

A Q saying (Lk. vii. 33f.=Mt. xi. 18f.) tells how the two men appeared in the eyes of their contemporaries:

'For John the Baptist is come eating no bread nor drinking wine; and ye say, He hath a devil. The Son of man is come eating and drinking, and ye say, Behold, a gluttonous man and a wine-bibber, a friend of publicans and sinners.'

---

[1] See C. H. Dodd's article in *Expository Times*, June, 1932.

[2] 'Repent' means 'turn' in the prophetic sense. It denotes an act of the will, and in the parable of the Lost Son Jesus has given us a picture of it. 'It was not repentance when the Prodigal Son grew hungry,' Mrs. Booth is reported to have said, 'nor when he remembered his father's house, nor even when he said, "I will arise and go to my father"; you see repentance where it is said, He arose and came to his father.'

[3] J. S. Stewart, *Heralds of God*, 64.

The same contrast marked their disciples: those of John fasted and apparently wore the grave looks of men in deadly earnest about their religion; but the disciples of Jesus were like men at a marriage feast (Mk. ii. 18–20).

With this message of the inbreaking Reign of God Jesus began His Galilean ministry. At first He proclaimed it in the synagogues and elsewhere in the towns. But before long He clashed with the religious authorities, and had to seek the freer atmosphere of the Lake-side, whither, when His fame spread, the crowds resorted. There followed the third stage when He retired to the hill-country with a disciple-band. These disciples, after training, He sent out on a preaching and healing tour.

Before we fill in this rough outline, one general observation must be made. Under the influence of 'lives' of Jesus which took little account of the miracles, we have learned to think of the Galilean ministry as a great teaching tour. This is a one-sided view. In reality, as Mark shows, it rather resembled a campaign —a great campaign against the power of evil. 'We are apt,' says Micklem,[1] 'falsely to distinguish between the first part of the ministry in Galilee, as if it were a time of quiet preaching, from the last Judaean episodes which we call the Passion but might as truly call the Action. A distinction there may be in outward condition, but not in purpose; the campaign might fall into two parts, but it is one campaign.' This is well said, and this conception of the ministry as a great campaign is suggested by Jesus' own words: 'If I by the finger of God cast out devils, then is the Reign of God come upon you' (Lk. xi. 20=Mt. xii. 28, Q). 'I came to cast fire upon the earth, and how I wish it were already kindled!' (Lk. xii. 49, Q?) 'I beheld Satan fall like lightning from heaven' (Lk. x. 18, L). Most clearly of all, He describes His mission as that of the stronger man who despoils the strong man of his prey (Mk. iii. 27; Lk. xi. 21f.).

Now let us choose five salient features of His ministry. Of the call of His disciples, which we shall discuss later, let us note that there were three stages in the relationship between Jesus and His disciples. First, He summoned certain men from their daily tasks; then, when the number of His followers had grown, He chose twelve men to form the nucleus of the new Israel He was creating; finally, when these had been to school with Him, He sent them forth to preach and heal in His name and in the power of the Kingdom.

Second, we must observe the 'mighty works' which marked Jesus' ministry. (These we shall study in some detail later.)

[1] N. Micklem, *What is the Faith?*, 49.

Jesus announced the advent of God's Reign not in words only, but in deeds, as 'He went about doing good and healing all that were oppressed by the devil' (Acts x. 38). These mighty works were not accidental and incidental—the spontaneous reactions of His compassion to dire cases of human need, though of course the heart of Jesus was always moved at the sight of human misery. So far from being an *addendum* to the Gospel of the Kingdom, they were an integral part of it; they were, in one phrase, the Kingdom of God in action. Preaching and miracles alike were works in demonstration of the Reign of God— complementary parts in one great campaign against the dominion of evil.

Third, we notice Jesus' proclamation of the Reign of God to the common people. To them He spoke generally in parables, not, as Mk. iv. 11-12 suggests,[1] in order to blind and befog His hearers, but because 'truth embodied in a tale' is more telling and memorable; because also the parable teases into thought, awakens religious insight, sifts its hearers, challenges to decision. Mark records three of these parables: the sower, the seed growing secretly, and the mustard seed. To these we may add the parable of the Leaven from Q, where probably mustard seed and leaven formed a pair. All four parables imply, in one way or another, that the Reign of God is now in some sense a reality, a power of God already at work. Of course, the three parables Mark records do not represent the sum total of what Jesus said to the common people when He preached. Thanks to our other sources, we can form a better idea of the manifold ways in which Jesus presented the claims and challenge of the Kingdom of God. Thus, we can hear Him in the synagogue at Nazareth quoting the great

[1] The meaning of Mk. iv. 11-12 seems to be that Jesus used parables in order to blind and harden the people. This is absurd. There are four possible solutions of the difficulty:

(1) The words are later Church theology—an attempt to explain why the Jews as a whole rejected the Gospel.

(2) They are a piece of Semitic determinism on the lips of Jesus—spoken perhaps ironically. Cf. Rom. xi. 8.

(3) ἵνα 'that' is causal=ὅτι 'because' (Mt. xiii. 13 has ὅτι for Mk.'s ἵνα), i.e. 'those outside' lack spiritual insight. Therefore (says Jesus) I have to use parabolic language. For causal ἵνα see Rev. xiv. 13. For further examples see Pernot, *Expository Times*, December, 1926.

(4) ἵνα is a mistranslation of the Aramaic *de*. *De* was ambiguous. It could serve either as a relative pronoun ('who') or as a conjunction ('that'). Mark translated it 'that' when he should have written 'who.' In other words, 'those outside' are simply described as deficient in spiritual insight. (See Torrey, *The Four Gospels*, 76; T. W. Manson, *The Teaching of Jesus*, 74-80.)

I think our choice lies between (3) and (4). They come to much the same thing.

prophecy of Isa. lxi, 'The Spirit of the Lord God is upon me,' and summing it up with, 'To-day hath this scripture been fulfilled in your ears' (Lk. iv. 16-21, L). We can imagine Jesus closing a sermon on the Kingdom with the twin parables of the pearl and the hid treasure (Mt. xiii. 44-46, M), as though to say, 'How great is the joy of the Kingdom! Is not such blessedness worth any sacrifice?' One day, certain candidates for the Kingdom eagerly present themselves to Him, only to be warned to 'count the cost' (Lk. ix. 57-62, Q and xiv. 28-33, L). Another day, there are Pharisees within earshot who sneer at Him as 'the sinners' friend,' and He tells them the great parables of the lost (Lk. xv., L).

All through His preaching there must have sounded a note of terrible urgency (see Lk. xiii. 1-5, L). The Reign of God was now in their midst, for blessing or judgement; a great crisis was upon them; and unless they repented, there was only doom and disaster for the people of Israel.

Fourth, we observe the effect of Jesus' ministry on the people. Without doubt His mission deeply stirred the people of Galilee and beyond. After the wonderful Sabbath in Capernaum the disciples could say to Jesus who had sought retreat, 'All are seeking thee' (Mk. i. 37). We read of a great multitude following Him to the Lake of Galilee—so great that He had to have a small boat standing by lest He be mobbed (Mk. iii. 7-10). And there were, on a very rough computation no doubt, five thousand men in the desert place where, at the height of the Galilean ministry, He fed them (Mk. vi. 44). For their part, the people found the teaching of Jesus altogether 'new,' for He spoke with conscious authority and not as their scribes did (Mk. i. 22, 27).[1] Layman as He was, there was a wonderful 'wisdom' about His words—a depth and insight unique in their experience (Mk. vi. 2). And with this authority and wisdom went a 'winsomeness'—a grace, a charm that thrilled them (Lk. iv. 22). Jesus, however, was not deceived by this popular enthusiasm: not all, He knew, would receive the glad tidings of the Kingdom; and in that simple story of a farmer's fortunes which we call the parable of the sower we hear Him thinking aloud about His work in Galilee, with its mixture of failure and success (Mk. iv. 3-9).

For—and this is the fifth feature—side by side with the popular enthusiasm there was growing up hostility among the scribes and Pharisees. At the causes of this hostility it is not hard to

[1] 'The rabbis taught, and nothing happened. Jesus taught, and all kinds of things happened. He declared sins forgiven and they were forgiven; a paralysed man arose to his feet and walked.' W. Manson, *Jesus the Messiah*, 53.

guess. There was His frank and fearless criticism of them (Lk.
xi. 42–52, Q), but there were other things no less galling; His
attack on their 'tradition' (Mk. vii. 6ff.); His highly irregular
attitude to fasting (Mk. ii. 18f.); His healing on the Sabbath with
which was conjoined a mysterious claim to be 'Lord of the
Sabbath' (Mk. iii. 1–6; Lk. xiii. 10–17, L, etc.); His unpatriotic
commendation of Samaritans and Gentiles; His claim to forgive
sins which was in effect a claim to be the divine pardon incarnate
(Mk. ii. 10); His consorting with social pariahs and outcasts like
customs officers, harlots and the rest. All these served to arouse
the antagonism of the scribes and Pharisees and to hasten the
inevitable conflict.

During this time Jesus made no public claim to be the Messiah.
If He used a title for Himself, it was the Son of man—a title
which was at once mysterious and non-committal. To have made
an overt claim to be the Messiah would have wakened wrong
hopes in Jewish breasts and would have attracted on Himself
the attention of Rome, whose *Realpolitik* found swift ways of
suppressing possible Messiahs. If certain demoniacs guessed at
His messianic rank, only to be sternly silenced by Jesus (Mk. i. 24,
iii. 11, v. 7), we must remember the current messianic excitement
and attribute their 'inspired guesses' to spiritual clairvoyance
in these psychic sensitives.

All this activity of Jesus may have lasted from one spring to
another. The Twelve were sent out on their mission. On their
return Jesus took them into retreat. But the crowds followed, and
in a desert place He fed them (Mk. vi. 30–44).

We call this event 'the feeding of the five thousand,' laying
all the emphasis on the miracle. But we might equally well
name it, 'the Galilean Lord's Supper.' Let us recall that Jesus,
in the manner of the Old Testament prophets, made free use of
symbolic action. Let us also remember that He once told a
parable of the Kingdom under the figure of a great feast (Lk.
xiv. 16–24, Q; cf. Mt. xxii. 1–10, M)—a feast to which guests
were invited with the words, 'Come, for all things are now
ready.' We may then say that when Jesus 'made the men all
sit down' and gave them food by the hands of His disciples, He
was acting out His own parable, signifying by word and deed
alike that the new life of the Kingdom was now available for
men. (It is significant that St. John follows up his version of the
feeding with a discourse on 'the Bread of life.')

VII

SKETCH OF THE MINISTRY: (2)

The Travel Period (Mk. vii. 24–ix. 29)

Jesus now left Galilee (Mk. vii. 24) and for a time abandoned His public ministry. St. Mark goes on to describe a period of travel in the north-west; there follow Peter's confession at Caesarea Philippi, the Transfiguration and the last journey to Jerusalem.

With the data at our disposal, we cannot reconstruct Jesus' itinerary during this period of travel. The vague phrase 'the borders of Tyre and Sidon' does not necessarily mean that He set foot in Phoenicia. Moreover, the other Synoptists give us no help. Luke omits the travel period and replaces it by his 'central section' (Lk. ix. 51–xviii. 14)—a vague narrative of journeyings towards Jerusalem, with hints of contacts with Samaria. Matthew well-nigh eliminates it. John has nothing to say about it. Why does Mark insert it? Bacon's guess that it was meant to justify the extension of the Gospel to the Gentiles is just a guess, and an unlikely one. Admittedly, the section in Mark is difficult: e.g. the feeding of the four thousand looks like a doublet, or variant version, of the feeding of the five thousand. But there is no good reason for doubting that Jesus did travel for a time in the north-west outside of Galilee. To this period Mark assigns the cures of the Syro-Phoenician woman's daughter, the deaf-stammerer and the blind man of Bethsaida.

Why did Jesus seek the north-west regions for a time? A common view is that the people failed to respond to His message, or responded in the wrong way; and that Jesus, seeing His cause lost in Galilee, withdrew for a time. Burkitt, however, held that Jesus left Galilee to avoid the hostile designs of Herod Antipas—the time of travel being a time of flight—and appealed to Lk. xiii. 31f., L as evidence:

'In that very hour there came certain Pharisees, saying to him, Get thee out, and go hence: for Herod would fain kill thee. And he said unto them, Go and say to that fox, Behold, I cast out devils and perform cures to-day and to-morrow, and the third day I am perfected.'

This cry of cool defiance does not sound like that of One who feared what men, even Herod, could do. Schweitzer protests vigorously against the theory of a 'flight,' declaring that it has no basis in the text. In default then of clear evidence we must

48

be chary of propounding theories. Possibly the menaces of Herod
had something to do with the withdrawal, resolved as Jesus was
to finish His course in Jerusalem. Possibly the wrong response of
the Galilean crowds must also be taken into the reckoning.
But possibly the motive of Jesus may simply have been a longing
for rest coupled with the desire to train the Twelve before they
turned south for Jerusalem.

Caesarea Philippi (Mk. viii. 27–33 and parallels; Mt. xvi. 17–19, M)

'And Jesus went forth, and his disciples, into the villages of
Caesarea Philippi' (Mk. viii. 27). In the neighbourhood of
Caesarea Philippi, a region of deep solitude and romantic beauty,
almost in the shadow of snow-capped Hermon, Jesus put (as
we should say) the great Christological question to the Twelve,
'Who do men say that I am?' They replied, in effect, that popular
speculation took different forms: the Baptist risen from the
dead, Elijah (who was expected to return to herald the Messiah)
or someone in the same spiritual line as the old prophets. Then
Jesus pressed the question down on them squarely: 'But you—
who do you say that I am?' The answer was critical for Jesus
as well as for the Twelve. If they had penetrated no more deeply
into His secret than the common people, He must still have
stayed His advance. Peter, however, at once spoke out the
conviction that was in all their minds, 'You are the Messiah'
(Mt. has 'the Messiah, the Son of the living God'; Lk. 'the Messiah
of God'). He was more than the prophet of Nazareth; He was
the Anointed of God, the Coming One, the Bearer of God's
Rule to men.

According to Matthew (Mt. xvi. 17f., M) Jesus at once felici-
tated Peter, 'Blessed art thou, Simon Bar-jonah!': his confession
was no mere human deduction but a revelation from on high.
Mark has nothing of this. On the contrary, Jesus (says Mark)
at once commanded silence on the Twelve. Messiah He was,
but such a Messiah as no Jew had ever dreamed of; for as He
told them frankly, 'The Son of man must suffer many things,'
must be rejected by the authorities and die, before He came to
His triumph. And the words which He used echo the fifty-third
chapter of Isaiah. So, hard on Peter's confession of His Messiahship—a confession which Jesus tacitly accepted—came the still
more staggering truth that Jesus, in His vocation as the Son of
man, must go the way of the Suffering Servant of the Lord.

We do not wonder that the paradox of a suffering Messiah
swept Peter out of his spiritual depths; he reproved Jesus (not
knowing what he said) only to be in turn reproved with awful

D

severity, 'Out of my sight, you Satan! Your outlook is not God's but man's.' As Jesus listened to Peter's protest, there came back to Him in all its grimness His conflict in the wilderness. Satan was speaking through Peter's lips, tempting Him to follow a worldly course, tempting Him to saviourhood without a cross.

It is fashionable to describe Peter's confession as 'a turning-point' in the story of Jesus. The assumption is that the central point in the narrative is the disciples' realisation of Jesus' Messiahship. One cannot help wondering if this is a right view. Must we say that not till Caesarea Philippi did the Twelve divine that Jesus was the Messiah? We may well admit that this may have been the first occasion on which they put their thoughts into words; but it seems likely that long before this something of the truth must have dawned upon them.

Jesus' question, says Bowman, 'did not, so far as he was concerned at any rate, come "out of a clear sky," so to speak. These disciples had been with him over a period of months, possibly of several years. They had seen his marvellous works; they had heard his teachings; they had heard the command, Follow me; they had been challenged at every point to open their eyes and their ears, to see and hear. They had heard him say that with his healing activity the Kingdom of God was present in their midst. . . . No doubt on more than one occasion such experiences had brought the question to their lips, "Who then is this?" . . . When therefore at Caesarea Philippi our Lord asked them the startling question, "But who say ye that I am?" they were ready with the answer, for that was exactly the question they had been asking themselves all through the months previous. "Thou art the Messiah," said Peter for the band.'[1]

We will only add that the idea that He was the Messiah could hardly be new: it had occurred to the Baptist.

The more we reflect on it, the likelier it appears that the sovereign truth disclosed at Caesarea Philippi was not so much that Jesus was the Messiah as that He was a Messiah who must go to His triumph by way of a cross.

The Transfiguration (Mk. ix. 2–8 and parallels)

A week after Peter's confession and the announcement of the coming cross there came the Transfiguration:

'And after six days Jesus taketh with him Peter, and James and John, and bringeth them up into a high mountain apart by themselves: and he was transfigured before them: and his

[1] *The Intention of Jesus*, 180.

garments became glistering, exceeding white; so as no fuller on
earth can whiten them. And there appeared unto them Elijah
with Moses: and they were talking with Jesus. And Peter answer-
eth and saith to Jesus, Rabbi, it is good for us to be here: and
let us make three tabernacles; one for thee, and one for Moses,
and one for Elijah. For he wist not what to answer; for they
became sore afraid. And there came a cloud overshadowing
them: and there came a voice out of the cloud, This is my
beloved Son: hear ye him. And suddenly looking round about,
they saw no one any more, save Jesus only with themselves.'

There are some interesting additions in the Lucan account.
Luke tells us (1) that the event happened 'eight days' after the
confession; (2) that Jesus went up to the mountain 'to pray';
(3) that the conversation of Jesus with Moses and Elijah concerned 'the *exodus* which he was about to accomplish at Jerusalem'; (4) that the three disciples were 'heavy with sleep' (as
though it were night); and (5) that the words of the heavenly
voice were, 'This is my Son, the Chosen: hear ye him.' We do
not know whence Luke derived these details; but they help us to
understand this strange story.

Two preliminary observations are in place. First, it is best to
regard this narrative as the story of a vision, as indeed Matthew
calls it (Mt. xvii. 9). Second, the story is told from the point of
view of the disciples. Indeed, we may regard the Transfiguration
as the counterpart in the disciples' experience of the Baptism in
the experience of Jesus. As at the Baptism Jesus saw a vision
and heard a voice, which proclaimed Him the Messiah, so here
the disciples see a vision and hear a voice which says, 'This is
my Chosen One.'

We may now try to ask and answer three questions:

> What happened to our Lord?
> What was the experience of the disciples?
> Was the vision genuine?

The answer to the first question is that we know very little
about Jesus' experience on this occasion. It is not only that we
cannot penetrate far into the religious experience of our Lord's
humanity, but we cannot appraise with any scientific precision
the strange sight which the three disciples saw as they watched
their Master rapt in prayer. But this much we may venture.
It was a critical time in His life. In a day or two He would turn
south for Jerusalem and death. May we not surmise that, at
such a time, with His unique nature completely fixed on God,
the supernatural dominated His whole person in some—to us—

inexplicable way which His disciples perceived with an awe
heightened by the magnificence of the mountain surroundings?
And may we not say that Jesus went through an experience of
self-dedication to His Father's will as He now saw it in all its
sombre significance? ('They spoke of the *exodus* that he was
about to accomplish at Jerusalem.') We need only add that
there are many recorded observations of a luminous glow trans-
figuring the faces of saints at prayer.[1]

What of the disciples' experience? It was only a week after
Peter's confession. They knew that He was the Messiah; but
along with that realisation had come another disclosure still
more startling—the doctrine of the Cross. If, in one way, the
mystery of Jesus' person had been illumined for them, in another
way it had been deepened and intensified. The disciples were in
a state of tension. They were also 'heavy with sleep.' May we
not say that an imaginative release of this tension was inevitable
and that it expressed itself in vision and audition? In this vision
and audition the imaginative materials in their minds—their
conviction of Jesus' Messiahship, His place in the divine economy
of history, His relation to the Law (Moses) and the Prophets
(Elijah)—were projected outwards. They saw Moses and Elijah
with Jesus. They heard a divine endorsement of Jesus as God's
Messiah.

Was the vision genuine, and if it was, what did it signify?
The criterion of the genuineness of any vision is not in its form
but in its spiritual content. That this was a genuine, a divinely-
caused vision, no Christian will deny. In it God set the seal on
Peter's confession, confirmed the truth of Jesus' Messiahship to
the disciples, even if the doctrine of a suffering Messiah was to
remain for them a great stumbling-block (Mk. ix. 30–32).

(The alternative to this explanation in terms of the psychology
of mysticism seems to me to be that in terms of spiritualism.
So Conan Doyle in *The New Revelation*, p. 79, speaks of 'the
materialisation of the two prophets on the mountain' and says
that Peter, James and John 'formed the psychic circle' through
which the miracle was done. He adds that the high pure air of
the mountain and the shining robes consist well with his explanation.)

As they descend from the mountain, Jesus bids the disciples
be silent about their experience till the Son of man be risen
from the dead. The disciples are puzzled. Had He said 'till

[1] A friend of Sadhu Sundar Singh noted 'a faint luminosity' about the
Sadhu's face as he prayed alone. See Leslie Weatherhead, *His Life and Ours*,
108.

Resurrection Day,' they would not have been so. What puzzled them was what this resurrection from the dead could mean and why scripture could say that so glorious a figure as the Son of man must suffer. 'Must not Elijah come first, as the scribes say?' they asked Jesus. 'Yes,' He replied, 'Elijah must first come. But, in fact, Elijah has already come, and they have served him, as scripture said they would' (1 Kings xix. 2, 10). John had found his Jezebel in Herodias.

There follows the story of how Jesus on His descent from the mountain cured an epileptic boy (Mk. ix. 14–29).

VIII
THE MIGHTY WORKS

If we were writing a philosophical treatise on miracles, we might begin, as Mr. C. S. Lewis does,[1] with a bold definition: 'I use the word *miracle* to mean an interference with Nature by supernatural power,' and prepare to meet the objectors. Our purpose is more modest; and it will suffice to say, at the outset, that in the New Testament miracles are regarded not as 'interferences' but as tokens of a new order of life inaugurated by the coming of Christ. In this way, we shall get the Gospel miracles in their proper perspective.

The Gospels assert that Jesus wrought many wonderful cures on men's bodies and souls, and exercised on occasion an extraordinary control over what we call 'inanimate nature.' These exhibitions of extraordinary power are called in the Synoptic Gospels 'mighty works' (δυνάμεις) and in the Fourth Gospel 'signs' (σημεῖα), the last word underlining the spiritual significance of the 'mighty work.'

Miracles bulk large in the Gospels. Moreover, we find the miraculous element in the Gospel tradition as far back as we can go. In Mark, the earliest Gospel, 209 verses out of a total of 661 deal, directly or indirectly, with miracle, i.e. over 31 per cent. If it be objected that our other primary source, Q, contains only one or two miracles, the explanation is that Q was not a Gospel but a collection of Jesus' sayings. Furthermore, the teaching of Jesus in Q implies miracle. We need look no further than Jesus' reply to the Baptist's question: 'Go your way and tell John what things ye have seen and heard; the blind receive their sight, the lame walk, the lepers are cleansed, and the deaf hear, the dead are raised up, and the poor have good tidings preached to them' (Lk. vii. 22=Mt. xi. 4f.). In short, the story of Jesus was told from the very beginning as the story of One who wrought miracles. Miracles are not accidental but integral to the Gospel tradition. We can no more eliminate them from the record than we can remove a watermark from a sheet of paper.[2]

---

[1] *Miracles*, 15.

[2] My count of the miracles of Jesus, according to sources, yields these statistics: Mark, 17; Q, 2; L, 6; and M, 1. There are also a few references to mass healings. 'Miracle,' writes Dr. W. Manson, 'is not a late importation into the tradition of Jesus, but constitutes the primary stratum' (*Jesus the Messiah*, 45f.).

THE SIGNIFICANCE OF THE MIRACLES

What is the place and purpose of miracles in the story of Jesus?

The traditional theory is that their purpose was evidential. They were designed to prove the heavenly origin of Jesus, to accredit Him as the divine Son of God.

This view is open to serious objections. To begin with, Jesus did not work miracles in order to call attention to His message, or credentials. On the contrary, He deliberately refused to give signs. 'There shall no sign be given to this generation' (Mk. viii. 12; Lk. xi. 29, Q). Moreover, this theory does violence to the close connection between miracles and faith. Worst of all, it portrays Jesus as a sort of 'heavenly bellman,' calling attention to His divinity by His miracles. Yet, as we shall see, the miracles of Jesus were signs—Messianic signs—for those who had eyes to see.

Very different is the modernistic approach to the miracles, of which we may take the German scholar Harnack as example: 'We are firmly convinced,' he says, 'that what happens in space and time is subject to the general laws of motion, and that in this sense, as an interruption of the order of nature, there can be no such things as miracles.'[1]

The modernist tends to see miracles as interruptions of the sacrosanct order of nature, intrusions into a world which is 'a closed system' of cause and effect. Not surprisingly he shares Matthew Arnold's view that 'miracles do not happen' and tends to dismiss the mighty works of Jesus, and especially the nature-miracles, as legendary accretions to the story which arose, intelligibly enough, in a miracle-mongering age.

The only difficulty about this view is that it assumes the answer to the one question that really matters, Is nature a closed system, quite impervious to intrusions from super-nature? To this point we shall come back. Meantime, we must say that neither of these views will do. The miracles of Jesus are not seals attached to the document (as the traditionalist avers) but part of the document itself. Nor are they (as the modernist avers) a semi-legendary frame to be discarded, but part of the picture itself.

How then are miracles regarded in the Gospels themselves? Modern scholarship yields a truer view. The miracles (it says) are not a mere addendum to the message of Jesus but an integral part of it. They are tokens of the coming of God's Reign in Jesus. They are the Kingdom of God in action—God's sovereign grace

[1] *What is Christianity?*, 28f.

and forgiveness operative in Christ. 'If I by the finger of God cast out devils,' says Jesus, 'then is the kingdom of God come upon you' (Lk. xi. 20=Mt. xii. 28, Q; cf. Mk. iii. 22–30). The miracles are signs, after all, but only signs for those whose spiritual insight enables them to discern the sovereign saving activity of God in Jesus.

THE CHARACTERISTICS OF THE MIRACLES

Looking at the miracles from the human side, we observe, first, the emphasis which Jesus sets on faith as the pre-condition of these miraculous events. Faith in Jesus' God-given power to heal is their pre-requisite; and where such faith is lacking, as at Nazareth (Mk. vi. 5), miracles are not easily wrought. 'Thy faith hath saved thee,' Jesus tells the woman with the issue of blood and Bartimaeus. 'Fear not, only have faith,' is His word to Jairus. 'All things are possible to him who has faith,' He assures the father of the epileptic lad. And so on. It is also noteworthy that both the tragic realm within man and the tragic element in human life—disease and disorder of every kind—are alike regarded as spheres of conquest for the victorious energy of faith.

Second, we note the emphasis Jesus sets on the power of prayer. We moderns impressed by 'the steel-and-concrete' order of nature, timidly ask, 'What may we pray for?' 'All things,' says Jesus, 'whatsoever ye pray and ask for, believe that ye have received them, and ye shall have them' (Mk. xi. 24). We wonder whether we may dare ask for material blessings. Jesus, in the disciples' prayer, includes a petition for 'daily bread.' Clearly He believed in the power of prayer to influence the circumstances of life.

But faith and prayer are only one half—the human half—of the secret of the miracles. What shall we say of the divine side? Jesus' own answer can be put in one phrase, 'By the finger of God.' His mighty works are the tokens or signs of the Divine Spirit working in all its plenitude through Him. At His Baptism Jesus knew Himself to be 'the anointed of the Spirit.' Whatever else that meant, it meant equipment with divine power. Except on that assumption the story of the Temptation does not make sense. His words in the Nazareth synagogue point in the same direction. 'The Spirit of the Lord is upon me,' He quotes, 'because he anointed me to preach good tidings to the poor: he hath sent me to proclaim release to the captives, and recovering of sight to the blind, to set at liberty them that are bruised, to proclaim the acceptable year of the Lord' (Lk. iv. 18f., L).

If we take this passage in the context of His ministry, we see that Jesus regarded not only His 'teaching with authority' but also His 'mighty works' as wrought by the Spirit of God through Him. His 'powers' are manifestations of the Supreme Power. His signs are the creative works of the Spirit operating through Him to save sick and sinful men and women. 'The Father that dwelleth in me,' Jesus says in the Gospel according to St. John (Jn. xiv. 10f.), 'he doeth the works.' (Note that in the Apostolic Church also miracles were regarded as manifestations of the Holy Spirit, and see especially Rom. xv. 18f. and Heb. ii. 3f.)

THE CREDIBILITY OF THE MIRACLES

We come, last of all, to the question of the credibility of the miracles. Can a modern Christian who values his intellectual integrity accept them?

Before we attempt an answer to this question, there are two important things to be said.

First of all, and granting for the moment the possibility of miracles, we must say that in every case it is a matter of historical evidence. Before we can accept any particular miracle, we must satisfy ourselves that there is sufficient historical evidence for it. After all, a miracle, on any definition, is an abnormal event. It needs good evidence. (Thus, we should need only slight evidence if anyone told us that he had seen King George VI riding in Windsor Great Park. But we should require quite over-whelming evidence if a man told us that he had seen Charles I riding in the Park with his head underneath his arm.[1]) Further-more, to be good evidence, it needs to be early evidence—evidence not too far removed in time from the event, and evidence given by a competent witness. If we use this criterion, it is obvious that some of Jesus' miracles are better attested than others. For example, the feeding of the multitude which occurs in all four Gospels and, in Mark, takes us back to about a generation after the actual event, is better attested than the turning of water into wine which occurs only in the Fourth Gospel, written two generations after the ministry of Jesus. Furthermore, doubt about any miracle does not discredit all.

The second thing to remember about the miracles of Jesus is that they belong to an age which had no doctrine of 'secondary causes' and sought a supernatural explanation for any event that baffled popular understanding. We, who have a better understanding of such secondary causes, are therefore entitled to

---

[1] I owe this illustration to Harold Anson.

rationalise the miracles of Jesus, provided that our 'explanation' does not caricature the historical evidence. Thus, to pick two examples from Mark, we may take quite literally Jesus' words about Jairus's daughter, 'The child is not dead but sleepeth' and explain this as a case of coma. Or in the story of the Gerasene maniac we may reasonably question Mark's statement that Jesus transferred the evil spirits to the swine (as being something quite 'out of character' in Jesus) and, while refusing to doubt that Jesus cured the maniac, hold rather that the wild gesticulations of the maniac sent the swine into a headlong panic.

With these two observations, we may now essay a general answer to the question of credibility.

It is true to say that the healing miracles of Jesus impose no real strain on a Christian's faith. We are beginning to remember that man is 'psychosomatic' and to recognise the potent part played by the mind in the cause and cure of disease. We all know something of the achievements of modern psychotherapy in cases of blindness, paralysis and various nervous disorders. And there is the ever-accumulating evidence of spiritual healing. All these things conspire to bring Christ's healing miracles within the range, if not of our powers, at least of our credence. To be sure, we cannot match the speed of His cures, nor can we heal at a distance. But when (to put it at the lowest) we remember the extraordinary personality of Jesus, we shall wisely refuse to say that we will accept only those healing miracles which we, with our present knowledge and skill, can accomplish. And the secret of His cures at a distance (the Syro-Phœnician woman's daughter and the centurion's servant) is surely to be sought in the person of Jesus and the realm of prayer.

Ultimately, it is the nature miracles (the feeding of the multitude, the stilling of the storm, and the walking on the water) which make men hesitate. Here we may try rationalisation. Thus, it may be that the feeding was simply a sacramental meal and that the whole story is historical except the statement that 'all were filled.' It may be that instead of walking on the water Jesus was actually only wading in the surf, as St. John's account may well be taken to mean.[1] And it may be that what Jesus stilled was not the gale of wind on the Lake but the storm of fear in the disciples' hearts.

There may be truth in the first two suggestions, but the third is an obvious caricature of the evidence. Rationalisations of this kind always leave us with the feeling that, if this was all that happened, the story would never have been told. In the

[1] 'In John there is no miracle whatever' (Bernard, *St. John*, 185).

last resort, therefore, our verdict on the miracles will depend on two things.

The first is our world-view. Here it must be allowed that the last fifty years have seen a great advance. Those days are gone in which scientists could affirm downrightly that events like nature miracles, being flagrant interruptions of the immutable reign of natural law, were impossible. The 'laws of nature' are now seen to be merely convenient summaries of existing knowledge; and the discoveries of the last few decades (wireless waves, the splitting of the atom and so forth) have shown us that reality as perceived by us is by no means identical with reality in itself. In fine, our men of science have grown much more modest, are readier to avow human nescience in the face of ultimate mysteries, and are willing to admit that there are more things in heaven and earth than they hitherto dreamed. Beyond doubt, this change in the intellectual climate has made the case against the nature miracles less formidable.

This brings us to the second and fundamental thing: our estimate of Jesus. In the last resort, all turns on what we think about Him. If a man can see in Jesus only a prophet, then, while he may accept the healing miracles—or many of them—he will reject the nature miracles. But if Jesus was, and is, what Christians have always believed Him to be, the Son of God in a unique and lonely sense; if in Him the Spirit of the living God was uniquely incarnated; if His will was completely synonymous with the divine Will; then there is nothing inherently absurd or incredible in the supposition that such a one must have had control over the great frame of Nature itself. In other words, grant 'the Grand Miracle' of the Incarnation, and the main objection to the other miracles falls to the ground. The issue has been memorably put by a recent writer with whose words we may close this discussion:

'If the universe is dominated by a Spirit, miracles are possible; if by a Spirit that is Love, probable; and if that Spirit has become incarnate, this miracle would make further ones very probable indeed.'[1]

[1] T. E. Jessop, *The Christian Faith*, 15.

IX

THE TRAINING OF THE TWELVE

In his essay, 'The Twelve Men,' dealing with the British jury, the late G. K. Chesterton wrote: 'Whenever our civilisation wants a library to be catalogued, or a solar system discovered, or any other trifle of that kind, it uses up its specialists. But when it wishes anything done which is really serious, it collects twelve of the ordinary men standing round. The same thing was done, if I remember right, by the Founder of Christianity.' It is Jesus' choice and training of these twelve 'ordinary men' which we are now to study. 'Disciples' we call them, but it may be that, as Professor T. W. Manson has suggested, the Aramaic word Jesus used meant not 'student' but 'apprentice,' and 'their discipleship was not matriculation in a rabbinical school but apprenticeship to the work of the Kingdom.'[1]

THE THREE STAGES

We can trace three stages in Jesus' relations with His disciples which we may alliteratively style their call, their choice and their commission.

First comes the call, probably near Capernaum, of two pairs of brothers—Peter and Andrew, James and John—from their fishing-nets (Mk. i. 16–20; cf. Lk. v. 1–11, L and Jn. i. 35ff.). The only other call singled out by Mark for description is that of Levi, or Matthew ('gift of God'), perhaps the name given him by Jesus (Mk. ii. 14; cf. Mt. ix. 9). No doubt these calls were typical of others unrecorded. The call is 'Follow me' and the promise is that He will make them 'fishers of men.' The dramatic suddenness of the call does not mean that the two pairs of brothers had no previous knowledge of Jesus (cf. Jn. i. 35ff.), nor does Mark's record say expressly, though it may imply it, that the hour of the Lake-side call meant the irrevocable abandonment of their old trade.

The next stage—the choice—is recorded in Mk. iii. 13f.: 'And he goeth up into the mountain [perhaps, more generally, "the hill-country"] and he calleth unto him whom he would, and they went unto him. And he appointed twelve that they might be with him, and that he might send them forth to preach and to have authority to cast out devils.' Thus the second stage of

---

[1] *The Teaching of Jesus*, 237–240.

close discipleship points forward to the third stage, apostleship. This call of twelve men, the number of the tribes of Israel, was an acted parable in the manner of the old prophets. By His choice of twelve men Jesus proclaimed His intention to create a new Israel; and wherever He appeared with His twelve men the number itself would say to all men of insight, 'This is the Messiah and the new People of God.'

Twelve men formed the inner circle of disciples, and within that circle there was a still smaller one—Peter, James and John, 'elect of the elect.' We are not sure of all their names—see Mk. iii. 16–19; Lk. vi. 14–16; Mt. x. 2–4 and Acts i. 13—and know little about most of them:

Peter and Andrew, James and John, Matthew (Levi) and Thomas, Philip and Bartholomew, James the son of Alphaeus and Thaddaeus, Simon the Zealot and Judas Iscariot. For Thaddaeus in this list (which is Matthew's and Mark's) Luke has 'Judas, the son of James' (cf. Jn. xiv. 22, 'Judas, not Iscariot'). Possibly they are one and the same person (Thaddaeus= Theudas=Judas?).

Of Peter we know most, for he was the spokesman of the Twelve. His nickname, *Cephas*, is something of a puzzle. Was it given him at his call, or at the choice of the Twelve, or at Caesarea Philippi? And why did Jesus call him a 'rock'? In the Gospels he is hardly rock-like. Was the name given in order to steady him, or did Jesus who 'knew what was in man,' foresee his ultimate staunchness and fidelity (cf. Lk. xxii. 31f., L)?[1]

The other nickname *Boanerges* bestowed on James and John is also puzzling. Does it mean, as Lk. ix. 54, L suggests, that there was something of the thunderstorm in their nature? Or does the title playfully refer to their place in the New Order? (Cf. Mk. x. 37 and Bengel's comment: 'Jesus alludes to two scribes who were accustomed to sit in the Council, the one counting the suffrages of those who were to be acquitted, the other of those to be condemned?') Or can it be that *Boanerges* is *Benē Regesh*, i.e. 'sons of perception,' or, as we should say, 'men of insight,' James and John, with Peter, being chosen to accompany our Lord on certain high and searching occasions like the Transfiguration and the Agony?

The other Simon in the band, Simon the Cananaean or

[1] Cf. Temple, *Readings in St. John's Gospel*, 29. '*Thou art Simon.* You are the man we know well; and what we know is that you are eager, impulsive, generous, loyal and essentially unreliable. But that is going to be altered. One day you shall be called by a name that no one would give you now— Rock-man.'

Zealot, possibly belonged to the political party who later bore that name, and whose rallying-ground was Galilee.[1] Matthew (Levi) was one of the despised tax-gatherers and possibly a man of some education. Judas seems to have been the only non-Galilean in the band, if, as his second name seems to mean, he was 'a man from Kerioth.'

Twelve men, then, belonging to what we might call the lower middle-class—a tax-gatherer, a revolutionary, four fishermen, and the rest we know not what—such were the Twelve whom Jesus chose. More than twenty years later St. Paul could describe the Christians in Corinth as 'not many wise men after the flesh, not many mighty, not many noble' (1 Cor. i. 26); but it had been true in the first place of the men whom Jesus called to be the nucleus of the new Israel.

The third stage of the story of the disciples was the Mission. (See Mk. vi. 7–13, 30; Mt. x. 1–42; Lk. ix. 1–6 and x. 1–20. Since all four Gospel sources—Mk., Q, M and L—had a version of the Mission 'charge,' we may call it one of the best-attested facts in the life of Jesus. Notice that Luke has two missions and two charges. The first, Lk. ix. 1–6, comes from Mk. vi. 6–13. The second, Lk. x. 1–20, a mixture of Q and L, is associated with the mission of the Seventy. It may be that this latter is a doublet of the mission of the Twelve.)

The twelve disciples now become, for the time being at least, 'apostles,' i.e. envoys of Jesus. The time has come to test the results of their training (and to prepare them for future missions beyond the Cross). So Jesus sends them forth two by two, no doubt on the sound scriptural basis that 'two are better than one' (Eccles. iv. 8f.). If we ask what is the purpose of their mission, the answer is that it is to gather the People of God, to win men and women ready to accept the good news of the Reign of God which it is their calling to proclaim by word and deed. Jesus sends them out 'like men carrying the Fiery Cross through a Highland glen,' and before they go, He gives them their 'marching orders.'

First, they are to travel light. Dispensing with food, collecting bag, or money, they are to carry only a stick, a pair of sandals and one tunic. (Matthew denies them even sandals and stick, and Luke the stick. Mark must be right here.)

Second, they are to preach and heal. Mark tells us simply that they preached 'repentance.' But from Luke and Matthew

[1] Since the name Zealot was not used to describe a sect or party earlier than A.D. 66, Lake and Jackson think the title may describe not his politics but his character, i.e. 'Simon the zealous' or 'Simon the enthusiast.'

we learn that they were to preach the advent of God's Reign: 'Heal the sick and say, The Reign of God has come nigh upon you' (Lk. x. 9; cf. Mt. x. 7). This was the selfsame message as Christ's (Mk. i. 15). They were to be the messengers of the Kingdom; their credentials the power to exorcise and heal.

Third, they are to observe certain rules of hospitality. With well-wishers they are to stay; but, if others reject their message, they are to waste no time, but quit them with a solemn gesture ('the sacrament of failure,' as John Oman called it).

Fourth (and this point we derive not from Mark, but from Q), they are never to forget whose ambassadors they are. 'He who receives you, receives me; and he who receives me, receives him that sent me' (Mt. x. 40: Lk. x. 16; cf. Mk. ix. 37). They are the accredited envoys of Jesus, and, through Him, of the King of kings.

Then the curtain falls on their mission, save for one incident during the mission—the case of the strange exorcist (Mk. ix. 38ff.) which clearly belongs to a time when the Twelve were separated from Jesus; and we hear no more of the missioners until they return and report to Jesus.

Was the mission a success? We remember that later in His ministry Jesus was moved to lament that He had tried in vain to gather God's People together 'as a hen doth gather her brood under her wings.' Yet there is evidence enough that Jesus did not regard His sending out of the Twelve as a failure. 'I watched Satan fall like lightning from heaven' (Lk. x. 17ff., L; cf. Mk. vi. 30). Jesus saw in the mission a decisive crisis. The Power of Evil, He commented, is already toppling from his throne.

Call, Choice, Mission—these are the three stages in the relations of Jesus with His disciples. There was to be a fourth—what we may call the Consecration—in the Upper Room on the last night.

THE INSTRUCTION OF THE DISCIPLES

What did Jesus teach His disciples? According to Mk. iv. 11, He initiated them into 'the mystery of the kingdom of God,' i.e. the paradox that the Reign of God was already existent on earth for those who had eyes to see it. And after Peter's confession He laboured to initiate them into a still deeper mystery—that before that Reign could come 'with power' the Son of man must die. No doubt also He imparted to them something of His own unique knowledge of the Father who was King in the Kingdom, 'All things have been delivered unto me of my Father,' He said.

'and no one knoweth who the Son is, save the Father; and who the Father is save the Son, and he to whomsoever the Son willeth to reveal him' (Lk. x. 22=Mt. xi. 27, Q). So He said, and we cannot doubt that the disciples were of those to whom the Son willed to reveal the Father. (Dr. T. W. Manson[1] has argued that the Fatherhood of God was not part of Jesus' preaching to the general public but a mystery disclosed to the disciples. Centuries before Plato had said: 'To find the maker and father of this universe is a hard task, and when you have found him, it is impossible to speak of him before all the people.' So it was with Jesus. He did not speak publicly about God as Father, but privately to His close followers and friends. For them, He made the Father real not by argument or much speaking but because it was obvious that the Father was the supreme reality of His own life.)

He taught His disciples also what we call the Lord's Prayer but which would be better called 'The Disciples' Prayer' (Mt. vi. 9–13, M; Lk. xi. 2–4, L). In it He bade them pray for the hallowing of the Father's name, the fuller coming of His Reign, the doing of His will on earth as it is done in heaven; and then, turning from divine to human things, He bade them ask for sufficient bread for the coming day, for divine forgiveness for daily sins, and for deliverance from the power of evil.

Initiation into the mystery of the Kingdom and the Cross, some disclosure of the Divine Fatherhood, a pattern prayer—what else must we add to this summary of Jesus' instruction to His disciples?

Last of all, He gave them 'a design for life in the kingdom of God.'[2] The outline of this design has been preserved for us by St. Matthew and St. Luke in the Sermon which both of them record (Mt. v–vii; Lk. vi. 20–49. Observe that Luke's Sermon of some 30 verses probably represents the Sermon as it stood in Q. Matthew's Sermon on the Mount which runs to 107 verses contains some 45 verses from Q plus 62 from his special source, M. In what follows we shall follow the outline given in Matthew).

Here is an analysis[3] of the Sermon followed by a brief summary:

Design for Life in the Kingdom of God (Mt. v–vii)

A. The Life described:

    (*a*) its characteristics (the Beatitudes)   v. 3–12

    (*b*) its influence (salt and light)   v. 13–16

---

[1] *The Teaching of Jesus*, Chap. iv.   [2] The phrase is Professor Dodd's.

[3] Based on Votaw's analysis in *H.D.B.*, Vol. V.

B. Its Relation to the Old Order v. 17–20

C. Its Outworkings:
- (*a*) in thought, word and deed (6 antitheses)   v. 21–48
- (*b*) in worship (almsgiving, prayer and fasting)   vi. 1–18
- (*c*) in trust and devotion   vi. 19–34
- (*d*) in treatment of others   vii. 1–12

D. The Way of Life: profession and practice   vii. 13–27

The Sermon begins with a series of arresting paradoxes which we know as the Beatitudes. In them Jesus sketches, so to speak, the portrait of the man whose life illustrates the Reign of God. The men of the Kingdom will be as salt which purifies and as light which illumines a corrupt and dark world (v. 3–16).

The Messiah does not come to destroy the Law and the Prophets, i.e. the religion of the old order, but to fulfil them—to bring out their true meaning and purpose; and His followers' righteousness must surpass that of the scribes and the Pharisees (v. 17–20).

The will of God had been revealed to the men of the old order but their apprehension of it had been imperfect. So, in a series of antitheses, Jesus sets forth the way of life demanded of those who live under the new order of the Kingdom. It is a way of life in which not only the overt acts of murder, adultery, perjury and revenge but even the evil passions which inspire them—anger, lust, swearing and the wish to retaliate—have no place; in which the old *lex talionis* with its 'eye for an eye' is outmoded and transcended by forgiving love, a love which goes out, beyond neighbours, even to enemies, a love as catholic as the love of God Himself (v. 21–48).

When they give alms, pray or fast, the men of the Kingdom will aim at reality. These things they will do with utter sincerity towards God and with no thought for the glory these will bring them in the eyes of men; for ostentation of that kind brings no reward from the heavenly Father. In praying they will avoid all 'vain repetition' and 'much speaking,' taking as their pattern the Abba-Father Prayer which, putting first things first, begins with three petitions for the greater glory of God (the hallowing of His name, the coming of His Reign, the doing of His will) before going on to the needs of men (provision, pardon and protection) (vi. 1–18).

Furthermore, the new way of life demands detachment from earthly treasures: the only true treasures are the heavenly ones, and men must be single-minded in their devotion to God. Freedom from worry, born of a serene faith in God's over-ruling

E

Providence, must mark the men of the Kingdom (vi. 19–34).

The new way of life demands also an end to censorious judgement of our fellows. Holy things are not to be profaned. In prayer, they are to 'ask, seek, and knock,' assured that God will give good things to His children; and they are to find their whole duty to their fellow men epitomised in the Golden Rule (vii. 1–12).

Then, in the epilogue, by means of three illustrations (the two ways, the two trees and the two foundations), Jesus insists that practice must square with profession. The way to eternal life is strait and narrow, and many miss it. Let them beware of false guides in religion. These are to be known by their fruits. The true test is not that of merely verbal profession, but of readiness to do the Father's will. To hear Christ's words and to do them is to build on rock which will endure; to be a hearer only, and not a doer, is to build on shifting sand (vii. 13–27).

Such is Jesus' design for life in the Kingdom of God. How much of it is new and original? Jewish scholars often produce parallels to various sayings of Jesus from the sayings of the great rabbis like Hillel, and some declare, 'All of it is in the *Talmud.*' We may feel inclined to retort (with Wellhausen): 'All—and how much more!' But the fact of such parallels should not surprise or shock us, if indeed Jesus 'came not to destroy but to fulfil' and if, as Ambrose says, 'all truth by whomsoever uttered is of the Holy Ghost.' If truth is eternal, and if God is one, is not this just what we might reasonably expect? Nonetheless, after all parallels have been adduced, there remain passages in the Sermon, e.g. v. 38–48, which, as Montefiore and other Jewish scholars allow, go beyond anything in Judaism. And, by common consent, there is nowhere in literature a body of ethical teaching comparable with the Sermon on the Mount.

More important than the problem of originality is the problem of the place and purpose of the ethical teaching in the mission and message of Jesus. At the risk of repetition we must emphasise one or two points. The first is that the ethic of Jesus presupposes the Gospel of the Kingdom. 'The implied major premiss of all Christ's ethical sayings,' declares C. H. Dodd,[1] 'is the affirmation, The Kingdom of God has come upon you.' In other words, the way of life described in the Sermon is the way for those men who acknowledge one supreme loyalty, and in whose heart one supreme passion burns—loyalty to Jesus the Messiah and the passion for the Kingdom of God. What we have in the Sermon is not (as Tolstoi and others have thought) a new law to be

[1] *History and the Gospel*, 125.

literally fulfilled by all men in this world. The Sermon is essentially *disciple-teaching*, teaching for those who, though they must
live in this world, have their true citizenship elsewhere.

In the Sermon Jesus gave His disciples not so much a new
law (though Matthew's presentation of it may well give that
impression) as a design for living. In it He set them, as He sets
us, an ideal to aim at, and a standard to judge themselves by.
And what an ideal it is! No man measures up to it: the greatest
saints, judging themselves by it, know themselves to be sinners.
(In a sense then it is the greatest indictment of sin in literature.
There is no account of sin to match the Sermon.) Yet if neither
the first disciples, nor we, ever attained, or will attain, to the
moral heights to which God in Christ calls us in the Sermon, that
is but an illustration of the tension between the ideal and the
actual which must mark the lives of Christ's disciples, now as
then; for we have to live our lives at once as citizens of the
world, with all its trials and temptations, and as citizens of the
Kingdom of God.

'His ethic,' it has been said, 'stands for the unattainable which
yet we are bound to attain.'[1] Thus and thus, said Jesus in the
Sermon, God wills that His children should live as citizens of
the Kingdom. Though we, no more than the first disciples, can
ever hope to reach the ideal in this world, yet we are called on
day by day as Christ's disciples to make the effort. For it is the
design for life in the Kingdom of God.

[1] W. Manson, *Jesus the Messiah*, 85.

X

JESUS' TEACHING ABOUT
THE KINGDOM OF GOD

One phrase sums up the meaning of our Lord's mission and message. It is the Kingdom of God. If we can discover what Jesus meant by it, we have the key to the Gospels and, indeed, to the whole New Testament.

But the phrase is one thing, its interpretation quite another. The odds are that if we ask half a dozen men what they mean by the phrase, we shall get half a dozen different answers. Some will be in terms of natural evolution, others in terms of super-natural revolution. Every man is prone to read into the phrase his own dream of the Good Time Coming. The social reformer construes it in terms of some renovated social order to be built on 'the principles of Jesus'; the philosopher thinks of some ideal polity; the adventist dreams of some cataclysmic coming of Christ. Here are some definitions collected almost at random. The American Socialist Bouck White says: 'The modern reader can perhaps grasp the Kingdom of Heaven as Jesus used it by substituting for it in every case another term: the kingdom of self-respect.'[1] An Anglican preacher like the late Dick Sheppard can write: 'The Kingdom of God as our Lord intended it for us is the condition of living in which love spelt with a capital L really gets busy and wins through.'[2] The Methodist writer George Jackson defines it as 'a spiritual commonwealth embracing all who do God's will.'[3]

If we turn for light to the scholars and theologians, we do not find any greater unanimity. For Ritschl, the Kingdom of God was 'the organisation of humanity through action inspired by love.' But for his son-in-law Johannes Weiss it was some catas-trophic act of divine power which would make an end of the existing world and usher in miraculously the new order of God. For theological Liberals like Adolf Harnack or the late C. J. Cadoux, the Kingdom of God was essentially the Rule of God in the hearts of men, Cadoux defining it as 'men's loyal compliance with God's will.'[4] And for the Roman Catholic theologian, following Augustine, the Kingdom of God is to be identified

---

[1] Quoted by Dodd, *Parables of the Kingdom*, 35.
[2] In *Asking them Questions*, 24.   [3] *The Teaching of Jesus*, 87.
[4] *The Historic Mission of Jesus*, 115.

with the Church, and we need not ask which Church. *Regnum Dei* is *Ecclesia Romana*.

If, unbewildered by this variety of definitions, we are temerarious enough to ask how the Kingdom of God comes, we shall get all sorts of answers, from the unashamed synergism of W. P. Merrill's hymn—

> Rise up, O men of God,
>   His Kingdom tarries long,
> Bring in the day of brotherhood
> And end the night of wrong

to the rather cruel parody of the Barthian view produced by an S.C.M. student:

> Sit down, O men of God!
>   His Kingdom he will bring
> Whenever it may please his will.
> You cannot do a thing.

Amid this chaos of conflicting definitions our only remedy is to hark back to the Gospels and try to win an understanding of this all-important phrase.

THE MEANING OF *BASILEIA*

If there is one point on which our philologists agree, it is that 'Kingdom of God' is not a happy translation. The Hebrew *malkuth* (as also the Aramaic *malkutha*) does not mean 'kingdom' in the sense of a territory to be governed. It means 'sovereignty' or 'kingly rule.' We ought therefore to translate the *Basileia* of the Gospels by 'Reign' or 'Rule.' (It is a pity that among our modern translators only Moffatt has the courage of his scholarship to render the word usually by 'Reign.') Yet since a Reign or Rule does not operate in the void—since it implies a sphere of rule—since, moreover, in the Gospels the *Basileia* is something which a man can enter, from which he can be excluded, we may reserve the right (as Moffatt does) in a few passages to render *Basileia* by 'Realm.' But the dominant meaning is always that of God acting in His kingly power, exercising His sovereignty.

The other point on which there is agreement is that there is no difference of meaning between 'the Kingdom of God' (which is the usual phrase) and 'the Kingdom of heaven,' the phrase preferred by Matthew. Matthew's preference simply illustrates the pious Jew's avoidance of the ineffable Name. But mere linguistics will not take us to the heart of the matter.

THE JEWISH BACKGROUND

What did the phrase 'the Reign of God' mean for a Jew in our Lord's time?

For Jesus' contemporaries it might mean three things:

Eternal sovereignty   (*a*) God is now and always King: His Reign is eternal, and therefore beyond time. This is a thought that finds expression in the Psalms:

> Thy kingdom is an everlasting kingdom
> And thy dominion endureth throughout all generations.
>
> (Ps. cxlv. 13.)

Covenant Relationship   (*b*) God's Reign is, however, only partly recognised. Israel is His special People, and among them His Rule is realised in so far as Israel obeys His will revealed in the Law. Thus, according to the rabbis, if a man daily recites the *Shema* (Dt. vi. 4), he is said to 'take upon himself the yoke of the divine sovereignty.'[1]

Divine Intervention   (*c*) But there was a third sense in which they spoke of the Reign of God. God might be sovereign of the world in the *faith* of the pious Jew; but *in fact* He was not acknowledged as such. Amidst the evil and misery of the present the pious Jew dreamed of a blessed time when the living God would finally manifest His Rule, overthrow the powers of evil and show His grace and mercy to His faithful people. So Jews in the first century prayed, as they still pray, 'May He establish His Kingdom during your life and during your days, and during the life of all the houses of Israel' (from the *Kaddish*). And so a Pharisaic quietist, somewhere between A.D. 7 and 30 (according to Charles), wrote of the coming Kingdom:

> And then His Kingdom shall appear throughout all His creation
> And then Satan shall be no more,
> And sorrow shall depart with him. . . .[2]

These three senses we may call respectively: the eternal sovereignty, the covenant relationship and the divine intervention. We may sum them up in a single sentence: 'The eternal sovereignty of God, now acknowledged in Israel, will one day be effectively manifested in the world.'

[1] Dalman, *Words of Jesus*, 96f.
[2] *The Assumption of Moses*, chap. x, 1.

It is the third sense that matters now. In this sense the Reign of God is an eschatological idea. When we say 'eschatological,' we use the term not in the popular sense which seems to think only of post-mortem rewards in heaven and hell but in the Jewish sense. Eschatology means the doctrine of the End—*the eschaton*—the End conceived as God's age-long and final purpose destined to be realised in the future and to give meaning to the whole historical process. Now, in Jewish thought, the Reign of God (in this third sense) is the one great hope of the future—it is the *eschaton* with which all eschatology is concerned. It is another term for the Good Time Coming, the Messianic Age, and it connotes the whole salvation of God.

Before we turn to the New Testament, one thing more must be said. One of the most surprising features in recent New Testament research has been the scholars' return to the Old Testament as the key to the understanding of the New. After ransacking all sorts of sources, Jewish and Greek (and, we may add, starting all sorts of 'hares,' some of which have not run very well) they are re-discovering the truth of Augustine's *dictum*, 'The New Testament lies hidden in the Old, and the Old is made plain in the New.' In particular, they are learning how important for the understanding of our Lord's mission and message are the prophecies of Second Isaiah. Indeed, we might almost say that the Gospel is 'deutero-Isaianic.' Thus, it is in words from Isa. xlii that Jesus hears God speak to Him at the Baptism. His sermon in the synagogue at Nazareth takes up some great words from Isa. lxi and declares them to be now fulfilled. With words from Isa. xlix about the strong man and his spoils He replies to the charge of being in league with Satan. Above all, there is abundant evidence that Jesus consciously identified Himself with the Servant of the Lord by whose sacrifice 'the many' were to be redeemed (Isa. liii). Now we must add that it was from the same source that His whole Gospel of the Reign of God took its origin.

More than half a millennium before 'the fulness of the times' the great Unknown whom we call Isaiah of Babylon prophesied the return of the exiles. He saw them coming back triumphantly to Jerusalem with God in their midst and a herald going before them with a *euangelion*—a proclamation of 'good tidings.' Thrice in Isa. xl–lv there is the promise of 'one that bringeth good tidings'; but it is in the last of these passages that we see most clearly the nexus of New and Old Testaments. All Jerusalem is pictured on the walls when suddenly, on the hill-top, the herald appears:

> Look, 'tis the feet of a herald
> Hastening over the hills
> With glad, good news
> With tidings and relief
> Calling aloud to Zion,
> 'Your God reigns.'
> (Isa. lii. 7, Moffatt.)

So Isaiah foresaw the coming of the Reign of God. No doubt
he expected the glorious day to dawn soon. However, in the
providence of God, the stream of that great hope was to run
underground for more than five centuries till the decisive time
came. It came in the reign of the Emperor Tiberius when a
young man from Nazareth appeared in Galilee, saying (in
effect), 'The time which Isaiah foresaw is here. The good news
of the Reign of God is ringing out. Turn again to God and
accept this message as true.' The *eschaton* was becoming fact.
The Reign of God was breaking into history. The final purpose
of God was being realised.

REALISED ESCHATOLOGY

This is what we know nowadays as 'realised eschatology';[1] and,
however we may wish to qualify it, the phrase represents substantial truth. (Out of 27 references to the Kingdom of God in
the primary sources, Mark and Q, no less than 18 imply a
Kingdom that is already present.) 'Realised eschatology' means
two things. First, the Kingdom of God is to be interpreted not as
some moral disposition in the heart of man, or some far-off
earthly Utopia to be built by the effort of man, but as the
decisive intervention of the living God on the stage of human
history in order to 'visit and redeem his people.' Second, the
heart of Jesus' message was that this intervention was no longer
a shining hope on the far horizon but a *fait accompli*. The new
thing in Jesus' preaching (as Otto has said), was not the nature
of the Kingdom, but the fact that it had now come and men
must consider how to get into it.[2] In short, the eternal God was
now laying bare His arm and signally manifesting His sovereignty
in the person and work of Jesus. The Good News is not a pro-
gramme for human action but the proclamation of an act of
God in Jesus.

(*a*) Now let us marshal the evidence. First, there are direct
sayings like:

[1] The phrase was coined by C. H. Dodd.
[2] *The Kingdom of God and the Son of Man*, 47.

'If I by the finger of God cast out devils, then is the Reign of God come upon you' (Lk. xi. 20=Mt. xii. 28, Q).

'Heal the sick [says Jesus to His "missionaries"] and say, The Reign of God has come nigh upon you' (Lk. x. 9=Mt. x. 7, Q).

'The law and the prophets were until John: from that time the gospel of the kingdom of God is preached [lit., "the Reign of God is being gospelled"] and every man entereth violently into it' (Lk. xvi. 16=Mt. xi. 12f., Q).

'The Reign of God is in your midst [or "within you"]' (Lk. xvii. 21, L).[1]

'The publicans and the harlots go into the Realm of God before you' (Mt. xxi. 31, M).

To which we might add many passages which, from their use of the present tense, imply that the Kingdom has come: as Lk. vi. 20, Q, 'Blessed are ye poor, for yours is the Reign of God,' or Lk. ix. 62, L: 'No man, having put his hand to the plough, and looking back, is fit for the Kingdom of God.' Cf. Mk. iv. 11, xii. 34, etc.[2]

(b) Next, there are passages which, though they do not mention the Kingdom, sound the note of fulfilment:

'Blessed are the eyes,' says Jesus to the disciples, 'which see the things that ye see: for I say unto you, that many prophets and kings desired to see the things which ye see, and saw them not; and to hear the things which ye hear, and heard them not' (Lk. x. 23f.=Mt. xiii. 16f., Q).

Or 'the queen of the south shall rise up in the judgement with the men of this generation, and shall condemn them: for she came from the ends of the earth to hear the wisdom of Solomon; and behold something greater than Solomon is here. The men of Nineveh shall stand up in the judgement with this generation, and shall condemn it: for they repented at the preaching of Jonah; and behold, something greater than Jonah is here' (Lk. xi. 31f.=Mt. xii. 41f., Q).

[1] I prefer the rendering of R.V.mg. See the admirable note on the passage in *The Sayings of Jesus*, 303.

[2] In Mk. i. 15 Jesus says, 'The Kingdom of God has drawn nigh (ἤγγικεν).' *Prima facie*, this might sound as if the Kingdom were 'just round the corner.' The Greek verb, however, probably means, 'has come,' as witness:
(1) The immediately preceding words, 'The time is fulfilled.'
(2) The many other passages implying a present kingdom.
(3) In the LXX ἐγγίζειν is often used to render the Hebrew *naga'* and the Aramaic *m'ta*, both of which mean 'reach' or 'arrive.' The same two verbs are also translated by the aorist of Φθάνειν, 'has come,' which is used in Lk. xi. 20: Mt. xii. 28. No difference of meaning is therefore intended between Ἔφθασεν ἐφ'ὑμᾶς ἡ βασιλεία τοῦ Θεοῦ and ἤγγικεν ἡ βασιλεία τοῦ Θεοῦ.

In the first of these sayings Jesus says that what for all former generations lay still in the womb of the future is now a blessed reality—for those who have eyes to see. In the second, the 'something greater' which is now here, is beyond any doubt the Kingdom of God.

The same note rings through Jesus' reply to the Baptist's question from prison: Lk. vii. 22f.=Mt. xi. 4f. Jesus answers John with a list of tokens of the actual presence of the Kingdom. Cf. Lk. iv. 17–21, L.

(c) Finally, we may point to the parables of growth which imply, in one way or another, the fact of a present Kingdom. Of the parables in Mark iv, Bacon has written:

'All four comparisons have a common object, to confirm the glad tidings of a coming kingdom as a power of God already at work. . . . In the group of parables (the Sower, the self-growing Seed, the Mustard Seed) the chief lesson is the present inward working of God's Spirit unseen by dull or hostile eyes, a Kingdom of God which is already in the midst, silent, omnipotent, over-taking unawares those whose spiritual eyes are closed.'[1]

Elsewhere the same truth is implied. The Reign of God is like leaven working among a mass of dough; it is like a Drag-net gathering into its meshes all sorts of fish; it is like a great Supper to which the invitation goes out, 'Come, for all things are now ready.'

We need not multiply the evidence. The conclusion is inescapable. In some decisive sense, the Reign of God has come in the person and work of Jesus. And here we may set the miracles of Jesus in their true light. They are not mere acts of wonder-working such as were sometimes ascribed to thaumaturgists, whether Jewish or Gentile. They are 'the baring of the arm of the Lord for the salvation of men.' Not seals attached to the document, as the traditionalist avers, but part of the document itself; not, as the modernist avers, a semi-legendary frame to be summarily discarded, but part of the picture itself. They are tokens of the inbreaking Reign of God. They are the Kingdom of God in action.

THE KINGDOM AND THE FUTURE

The Reign of God had come. Did Jesus ever say that it would come in the future, and if He did, in what sense?

The relevant passages here are as follows:

[1] *The Story of Jesus*, 212.

Mk.: ix. 1 and xiv. 25.

Q: Mt. viii. 11=Lk. xiii. 28f.

L: Lk. xi. 2, xxii. 16 and xxii. 29f.

M: Mt. vi. 10.

(We have excluded three M sayings: Mt. v. 19f. and xiii. 43, because their authenticity is widely doubted, and Mt. vii. 21, because the Lucan version, 'Why call ye me Lord, Lord, and do not the things which I say' (Lk. vi. 46), which is considered more original, contains no reference to the Kingdom.)

Mk. ix. 1, correctly translated, reads: 'There are some of those standing here who will not taste of death till they see that the reign of God *has come* with power.' The saying contrasts a Kingdom already come with one to come 'with power,' or 'with a miracle.' The clue to its interpretation is in Rom. i. 3f., where Paul says that by the Resurrection God 'appointed' Jesus as the Son of God 'with power.' When therefore Jesus says that the Reign of God will, at some not far distant date, come 'with power,' He is referring to His triumph in the Resurrection and what followed it.[1]

Mk. xiv. 25 is Jesus' saying at the Last Supper: 'I will no more drink of the fruit of the vine until the day when I drink it new (καινόν) in the Kingdom of God.' Here the mention of wine of a new kind—compare the use of 'new' in Rev. xxi. 1—points unmistakably to the transcendent order beyond time and space—to 'a better world than this.' Of the same sort are the two L sayings: Lk. xxii. 16 (probably the L version of the saying we are discussing) and xxii. 29f.: 'Even as my Father appointed a Kingdom for me, I appoint that you may eat and drink at my table in my Kingdom.'[2]

The solitary Q saying, in Matthew's version, reads: 'Many will come from east and west and sit at meat with Abraham, Isaac and Jacob in the Kingdom of heaven.' There is no reference here to a 'coming' of the Kingdom. Moreover, Abraham, Isaac and Jacob, so far as their mortal bodies were concerned, were long dust. The reference is not to any Kingdom destined to come on this earth, or this side eternity, but to the heavenly Kingdom where God's Reign does not come or go but is eternally present.[3]

[1] See Dodd, *Parables of the Kingdom*, 53; Swete, *St. Mark, ad loc.*; and Sanday, *Life of Christ in Recent Research*, 115ff.

[2] Westcott and Hort's punctuation. This translation is adopted by the American R. S. V., Moffatt, Creed, V. Taylor, etc. For 'in *my* Kingdom' we should probably read (with D, some old Latin versions and Syr. Cur.) 'in the Kingdom.'

[3] The reference in Lk. xvi. 22 to 'Abraham's bosom' implies that the patriarchs were already in the heavenly Kingdom.

But did not Jesus bid His disciples pray, 'Thy Kingdom come' (Mt. vi. 10, M, and Lk. xi. 2, L)? And what did He mean by it? In interpreting this petition, we must first lay account with the many sayings which imply, or declare, that in the ministry of Jesus the Kingdom had already, in some sense, come. The prayer must then be for a fuller coming of the Reign of God. If so, we may say that it was in part fulfilled in the Resurrection, Pentecost and the rise of the Church. The other thing to be said is that in the twin parables of the mustard seed which grows into a tree and of the leaven which permeates the whole lump, we have Jesus' own pictorial exegesis of the petition. He bids His disciples pray for a time when the Reign of God will extend its sphere over the earth. And may we not say that in the growth of the World Church, the People of God living under that Reign, we are seeing a further fulfilment of that Prayer?

THE KINGDOM OF GOD

We may now essay an answer to our initial question, What is the Kingdom of God?

It is not a renovated social order built by men, or a cataclysmic end of the world. It cannot be equated with some earthly Utopia or the evolutionary process. Nor can the Kingdom of God be identified with the Church, though the Rule of God implies a people living under that Rule.

It is a divine act, not a divine demand. It is the sovereign saving activity of God. It is His Reign becoming manifestly effective in the world of human experience. It is God in action, God in conflict with evil, through Jesus, for men's salvation. If we say that the Kingdom is 'eschatological'—in the sense of being 'the ultimate thing' in God's ordering of history—we shall be right; but it is *realised* eschatology. If we say that the Kingdom is supernatural, we shall be right again; for it is the living God intervening in history to 'visit and redeem his people.' It is a divine crisis—nay, the divine crisis—in the affairs of men, the crisis which gives meaning to all history before and after it, so that the division of history into B.C. and A.D. is seen to be the only accurate statement of the facts.

Moreover, the Kingdom is God's gift: something God gives, man does not build (Lk. xii. 32, L). ('Our modern idea of labouring for the coming of the Kingdom,' says Vincent Taylor,[1] 'is a noble conception, fully baptised into Christ and expressive of His spirit; but it is not His teaching regarding the *Basileia*.')

[1] *Jesus and His Sacrifice*, 10.

Men receive the Kingdom like little children—as a gift of God's pure grace (Mk. x. 15). Yet it calls for decision. Confronted by it men must make their own choice, and no man who sets hand to the plough and looks back is fit for it (Lk. ix. 62, Q?). Riches are a hindrance to entering it (Mk. x. 23). Yet no sacrifice is too great in order to win its wealth (Mt. xiii. 44–46, M). Indeed, a man must be ready to renounce even hand and foot in order to win 'life' or 'salvation' which is just another name for the Kingdom of God (Mk. x. 17–21).

What then is the relation of the ethical teaching of Jesus to this preaching of His about the Kingdom of God?

Albert Schweitzer, it will be remembered, called the moral teaching of Jesus 'an ethic of the interval'—a code of emergency regulations valid only for the short interval between the preaching of the Gospel and some impending *Parousia* which would end the world-order. The ethical teaching of Jesus is not an interim ethic in Schweitzer's sense. To import a reference to the *Parousia* into Jesus' words about prayer, or forgiveness, or humility, or truthfulness, or trust in God is to read into the Gospel record what is simply not there. Jesus did not say, 'Love your enemies, because the end of the world is at hand.' He bade men love their enemies that, by so doing, they might become sons of their heavenly Father (Mt. v. 44f.=Lk. vi. 35, Q). Yet the ethics of Jesus are eschatological ethics in the sense that they grow out of Jesus' eschatology. But the eschatology is 'realised eschatology,' and the major premiss of Jesus' moral teaching is, 'The Reign of God has come upon you.' In other words, the ethic of the Sermon on the Mount is *the moral ideal* of the Kingdom of God. It is the new way of life for those who live in the new age which has come with the coming of the Kingdom and the King.

THE KINGDOM AND THE CROSS

One big question remains. What is the connection between the Kingdom and the Cross?

Obviously, if the Kingdom of God has, in a real sense, come in the ministry of Jesus, we may not say that Jesus died to bring in the Kingdom of God. The Cross must fall *within* the Kingdom— must be part of the redeeming Rule of God—its burning focus and centre. And here we may ask, Where in scripture is it laid down that the Reign of God involves a Cross? Once again we find the answer in Second Isaiah. If the word 'gospel' as Jesus used it and the message of the Reign of God as He preached it,

have their roots in Isa. lii, where else shall we look for 'the word
of the Cross' but in Isa. liii?

If now we assume that the Cross falls within the Kingdom,
we may say that, for our Lord, the Cross was the condition not
of the initial coming of the Kingdom but of its 'coming with
power' (Mk. ix. 1). Nor is this only a speculation, for there is
another remarkable saying which links up with Mk. ix. 1:

'I came to cast fire on the earth,' said Jesus, 'and how I wish
it were already kindled! But I have a baptism to be baptised
with, and how am I straitened until it be accomplished!' (Lk.
xii. 49f., Q?).

The 'fire' must be the fire of the Gospel,[1] as the 'baptism' is
undoubtedly His Passion. And the thought in our Lord's mind
is this: 'My mission is to kindle the divine fire in the world.
But only by my dying can it be kindled, and the Reign of God
come with power.' Jesus is the new Prometheus, and He must
pay the same price. 'The planted seed,' as Glasson finely says,[2]
'must be watered by the bloody sweat of his Passion.' If this be
true to the mind of Jesus, then in the Cross and Resurrection
the Reign of God 'came with power' and on the day of Pentecost
(as Bengel said[3]) 'the fire was lit.'

All we have said must have suggested a close connection
between Jesus and the Kingdom of God. Thus, to become a
disciple of Jesus is equivalent to being in the Kingdom. If Jesus
exorcises evil spirits, the Reign of God comes upon men through
Him. Where He is, there is the Rule of God. Clearly the Kingdom
is bound up with the person of Jesus, the message with the
messenger. Long ago Marcion discerned this when he said, 'In
the Gospel the Kingdom of God is Christ himself.'[4] Who then
is Jesus, and what does He teach about Himself? This is the
question we must face in the next chapter.

NOTE

In the Synoptic Gospels 'the Kingdom of God' is the central
theme of all preaching. When we turn to Paul's epistles, we read
about the 'preaching of Christ.' In the Acts of the Apostles we
read now of 'preaching the Kingdom of God' and now of
'preaching Christ.' What is the explanation of this apparent
change in the theme of the preaching? Why has 'the Kingdom'

---

[1] Cf. Jer. xx. 9 and xxiii. 29 for the Word of God as 'a fire.'

[2] *The Second Advent*, 115.   [3] *Gnomon, ad loc.*

[4] Quoted by K. L. Schmidt in article on *Basileia* in Kittel's *Theologisches
Wörterbuch.*

fallen out and been replaced by 'Christ'? The closing sentences of our last chapter point the way to the answer. The Kingdom is Christ, or, as P. T. Forsyth put it in a memorable passage:

'The Gospel of Christ replaced the Gospel of the Kingdom because by His death He became the Kingdom, because He became all that the Kingdom contained. . . . The Testimony of Jesus is the Spirit of the Kingdom. The Kingdom was great with Him. The Gospel of the Kingdom was Christ in essence; Christ was the Gospel of the Kingdom in power. The Kingdom was Christ in a mystery; Christ was the publication, the establishment of the Kingdom. . . . He was the truth of His own greatest Gospel. It is wherever He is. To have Him is to ensure it' (*The Person and Place of Jesus Christ*,' 4th ed., 122).

XI

JESUS' TEACHING ABOUT HIMSELF

In the last chapter we saw that the Kingdom of God is bound up with the person of Jesus Himself. This appears, perhaps even more impressively, in sayings of Jesus where no titles come into the picture at all. But before we study them, we must say something about the titles used by Jesus of Himself.

We begin with a general word about them. As we read the Gospels, we note that Jesus sometimes calls Himself 'the Son' (of God) and often 'the Son of man,' that on at least one occasion He accepts the title 'Messiah,' and that, though He never uses the actual words, the title 'Servant of the Lord' often trembles on His lips.

Now this diversity of self-designation may easily mislead; for these titles sound, at first, distinct, unrelated, even discrepant. (Do we not in popular sermons commonly set the titles 'Son of God' and 'Son of man' in contrast?) But this is really not so. Beneath this titular diversity there lies a deeper unity, as Dr. William Manson has convincingly shown. Thus, if we will take the trouble to compare the attributes and functions of the Messiah as sketched in Ps. ii. 6–8 with those of the Servant of the Lord in Isa. lii. 13, liii. 9, 12 and again with those of the Son of man as set forth in Dan. vii. 13–14, we shall find that all three are really 'variant phases of one Messianic idea'—Israel's age-long and unquenchable hope of a Saviour:

'All three are invested with the same attributes of wisdom, judgement, righteousness, and the possession of the Spirit of God. All three are a light to the Gentiles. All three are associated with a "covenant" which God makes with His people. All three receive the homage of "kings" and raise the mighty from their seats.'[1]

Thus, we might almost say of these titles: *Plus ça change, plus c'est la même chose.* Son of God, Servant of the Lord, Son of Man—so, in one picture after another, seer and prophet in Israel foreshadowed the coming Messiah. And when He came, we find these titles focused and fulfilled in Jesus. Was not this thought in St. Paul's mind when he wrote: 'How many soever are the

[1] W. Manson, *Jesus the Messiah*, 99. Dr. Manson gives much fuller evidence in Appendix C of his book.

promises of God, in him is the Yea' (2 Cor. i. 20). To the prayers and hopes of Israel that found expression in Psalm ii and Isaiah liii and Daniel vii Jesus the Messiah is 'God's Yes.'

We may now consider in turn the three titles: Messiah, Son of God and Son of man. (The place of the Isaianic Servant of the Lord in Christ's thought will concern us in the next chapter.)

The Messiah

Before we consider the evidence of the Gospels, we must briefly consider the history of the idea.

Messiah is a Hebrew word meaning 'anointed,' which in Greek becomes 'Christos' and in English 'Christ.' More important than the word is the idea. We trace its origin in the Old Testament use of the word 'anointed' to denote offices of divine appointment, whether it be Israel as the elect people *generally "anointed"*

> Thou wentest forth for the salvation of thy people,
> For the salvation of thine anointed (Hab. iii. 13);

or the king as pre-eminently the Lord's anointed, as in 2 Sam. i. 14: 'How was thou not afraid,' says David to the Amalekite who had slain Saul, 'to put forth thine hand to destroy the Lord's anointed?'; or even a pagan ruler like Cyrus raised up to do God's will in history—

> Thus saith the Lord to his anointed, to Cyrus (Isa. xlv. 1).

The word, however, soon acquired a special sense. In the Good Time Coming God would raise up an ideal anointed King who would deliver Israel and reign in righteousness. Prophecies like Isa. ix. 2–7 and Psalms like Ps. ii which may originally have had another application, came to be read in the light of this great hope. Nor did the exile quench it, as Ps. lxxxix shows. A fourth-century prophet painted a new and noble picture of the Messiah as 'lowly and riding upon an ass' who should 'reign from the river unto the ends of the earth' (Zech. ix. 9f.). And in the century before Jesus came,[1] a seer who wrote the apocalyptic *Similitudes of Enoch* pictured the Messiah as a superhuman personage, pre-existent with God, who would be manifested as judge at the close of history. There was no uniform picture of the Coming One. A second and greater David, as in Ps. lxxxix or the so-called *Psalms of Solomon*, was perhaps the commonest view. Others perhaps expected a warrior Messiah, a second and greater Judas Maccabaeus. Others dreamed of a supernatural *Particularly "the Future Deliverer"*

---

[1] This is Charles's dating. Others put it in the first century A.D.

F

den head of
god's People

god's Ruler.

saviour from another world. Yet, as we have said, the essential attributes of the Messiah were not so very different, and there was one basic idea in all these various conceptions—that the Messiah, when he came, was to be the divinely appointed Head of the People of God and the Bearer of His Rule to men.

We may now turn to the Gospels asking the question, Did our Lord claim to be the Messiah? Q does not mention the word, and once only in Mark does Jesus lay clear claim to the title: 'The high priest asked him, Art thou the Messiah, the Son of the Blessed? And Jesus said, I am' (Mk. xiv. 61f.). Not surprisingly therefore some scholars (e.g. Wrede) have denied that Jesus ever made the claim. This denial, however, involves casting wholesale doubt on the Gospel records, which are unintelligible unless He was the Messiah. The messianic claim is implicit in the stories of the Temptation and the Baptism. At Caesarea Philippi Peter confessed Him to be the Messiah, and Jesus did not disavow it. The Entry into Jerusalem is messianic, and, as Otto says downrightly, 'he was crucified as a messianic claimant, and without the messianic claim the crucifixion of Jesus is meaningless.'[1]

X made a
Messianic
claim.

Messianic
secret

Nevertheless, there was 'a messianic secret.' If Jesus knew Himself to be the Messiah, He did not blazon the fact abroad. He deliberately veiled it (recall His answer to the Baptist), and silenced all who would have sent the messianic rumour flying through Galilee (Mk. i. 34, iii. 12, viii. 30, etc.). He had good reasons. For one thing, Jesus knew that He was not the Messiah whom the people expected. If Peter did not like Jesus' conception of Messiahship, can we suppose that the multitude would have liked it any better? Moreover, if Jesus, or His disciples, had published His Messiahship abroad, the claim would have been construed, willy nilly, in a political sense, and Rome, with her 'Argus-eye' ever open for movements of this kind, would have taken her own swift way of suppressing it.

Spiritual &
Eschatological
Messiah.

To sum up. Jesus knew Himself to be the Messiah, albeit in humiliation, during His Ministry. What does this mean? This at least—that He was the Person through whom God's Rule was being realised and the ancient promises fulfilled. But in the mind of Jesus all political suggestions fall away: His Messiahship is conceived in purely spiritual and eschatological terms. Perhaps we get the clearest look at what our Lord's Messiahship meant to Him in the reply which He sent to John the Baptist. If we would learn more concerning His own view of Himself, we must study the other titles.

[1] *The Kingdom of God and the Son of Man*, 228f.

The Son of God

Ref to: Israel kings Angels Messiah.

In the Old Testament the phrase 'son of God' is variously applied to Israel (as in Hos. xi. 1), to kings (as to Solomon in 2 Sam. vii. 14), to angels (as in Job i. 6) and to the Messiah. This last application is the one that matters most here. Thus Ps. ii. 7—

> The Lord said unto me, Thou art my son:
> This day have I begotten thee,

may have originally applied to an actual king, but it was messianically interpreted in our Lord's time. The apocryphal book known as 4 Ezra, written towards the end of the first century, calls the Messiah 'the son of God,' and the Gospels themselves confirm this usage in passages where 'Messiah' and 'son of God' lie in cheek-by-jowl equation: 'Thou art the Messiah, the son of the living God' (Mt. xvi. 16); 'Art thou the Messiah, the son of the Blessed' (Mk. xiv. 61); cf. Lk. iv. 41.

With this brief summary let us turn to the Gospels. In the relevant Gospel passages (all in Mark and Q) we must distinguish between others' use of the title and our Lord's own employment of it. Thus, demoniacs (Mk. iii. 11, v. 7), the high-priest (Mk. xiv. 61), and the centurion at the Cross (Mk. xv. 39) all designate Jesus 'the son of God.' In such cases the wisest course is to regard 'son of God' as a synonym for the Messiah, though in the last passage it may mean no more than 'a righteous man.'[1] When we turn to study the passages where the phrase occurs on our Lord's lips, we come first to the stories of the Baptism and the Temptation. 'Thou art my beloved son' says the heavenly Voice at the Baptism, echoing Ps. ii. 7. 'If thou art the son of God . . .' says the Tempter to Jesus in the wilderness. These two passages certainly attest a messianic consciousness in our Lord. But is this an exhaustive description of His self-awareness? Does His description of Himself as 'son' in relation to God mean no more than 'Messiah'?

When we recall the boy Jesus' question, 'Wist ye not that I must be about my Father's business?' and His later mode of addressing God as *Abba*, must we not say that 'son' on His lips means at least 'Messiah plus'? There is here something more than simply a consciousness of being Messiah.

Happily we can shed light on that 'something more.' Three passages, all in our primary sources, hint at something uniquely filial in our Lord's self-consciousness.

[1] Cf. *The Wisdom of Solomon*, ii. 18, 'For if the righteous man is God's son, he will uphold him,' and Lk. xxiii. 47.

a) **Mk 12¹⁻⁹**

There is, first, the parable of the wicked husbandmen (Mk. xii. 1–9), a parable whose authenticity there is no good reason to doubt. Here all God's previous messengers to Israel are 'slaves': Jesus is not a slave but a son. Nay, He is not a son, but the 'one beloved Son' of the Father; He is 'the heir'—all that is the Father's is His.

b) **Mk 13³²**

Second, we note Mk. xiii. 32, a saying, as even Schmiedel admits, beyond the power of the early Church's invention. 'But of that day or that hour knoweth no one, not even the angels in heaven, neither the Son but the Father.' Here the Son occupies a place of lonely splendour, above both men and angels, subordinate only to God Himself.

c) **Mt 11²⁷**

Most conclusive of all (it is the most important Christological verse in the New Testament) is the second stanza of the Great Thanksgiving:

> All things have been delivered unto me of my Father,
> And no one knoweth the Son, save the Father;
> Neither doth any know the Father save the Son,
> And he to whomsoever the Son willeth to reveal him.
>
>   (Mt. xi. 27=Lk. x. 22, Q).

No saying of our Lord's has been put oftener under the critical microscope. It has been called 'a bolt from the Johannine blue,' and radical critics have made desperate attempts to get rid of it.[1] There is no good reason for doubting its genuineness: it has as high a documentary claim to authenticity as any in the Gospels. And what a majestic light it throws on Jesus' estimate of His own person! He claims not only that He is the organ of God's self-revelation, but that He alone knows God truly as Father and for that supreme knowledge all men must become debtors to Him. This is 'unshared sonship.' We do not wonder that later St. Paul was to call Jesus 'the son of His [God's] love.' Nothing less is adequate to Jesus' own consciousness. 'A filial relationship to the Father, to which there is a parallel nowhere else, is the secret of the work and ministry of Jesus.'[2]

× claimed unshared sonship.

The Son of Man

If our Lord accepted the title Messiah, the title that He claimed was 'the Son of man.' In the Synoptic Gospels it occurs some seventy times. If we discount the textually doubtful cases and

[1] Harnack thought the utterance authentic except the clause about the Father's knowledge of the son, which was an interpolation. I can see no good reason for surrendering even this.

[2] V. Taylor, *Jesus and His Sacrifice*, 38.

those which Matthew and Luke borrow from Mark, there remain *x and this* *title.* about three dozen examples (Mk., 14; Q, 11; L, 5; M, 6). It is found only on the lips of Jesus, and in most cases refers clearly to Himself. Some of the examples are of a general tenor, as 'The Son of man came eating and drinking' (Lk. vii. 34=Mt. xi. 19, Q); but, for the most part, they group themselves round *a) humiliate* two motifs: (a) humiliation, as 'The Son of man must suffer many things' (Mk. viii. 31), and (b) exaltation, as 'Ye shall see *b) exaltation* the Son of man sitting on the right hand of power and coming with the clouds of heaven' (Mk. xiv. 62).

Some fifty years ago Lietzmann startled the theological world by asserting that Jesus never applied the title to Himself, because in Aramaic the title could not have existed. His argument was that in Aramaic 'the Son of man' becomes *barnasha* which means simply 'the man' (in the generic sense), and that therefore Jesus could not have used it in the titular sense demanded by the Gospels. The great Aramaic expert Dalman at once joined issue with him. He pointed out, among other things, that it was possible in Old Syriac (a language closely akin to our Lord's Aramaic) to distinguish between the generic and the titular sense.[1] And in the end scholars generally resiled from Lietzmann's view. In a few passages 'man' rather than 'Son of man' may give the true sense; in most, the meaning 'man' is quite inept, and we may be sure that the titular use was possible.

What then is the source of our Lord's title? In the Old Testament 'son of man' is often a poetical synonym for 'man.' It is so in Ps. viii. 4, and in Ezekiel (some 87 examples) it describes the prophet as a frail human creature in the sight of the almighty God. Most modern scholars, however, agree that the source of our Lord's title must be either Dan. vii. 13 or that part of the book of *Enoch* known as 'The Similitudes' (Enoch xxxvii–lxxi), a document commonly held to belong to the first century before Christ. In this book 'the Son of man' is a name for the Messiah regarded as a supernatural being predestined by God to be judge at the end of history. But since (a) the pre-Christian date *title from* of the *Similitudes* is not certain; (b) no one has yet proved that *Dan 7 13 ff* Jesus knew them; and (c) He certainly knew Daniel,[2] we may follow most scholars in deriving the title from Dan. vii. 13f. This chapter describes the seer's vision of the four beasts, then it goes on: 'I saw in the night visions, and behold, there came with the clouds of heaven one like unto a son of man, and he came even unto the ancient of days, and they brought him near

[1] B'reh d' nasha.

[2] There are echoes of Daniel in Mk. iv. 32, xiv. 62 and Lk. xii. 32.

before him. And there was given him dominion and glory and a kingdom, etc.' Later follows the interpretation: the four beasts signify four kings, the heads of four empires. The 'one like unto a son of man' represents 'the saints of the Most High,' i.e. the People of God.

Now it seems clear that Jesus regarded Himself as that 'someone,' who was destined to receive from God 'dominion and glory and a kingdom.' The 'someone' was Himself, the Messiah. If so, an interesting corollary follows. In Daniel the symbolic 'son of man' represents 'the saints of the Most High': in technical language, he is 'a societary person.' Jesus must therefore have regarded Himself as the representative, or head, of the People of God. His task then, as the bearer of God's Rule, was to create this People; and for Him the Twelve (significant number) was its nucleus. (This seems to us the valuable truth in T. W. Manson's collective interpretation of the phrase, *The Teaching of Jesus*, Chap. viii.)

How did Jesus use the title? Of the fourteen uses of the title in Mark, twelve fall after Peter's Confession. Many have therefore inferred that Jesus used the title only after that event. This is a precarious conclusion. It compels us to take the two early examples in Mark (ii. 10, 28) in the sense of 'man'—a difficult business— and it assumes that all the non-Marcan examples fall after the episode at Caesarea Philippi; or, if some, like Lk. vii. 34, are plainly earlier, they must be explained away. It is surely wiser not to trim the evidence in the interests of a neat conclusion. If, as many scholars say, it was not a current messianic title, why should Jesus not have used it before Caesarea Philippi? To be sure, He avoided the title Messiah; but for that He had good reasons. There seems to be no cogent reason why He should not have chosen from the beginning (as Mark asserts) another title to express His unique relation to the Kingdom. That title lay to hand in the Son of man. It was not a familiar messianic title. It was non-political. And in virtue of its mysterious nature Jesus could use it, even before Peter's Confession, without the disciples finally concluding that He was the Messiah.

The dominant idea in the title seems to be that of sovereignty.[1] Thus, in Dan. vii. 14, the 'one like unto a son of man' receives a kingdom from God. He is the bearer of the divine rule. It is

[1] On the other hand, it seems likely that Jesus chose 'the Son of man Messiology' because it was 'weighted with a deeply human pathos,' because it suggested His kinship with humanity. 'It gave him back something of his own sense of oneness with the poor and unfriended, the sinful and unbefriended ostracised among his own people whom he came to save' (W. Manson, *Jesus the Messiah*, 118).

in accordance with this that in almost half the Gospel passages
Jesus associates the title with the thought of His ultimate exaltation and triumph. No matter what present appearances may be,
He as the Son of man is destined to triumph, and with Him the
cause of God's People.

But (and this is the startlingly original contribution of Jesus)
with sovereignty Jesus combined the idea of service and sacrifice;
'The Son of man must suffer many things' He said not once but
many times. 'The Son of man came not to be served but to
serve and to give his life a ransom for many' (Mk. x. 45). No
wonder that the disciples were appalled at this doctrine of suffering and sovereignty, that they were swept out of their spiritual
depths. It is a synthesis that can go back only to our Lord.
He knew Himself called of God to fuse in His own person and
destiny the two rôles of the Son of Man (Daniel) and the Servant
of the Lord (Isaiah). 'He was born to suffer, born a king.'

THE SELF-REVELATION OF JESUS

From titles we may turn now to 'testimonies.' 'The authority
which Jesus claimed,' says Sir George Adam Smith,[1] 'the
sufficiency for men of which he was conscious—these are his
own testimonies to what he was.' It is these testimonies—the
claims, the demands, the declarations which He made where
no titles are on His lips—which we must now examine. They
testify even more eloquently than any titles to the unique place
which Jesus knew Himself to hold in the purposes of God for
men.

We begin with the claim to forgive sin. In such a story as
that of the healing of the paralytic man in Mk. ii. 1-12, it is of
capital importance to note that the words, 'Child, thy sins are
forgiven thee,' are not merely declaratory but effective. Many
modern scholars evidently see in Jesus only a Galilean Heine
who says, 'God forgives you. That's His business': in other words,
Jesus simply announced, as any pious Jew might, that if the man
were penitent, God would not reckon his sins against him. This
is to miss the whole point of the story. Jesus claimed power
actually to forgive sins; and the scribes were quite right in
assuming that He exercised the prerogative of pardon—a prerogative belonging to God alone. This was the head and front of
His offending—that He claimed power to work a spiritual as
well as a physical miracle. We are dealing not with a declaration
but with an achievement. Who then is this who can come forward

[1] *Jerusalem*, ii. 555.

as the <u>divine pardon incarnate</u>, proclaiming His power to lead
sinful men there and then into God's presence?

Not less remarkable, if we reflect on them, are the demands
which Jesus makes. These are not simply for ethical obedience;
they are for utter self-committal to Himself. They represent the
'totalitarian' claim of Jesus. Thus:

'Everyone who shall confess me before men, him will I also
confess before my Father who is in heaven' (Mt. x. 32=Lk.
xii. 8; cf. Mk. viii. 38).

Could language say more clearly than this that fidelity to
Jesus is that on which a man's final destiny depends?

'He that receiveth you, receiveth me; and he that receiveth
me receiveth him that sent me' (Mt. x. 40: Lk. x. 16; cf. Mk.
ix. 37).

Here is One who knows His cause to be the cause of God.

'He that loveth father or mother more than me, is not worthy
of me; and he that loveth son or daughter more than me is not
worthy of me; and he that doth not take up his cross and follow
me, is not worthy of me' (Mt. x. 37f.: Lk. xiv. 26f., cf. Mk.
viii. 34).

In such demands there speaks One who knows Himself to
be uniquely authorised by God. He acts for God: His doings
are God's doings. It is sometimes said[1] that Jesus never asks
men to believe in Him. So far as words go, this may be true.
How utterly untrue, in fact, it is! For in such phrases as 'Follow
me,' 'Learn of me,' 'Come to me,' 'Forsake all and follow me'
there is a demand for faith in Himself as insistent as Paul's
words to the Philippian jailor, 'Believe on the Lord Jesus Christ,
and thou shalt be saved.'

No less astounding are the 'I sayings' of Jesus. We are all
familiar with the 'I am' sayings in St. John, but we are apt to
forget that they are not absent from the Synoptic record. K. L.
Schmidt has rightly drawn our attention to the Synoptic sayings
in which the emphatic pronoun ἐγώ is found on the lips of
Jesus.[2] Those who do not read the Gospels in the original Greek
are apt to miss this remarkable feature; for it is not easily trans-
latable into English—an italicised 'I' is our best equivalent.
In Greek which does not insert such pronouns except for special
emphasis, this 'sovereign I' is infinitely suggestive of His self-
consciousness. Every reader of the Gospels has doubtless remarked
the imperious 'I' which sounds through the first part of the Sermon
on the Mount: 'Ye have heard that it hath been said by them of

[1] E.g. by Bousset, *Jesus* (Eng. tr.), 202.

[2] In *Le Problème du Christianisme primitif.*

old, but *I* say unto you.' But we find the same pronoun in other passages:

'It is *I* who send you forth' (Mt. x. 16).

'If *I* by the finger of God cast out devils, etc.' (Lk. xi. 20= Mt. xii. 28, Q).

'*I* will give you rest' (Mt. xi. 28, M).

'*I* will destroy this sanctuary . . .' (Mk. xiv. 58). Cf. also Lk. xxii. 29, L.

Very similar are the 'I came' sayings:

'I came not to destroy but to fulfil' (Mt. v. 17, M).

'I came not to call the righteous but sinners' (Mk. ii. 17).

'I came not to send peace but a sword' (Mt. x. 34, M).

'I came to cast fire upon the earth' (Lk. xii. 49, Q?).

These are amazing statements, to whose wonder only familiarity has dulled our ears: some of them remind us of detonating bombs. But one and all attest a mission to the world which moves any thoughtful reader to ask, 'Who then is this who knows himself so sent, so authorised by God?'

Finally, we must lay account with those declarations of Jesus in which, without ever mentioning the word 'Messiah,' He implies that with His own coming the messianic Age has come. Many we have already cited:—The sermon in Nazareth with the great words from Isa. lxi to which Jesus adds the comment, 'To-day hath this scripture been fulfilled in your ears'; His reply to the Baptist's question from prison which says, in effect, to John: 'I am the Messiah, but not the Messiah you expected'; His retort to those who charged Him with being in league with Satan, 'If I by the finger of God cast out devils, then is the kingdom of God come upon you.' Yet perhaps the most remarkable self-revelation of all is to be found in His words at the Last Supper. 'This is my body' is extraordinary enough; but the word over the Cup is even more so: 'This cup is the new covenant in my blood' (1 Cor. xi. 25; cf. Mk. xiv. 24). Centuries before, Jeremiah, at the nadir of his people's fortunes, saw their only salvation in the hope that God would yet make a new covenant— a 'new deal' with His people—a new order of things established not in stone but in the heart of man: in that day all would know God, and He would forgive their sins, and they would be in very truth His people (Jer. xxxi. 31ff.). Then what manner of man is this who knows that by His dying He will inaugurate this new and blessed order of relations between God and men? No mortal man makes such a claim, or we know him to be mad. We are driven back on the words of wise old 'Rabbi' Duncan: 'Christ either deceived mankind by conscious fraud, or he was himself deluded, or he was divine. There is no getting out of this trilemma.'[1]

Christians have never been in any doubt which of these propositions is true.

[1] *Colloquia Peripatetica*, 109.

XII

JESUS' TEACHING ABOUT HIS DEATH

What did Jesus teach about His death?

Let us begin by recalling two points made in preceding chapters. First, we saw that while it would hardly be true to say that Jesus died to bring in the Kingdom, the Cross was the condition of its 'coming with power.' The second was Jesus' startling reinterpretation of the rôle of the Son of man. The destiny of the Son of man was sovereignty; but, as Jesus saw it, it was a sovereignty which involved redemptive suffering. In other words, He knew Himself called of God to fuse in His own person the two rôles of the Danielic Son of man and the Isaianic Servant of the Lord. Keeping these two points in mind, let us proceed to our study.

Our sources yield about twenty independent sayings of Jesus about His death:

c20 sayings

Mark: Mk. ii. 19f. (the Bridegroom saying); viii. 31, ix. 31, and x. 33f. (three sayings about death and resurrection); ix. 12*b*; x. 38 (the 'cup' saying); x. 45 (the 'ransom' saying); xiv. 21 ('The Son of man goeth, etc.'); xiv. 22–25 (the Last Supper); xiv. 32–50 (Gethsemane); and xv. 34 (the Cry of Dereliction). Q: Lk. xii. 49f. ('I have a baptism') and Lk. xvii. 25. (Some scholars, because of their lack of Matthaean attestation, assign these passages to L.) L: Lk. xiii. 32f. (the Reply to Herod); Lk. xxii. 15f., 28–30, 37 (three Last Supper sayings); and xxiii. 32, 42f., and 46 (three words from the Cross).

+ 1 Cor. 11

To these we should add St. Paul's narrative of the Supper in 1 Cor. xi. 23–25.

WHY DID JESUS GO UP TO JERUSALEM?

Before we study these sayings, the general question must be raised, Why did Jesus 'steadfastly set his face to go to Jerusalem'?

Men have found out many answers to this question. Some have held that it was the inevitable conclusion to His life. We are to *not* infer that honour required it, as though He were the captain of *"honour"* some ship and must in duty bound go down with His vessel, even when He has the chance of escape. But this sentiment of honour finds no expression in the Gospels—unless it be in Jesus' reply to Herod, 'It cannot be that a prophet perish out of

Jerusalem.' (The point of this saying, however, is rather different.
There is irony in it: Jerusalem is the proper place for a prophet
to die, as history shows.) There are others who think that in
marching on Jerusalem and the Cross Jesus was deliberately
acting out His own precept of 'turning the other cheek' to the
smiter; that, by returning His best to His enemies' worst, He
hoped to win a wicked world by the sheer power of selfless love.
We must not speak lightly of such a conjecture; for it is an
empirical fact that the love of Jesus for His enemies has been,
in history, a great converting power. Yet, inspired as the conjecture is, we find little trace of it in the thought of Jesus recorded
in the Gospels. What the Gospels tell us is that Jesus saw His
death not as a glorious after-thought which would move men's
hearts by its splendour of self-sacrifice but as the very soul of
His vocation—the thing God sent Him into the world to do.

Others, again, have suggested that Jesus went up to Jerusalem
to offer Himself as the Messiah, hoping that He would be
accepted. But is it likely that Jesus, being the Messiah He knew
Himself to be, ever expected to be accepted? Having made trial
of the Galilean cities and found them impenitent, how could
He have the faintest reason for hoping that Jerusalem would
accept Him? Instead of the hope of acceptance, what we find is
predictions of the doom impending on Jerusalem, and for the
rest, all is solemnity and a settled foreboding of death.

HOW SOON DID JESUS FORESEE HIS DEATH?

This last conjecture raises the second important preliminary
problem. It is the problem of how soon Jesus foresaw the Cross.

There are those who believe that Jesus began His ministry
with brilliant hopes of success, and that only later, when these
hopes faded, did He bow to the inevitable and turn it to glorious
gain. In his learned book, *The Historic Mission of Jesus*, the late
C. J. Cadoux takes such a view. He tells us that we must divide
the ministry of Jesus into two periods: an earlier when, with
no prescience of rejection, He expected the people to respond
to God's call; and a later, when realising that, unless He fought
or fled, the opposition of His enemies would compass His death,
He accepted the Cross and explained it, believing that by His
death He would move men to penitence for their sin.

This sort of view, we are sometimes told, is necessary if we are
to preserve the reality of Jesus' human experience. Its advocates
will not admit that Jesus' experience could have been different
from our own. To hold the other view—that Jesus saw the Cross

from the beginning—is, they say, to impose a dogmatic and
therefore unhistorical theory upon the facts. In reality, however,
this so-called 'historical' reading of the Gospel story 'is as much
an a priori interpretation of the history of Jesus as if it were
derived from the Nicene Creed.' 'It is derived,' says Denney,
'from the word "historical," in the sense which that word would
bear if it were applied to an ordinary human life, just as abstractly
as another reading of the facts might be derived from the words
ὁμοούσιος τῷ πατρί. . . . The Christian religion rests on the
fact that there is not only an identity but a difference between
His life and ours; and we cannot allow the difference (and with
it the Christian religion) to be abolished a priori by a dogmatic
use of the term "historical." '[1]

But, leaving theorisings aside, let us look at the evidence. A
study of the Baptism makes it very hard to believe that Jesus
could have begun His ministry with cloudless prospects. In that
high hour of revelation there came to Him a heavenly voice
ordaining Him the Servant of the Lord. If it be said that the
words quoted from Isa. xlii contain no reference to death, we
must point out 'the tragic progress' of the Servant as Isaiah
delineates it. In the second of the songs his destiny is 'labour
in vain'; in the third, it is 'bitter persecution'; and in the fourth
and last, it is 'ignominious death.'[2] If Jesus knew Himself called
to fulfil the rôle of the Servant, the possibility of something tragic
in His destiny must have been with Him from the start of His
ministry.

We may pass over the Temptation story (though this too is
evidence that Jesus knew that the way to His triumph would
be no royal road) and turn to the saying about the removal of
the Bridegroom:

'But the days will come when the bridegroom shall be taken
away from them, and then they will fast in that day' (Mk. ii. 20).

This is an awkward bit of evidence for those who deny that
Jesus could have foreseen the Cross from an early date, and
they are at great pains to explain it away. One expedient is to
eliminate it as later Church theology. But in view of Vincent
Taylor's convincing defence in *Jesus and His Sacrifice*[3] it is hard
to doubt its authenticity. The other expedient is to say that it
is misplaced in Mark and must belong to a later period in the
ministry. This too is quite unconvincing. First, Mark who
presumably knew its proper setting in the life of Jesus better
than we do, put it early; and, second, the saying itself surely

---

[1] *The Death of Christ*, 12f.

[2] See Isa. xlix. 4, l. 6f., and lii. 13-liii. 12.

[3] Pp. 82-85.

cries out to be put early in the story, for it belongs to a time when the lightheartedness of Jesus' disciples betrays no apprehension of danger. In short, the saying proves that in the full tide of the Galilean ministry Jesus faced the probability of death.

There is a good deal of subsidiary evidence pointing in the same direction, e.g. the fate of the Baptist, Israel's treatment of her prophets, the beatitudes of persecution, Jesus' reply to Herod (which must belong to the Galilean ministry), the record as early as Mk. iii of the Pharisees and Herodians conspiring to destroy Him. The cumulative force of this evidence permits only one conclusion: that from the beginning Jesus laid account with the possibility of rejection and death in the fulfilment of His mission. Those who oppose this view generally point to two passages as proof that the Cross was taken up into Jesus' purpose only when His early hopes of success had been blighted. The first is Jesus' lament over Jerusalem (Lk. xiii. 34f.=Mt. xxiii. 37ff., Q); the other is the prophetic oracle preserved in Lk. xix. 42, L ('If thou hadst known,' etc.). On the strength of these passages we are asked to believe that Jesus hoped from the beginning for another and happier issue to His mission. But surely this is not the natural interpretation. Rather, both passages declare alike the inevitability of the doom overtaking Jerusalem and the natural heart-break of Jesus. The fact that Jesus knew Jerusalem's doom to be ineluctable did not preclude Him from at the same time uttering these cries of passionate regret for His people's impenitence.

We conclude that right from the outset of His ministry Jesus foresaw death as a probability inherent in His vocation as the Servant Messiah. Perhaps at first He was content to refer to it in language purposely vague—witness the Bridegroom saying. 'Just as a mother who knows herself smitten with a sickness which is unto death will sometimes try by shadowed hints to prepare her children for what is coming, while she yet veils its naked horror from their eyes, so did Jesus with his disciples.'[1]

THE MESSIAH WHO MUST SUFFER

By the time Caesarea Philippi was reached, death was no longer a possibility, or even a probability, but a certainty for Jesus: 'And he began to teach them that the Son of man must suffer many things . . .'(Mk. viii. 31).

We have seen already that the central point of this narrative was probably not the disciples' realisation of Jesus' Messiahship

[1] G. Jackson, *The Teaching of Jesus*, 54.

but the disclosure of a Messiah who must go to His triumph by way of a Cross. 'Jesus,' says Goguel, 'did not believe himself to be the Messiah *although* he had to suffer. He felt himself to be the Messiah *because* he had to suffer.'[1]

'The Son of man must suffer. . . .' The Greek for 'must' is δεῖ. What underlies it? Is it the 'must' of outward constraint? Did Jesus realise that His foes being what they were, must finally kill Him, if He remained true to God and Himself? Is it not far more likely that the 'must' is one of inward constraint, that the δεῖ is the 'δεῖ of divine necessity?' It was a necessity laid on Him by God. Jesus discerned in the historical necessity a divine necessity, saw that His Passion must become a great Action, the one indispensable Action if the Reign of God was to 'come with power.' This was why (in Masefield's words) He could not—

> return home
> Comfort his mother, live as other men,
> And taste the happiness of men on earth
> With wife and children, friends and fair old age.

'When Jesus unfolds Messiahship, it contains death.'[2] How did Jesus learn this? Some have suggested that it was His study of the Word of God in Isa. liii which first revealed to Him the necessity of dying in order to reign. It may be however that this terrible truth, so unwelcome to flesh and blood, was directly revealed to Him by His Father and then confirmed by the study of the scripture. Whichever it was, the fact is certain that most of His sayings about His death either echo Isa. liii or have its sombre music somewhere in the background. To be sure, it is only in Lk. xxii. 37 (L) that we find an express quotation:

'For I say unto you that this which is written must be fulfilled in me, And he was reckoned with the transgressors' (Isa. liii. 12), but in half a dozen other passages where He speaks of His Passion it is the merest scepticism to doubt that He has Isa. liii in mind. Does He speak of 'being delivered up' (παραδοθῆναι, Mk. ix. 31, x. 33, xiv. 21, 41; I Cor. xi. 23)? Then He is echoing Isa. liii. 12, 'Because his soul was delivered up unto death . . . and he was delivered up because of their iniquities' (LXX). Does He say that the Son of man must be 'rejected' and 'set at nought'? (See ἀποδοκιμασθῆναι in Mk. viii. 31 and Lk. xvii. 25 and ἐξουδενωθῆναι in Mk. ix. 12.) Then He is echoing Isa. liii. 3, 'He was despised and we esteemed him not.' Does He refer to His redeeming work as being for the sake of 'the many'?

---

[1] *Life of Jesus*, 392.   [2] Denney, *The Death of Christ*, 32.

(Note πολλῶν in Mk. x. 45, xiv. 24.) Then we recall the reference to 'the many' in Isa. liii. 11f., 'My righteous servant shall
(e) justify *many* . . . yet he bare the sin of *many*.' Does He say, in the
hour of His arrest, that the 'scriptures must be fulfilled' (Mk.
xiv. 21; cf. ix. 12*b*)? Who can doubt which scriptures He means?
Does He speak of His whole mission as one of 'service,' a service
(g) that must end in death (Mk. x. 45)? Then it can be only one
servant—the Servant of the Lord—whom He has in mind.

The conclusion is not doubtful. If we are to understand how
Jesus conceived of His Passion, we must begin with Isa. liii.
And the doctrine of Isa. liii is one of representative suffering,
with the idea of substitution well in the foreground.

THE PASSION SAYINGS

We may now review our Lord's chief sayings about His death.
First, Jesus sees His Passion as a 'baptism.' 'I have a baptism
to be baptised with, and how am I straitened (cramped) until
it be accomplished' (Lk. xii. 50, Q or L). 'Are ye able . . . to be
baptised with the baptism that I am baptised with?' (Mk. x. 38).
'Baptism' is a metaphor for suffering and here refers to His Death.
If we take the metaphor in its Lucan context, the meaning of
Jesus is: 'Before the fire of the Gospel can be effectively kindled,
there must come for the Kindler His own baptism of blood.'[1]

Second, Jesus speaks of His Passion as 'a cup' that God has
given Him to drink. 'Are ye able,' He asks James and John, 'to
drink the cup that I am drinking?' (Mk. x. 38). In Gethsemane,
He cries in agony, 'Abba, Father, all things are possible unto
thee. Remove this cup from me; howbeit, not what I will, but
what thou wilt' (Mk. xiv. 36). Now, in the Old Testament, of
twenty metaphorical uses of the word 'cup,' in seventeen cases
it is a metaphor for divinely-appointed suffering, even punishment.[2] (See especially Isa. li. 17, 22.) It describes God's punishment of human sin. If then we ask what Jesus meant by His
'cup,' we may put aside the idea that it was the actual physical
pain of the death that He had in mind. We should be nearer

[1] Beyond question, by 'baptism' in Lk. xii. 50 Jesus means His blood-
baptism, i.e. His death. The question is whether the word is only a vivid
metaphor for suffering, as in Pss. xlii. 7, cxlv. 4f., and Isa. xliii. 7, or is
something more. There is much to be said for the view that Jesus saw His
blood-baptism as *the means of initiation into a fuller and freer activity*. If so, He
was anticipating a time when, through death, He would be 'let loose in the
world, where neither Roman nor Jew could stop his truth' (Masefield).
See W. F. Flemington, *The New Testament Doctrine of Baptism*, 31f.

[2] See the valuable article by C. E. B. Cranfield in *Expository Times*, February,
1948.

the truth if we called it 'the cup of God's wrath against human sin.'

So Denney, writing of our Lord's cry in Gethsemane, says:[1] 'It is hard to believe that it was simply the anticipation of pain which made Christ cry, "O my Father, if it be possible, let this cup pass from me." It was the anticipation of that experience when, all sinless as He was, the Father would put into His hands the cup our sins had mingled.' This then was the 'cup' of Jesus— 'the cup our sins had mingled.' So closely had He associated Himself with those He came to save—so 'irrevocably had He betrothed Himself to the human race for better, for worse'[2]— that He tasted in all its naked horror the wrath of God against the sin of man.

Third, Jesus spoke of His passion as a road to be travelled. 'The Son of man,' He said, 'goeth, as it is written of him' (Mk. xiv. 21). We may paraphrase the saying thus: 'The Son of man travels the road mapped out for him in scripture.' And if we ask what road in scripture He means, there can be but one answer. It is that *via dolorosa*, that path of humiliation and death, mapped out five centuries before for the Servant of the Lord.

Thus, in His vivid picture-phrases—a baptism to be undergone, a cup to be drunk, a road to be travelled—Jesus sets forth the *necessity* of His Passion, with a hint, in the 'cup' saying, at something still more tremendous and profound. But there remain the two most important sayings of all: the Ransom saying and the Covenant saying.

The first of these is Mk. x. 45: 'The Son of man came not to be served but to serve, and to give his life a ransom for many.' Whatever else this means, it implies that Jesus saw His death as a price to be paid. Dead seas of ink have gone to the discussion of this saying, and every word of it has been weighed by the scholars. After all their study no one may claim to have fathomed all its depths, for

> none of the ransomed ever knew
> How deep were the waters crossed.

Yet, if we deal honestly with the saying, it must mean this at least, that by reason of their sins the lives of the 'many' had become forfeit, and that Jesus knew Himself called, as the Servant of the Lord, to release them from the doom that overhung them.[3] He was doing something for 'the many' (i.e. for the common deliverance), something which they could not do

---

[1] *Studies in Theology*, 123 (abridged).   [2] W. R. Maltby's phrase.
[3] The passages which shed light on Mk. x. 45 are Ps. xlix. 7-9, 4 Macc. vi. 28f. and xvii. 21f. and—above all—Isa. liii.

G

for themselves, something that He alone could do. It would be rash to find here a doctrine of the Atonement; yet the preposition used (ἀντί, 'instead of') clearly implies substitution, as the echoes of Isa. liii imply representative and redemptive suffering. At the very least, then, we must say (it seems to me) that the death of Jesus takes the place of 'the many'; and the most natural interpretation is that the death of the innocent One exempts the guilty.

The other saying is the Word about the Covenant uttered over the cup at the Last Supper.

In Mk. xiv. 24 it reads: 'This is my blood of the covenant which is shed for many.'

In 1 Cor. xi. 25 (where Paul is quoting something he 'received') the saying runs: 'This cup is the new covenant in my blood.' There is some variation here in the wording, and scholars have often debated the merits of the two versions, some arguing for the originality of the Marcan form and others for the Pauline. But the *essential* meaning of both is the same. Both speak of a covenant to be established by the 'blood' of Jesus (i.e. the life of Jesus sacrificially released by death), and of this the 'cup' is the symbol.

'Covenant' is not a perfect translation. It suggests a compact between equals. But the Hebrew word *berith* (which Jesus no doubt used) underlying the Greek διαθήκη lays the stress on the divine initiative. It denotes a reciprocal relationship in which the initiative is on the side of God. Its central idea is that of God entering history with a gracious purpose, to create a new order of relations between God and man.

What new order of relations, then, has Jesus in mind? Is there any Old Testament passage which provides a clue? There are three possibilities. First, Exod. xxiv. 8 describes the sprinkling of the sacrificial blood on the Israelites at Sinai in order to ratify their covenant with Jehovah: 'And Moses took the blood, and sprinkled it upon the people, and said, Behold, *the blood of the covenant* which the Lord hath made with you concerning all these words.' Mark's version of our Lord's saying seems to recall this passage and to combine it with Isa. liii. 12 ('which is shed for *many*'). Second, there is the great 'covenant of grace' which Jeremiah promised that the Lord would make with His people: 'Behold, the days come, saith the Lord, that I will make *a new covenant* with the house of Israel'—a covenant of which (he goes on to say) one prime blessing will be the forgiveness of their sin—'for I will forgive their iniquity, and their sin will I remember no more' (Jer. xxxi. 31–34). Paul's version with its allusion to a 'new covenant' is very reminiscent of Jeremiah. But there is a third possibility. In the Servant Songs of Second Isaiah there is a double mention of a covenant. The first is in Isa. xlii. 6, '*I will give you,*' says God to His Servant, '*for a covenant of the people,* (*) Isaiah's Servant. for a light of the Gentiles.' Cf. Isa. xlix. 8. Here it is expressly said that God will make His Servant to be the mediator of a covenant between Himself and His people.

It would be rash to decide downrightly that one, and one only, of these passages was in our Lord's mind. Most scholars think the primary reference is to Jeremiah. But it may well be that Jesus combined Jeremiah's prophecy of 'the new covenant' with Second Isaiah's prophecy of the Servant who was to be the mediator of the covenant. 'In His own mind Jesus blended these two ideas, knowing that by His passion and death they were being mingled and made one.'[1] If this be so, at the Last Supper, Jesus said (in effect): 'To-day are these ancient scriptures being fulfilled. In virtue of my death as the servant-mediator, men will be able to enter into the new covenant—the new order of relations between God and men—and to know the boon of sins forgiven and renewed fellowship with God.'

THE ATONEMENT

What do the Passion sayings of Jesus tell us? Are they simply a collection of scattered *obiter dicta*? Or do they add up to some theory of atonement?

We may admit that they do not yield a systematic doctrine. But should we expect one? Is it not true to say that Jesus came not so much to preach the atonement as that there might be an atonement to preach? Moreover, any proper doctrine must be founded not on a few isolated sayings but on the whole set of facts provided by the life and teaching of Jesus and on the experience of innumerable Christians since He died and rose. Nevertheless, Jesus had convictions about the necessity and the value of His sufferings and of the end they would achieve.

With which type of atonement theory do His sayings best agree? Aulén, in his book, *Christus Victor*, has divided all theories into three classes. There is, first of all, the humanistic theory— we should call it 'the moral theory.' Its basic idea is that Jesus on the Cross supremely reveals the love of God in conflict with sin, and by that revelation moves the hearts of sinful men to repentance. No Christian will speak scornfully of a theory which so sets the love of God in the forefront. Yet it must be said that

[1] R. N. Flew, *Jesus and His Church*, 103.

in Jesus' Passion sayings there is none which declares that He
dies to reveal the love of God.

The second type of theory Aulén calls the 'classical'—though
it might better be called the 'patristic' theory. Its cardinal idea
is that in His ministry and supremely on the Cross Jesus raided
the dark empire of evil, vanquished the devil, and led captivity
captive. The Cross is His death-grapple with Satan, a conflict
through which He emerges victorious by the Resurrection. We
may find evidence for this view in Christ's own words about the
despoiling of the Strong Man (the devil) and in such sayings as
Lk. xxii. 53 and Jn. xii. 31. But clearly this view is only a single
element, not the master-idea, in Jesus' thinking about the Cross.

The third type of theory Aulén calls the 'Latin.' We might
better call it the 'Penal' theory; for basic to it is the idea that
Christ's sufferings were, in some sense, penal—penal not in the
sense that God punished Jesus, but in the sense that Jesus
entered into the blight and judgement which men's sins must
incur at the hands of a God who is holy love. According to this
view, Jesus on the Cross offers an expiatory sacrifice for the sin
of men against the holy God, and the element of substitution is
never far away. Under this head we may include all theories
which deal in 'satisfaction' or substitution, or make use of 'the
sacrificial principle.' It is with this type of theory that the sayings
of Jesus seem best to agree. There can be little doubt that Jesus
viewed His death as a representative sacrifice for 'the many.'
Not only is His thought saturated in Isa. liii (which is a doctrine
of representative suffering), but His words over the cup—indeed,
the whole narrative of the Last Supper—almost demand to be
interpreted in terms of a sacrifice in whose virtue His followers
can share. The idea of substitution which is prominent in Isa.
liii. 6, appears in the ransom saying. And it requires only a little
reading between the lines to find in the 'cup' sayings, the story of
the Agony, and the cry of dereliction, evidence that Christ's sufferings were what, for lack of a better word, we can only call 'penal.'

No theory, of course—not all the theories put together—may
claim to preserve the whole truth of that Act in which God in
Christ 'took the responsibility of evil upon himself and somehow
subsumed evil under good.'[1] Yet enough survives in the Synoptic
record of our Lord's teaching to show why the first article in the
earliest Christian creed declared that 'Christ died for our sins
according to the scriptures' (1 Cor. xv. 3), and why it has been
the unanimous testimony of Christian souls all down the centuries
that 'He hath given us rest by His sorrow and life by His death.'

[1] *Letters of Principal James Denney to his Family and Friends*, 187.

XIII
JESUS' TEACHING ABOUT
THE FUTURE

Although Jesus knew Himself to stand in a relation to God which no prophet ever claimed, He did, like the Old Testament prophets, forecast 'the shape of things to come.' It is these predictions, some of a historical kind, others of a supra-historical nature, which we must now study.

What did Jesus foresee as He looked into the future? If He predicted doom for the Jewish Temple and people, what did He see lying beyond this time of disaster? What did He teach about the Day of Judgement? If He spoke of the coming of the Son of man, what did He mean by it? These are our main questions.

No part of our Lord's teaching is beset with greater difficulties, critical and exegetical. The critical troubles must be faced at once. The first concerns the trustworthiness of Matthew as a source for an enquiry of this sort. Years ago Streeter[1] showed that Q, Mark and Matthew furnish an ascending scale in their tendency to heighten our Lord's apocalyptic sayings. Beyond any doubt Matthew held strong beliefs about a Second Advent, or *Parousia*, and the Day of Judgement, and was prone to insert references to them in Christ's sayings where probably they did not originally exist.[2] A few examples will suffice. If we compare Mk. ix. 1 with Mt. xvi. 28, we find that 'the kingdom [having] come with power' has been changed into 'the Son of man coming in His kingdom.' In Mk. xiii. 1ff. where Jesus predicts the ruin of the Temple, the disciples ask, 'When shall these things be? and what shall be the sign when these things are all about to be accomplished?' In Matthew this has been altered to: 'What is the sign of thy *Parousia* and the end of the world?' (Mt. xxiv. 3). The same is true of certain references to judgement. Compare Mk. viii. 38 with Mt. xvi. 27. Furthermore, not only has Matthew a penchant for phrases like 'the end of the world' (five times in Matthew, but not elsewhere in the Gospels) and 'weeping and gnashing of teeth' (six times in Matthew, once elsewhere in the Gospels), but he has added allegorical doomsday explanations to the parables of the tares and the dragnet which hardly a

---

[1] *Oxford Studies in the Synoptic Problem*, 425-436.

[2] H. A. Guy, *The New Testament Doctrine of the Last Things*, Chap. iii, makes this point more fully.

single modern scholar will allow to go back to Jesus. We can
hardly be blamed therefore if we distrust Matthew as a guide
in the present enquiry.

The other crux is the use to be made of Mk. xiii.[1] It is now,
as Moffatt says, 'a *sententia recepta* of synoptic criticism' that this
chapter contains a Jewish Christian apocalypse, probably written
about A.D. 60, and that though the chapter contains genuine
sayings of Jesus, it does not, as it stands, give a true picture of
Christ's mind about the future. How much then of it has a
claim to go back to Christ? Most scholars accept 1–2 (ruin of
the Temple) and 28–37 (parables of the fig tree, the absent
householder, etc.). Of the remaining verses 9, 11–13 (disciples
in persecution) and 15–18 (which envisage the Roman assault)
may well be authentic. For the rest, we may be fairly sure that
24–27, which derive almost entirely from O.T. apocalyptic
passages, are not. With this provisional total of some twenty
genuine verses we may proceed to our discussion.

I

What historical predictions did Jesus make?

To begin with, it is plain that He forecast suffering for Himself
and His followers. All four sources preserve such predictions.

> Mk.: viii. 31–34, x. 39f., xiii. 11–13.
> Q: Lk. xii. 4–12, Mt. x. 28–33; Lk. xiv. 26f.=Mt. x. 37f.
> L: Lk. xxii. 35–38 (the two swords).
> M: Mt. v. 10 and x. 24f.

Sometimes Jesus speaks of 'bearing a cross'; at other times He
warns His disciples not to fear those 'who kill the body'; at
others, He foresees His disciples brought before the authorities.
Though the original setting of these sayings is not always certain,
Mark does record that on the last journey to Jerusalem Jesus
warned His disciples to be ready for suffering and that He once
vividly particularised it as 'a cross.'

The second sure conclusion is that Jesus predicted disaster
for the Jewish Temple and people. Again the evidence is impressive. There are explicit sayings like Mk. xiii. 2, 'There shall not
be left one stone upon another'; Lk. xiii. 35=Mt. xxiii. 38, Q,
'Your house [i.e. the Temple] is abandoned'; and Lk. xix.
41–44, L, 'If thou hadst known.' There are allusive warnings
like Lk. xiii. 1–5 ('Except ye repent, ye shall all likewise perish')

[1] The best modern discussion known to me is V. Taylor's article on the
subject in the *Expository Times*, January, 1949.

and Lk. xxiii. 28–31 ('Daughters of Jerusalem,' etc.), both L passages. And there are parables like those of the defendant (Lk. xii. 57–59=Mt. v. 25f.), the wicked husbandmen (Mk. xii. 1–9) and the barren fig tree (Lk. xiii. 6–9, L).[1] The disaster *clash with Rome.* which Jesus foresaw was clearly the fatal clash with Rome, and He prophesied that it would happen within the existing generation:

'Therefore also said the wisdom of God, I will send unto them prophets and apostles; and some of them they shall kill and persecute; that the blood of all the prophets which was shed from the foundation of the world, may be required of this generation; from the blood of Abel unto the blood of Zachariah who perished between the altar and the sanctuary: yea, I say unto you, it shall be required of this generation' (Lk. xi. 49–51 = Mt. xxiii. 34f., Q; compare Mk. xiii. 30, 'This generation shall not pass away until all these things shall be accomplished').

We have thus two well-attested predictions: one of suffering for Himself and His followers, the other of disaster for the Jewish Temple and people. How did Jesus connect the two coming events in His own mind?

We find the clue in Lk. xii. 49f., a passage usually assigned to Q: 'I came to cast fire upon the earth, and how I wish it were already kindled! But I have a baptism to be baptised with, and how am I straitened till it be accomplished! Think ye that I am come to give peace in the earth? Nay; but rather division.' And He goes on to predict the domestic and social chaos which will ensue.

Clearly Jesus expected His mission to issue in a great crisis in *fulfilment* human affairs and connected it with His own death, which He *not quite* called His 'baptism.' We trace a similar line of thought in the *in X's generation* parable of the wicked husbandmen (Mk. xii. 1–9) where the killing of 'the heir' is followed by the destruction of the tenants. All this Jesus said would happen in 'this generation.' If, in fact, the crisis came 35–40 years later, this is but a mild example of 'prophetic foreshortening of the historical perspective.' (Similarly, about 750 B.C. Amos had predicted, 'The end of my people is at hand.' In 721 the kingdom of Israel fell.)

These predictions all deal in doom and disaster. Was there

---

[1] We should perhaps add Mk. xiii. 28f. (parable of the fig tree) and compare Amos's parable of the basket of ripe fruit which he uses to predict the Assyrian destruction of Israel.

> 'And the Eternal said to me,
> So is the doom ripe for my people Israel'
> (Amos viii. 1f., Moffatt).

another and brighter side to the picture in our Lord's mind? Did He foresee a time of restoration beyond the coming tragedy?

We have already seen that He expected a coming of the Reign of God 'with power,' i.e. with some mighty (divine) act like the Resurrection, and that He also expected the sphere of that Reign to grow as the tiny piece of leaven gradually permeates the whole mass of dough, as the tiny mustard seed shoots up into a great plant (i.e. in terms of growth, not of catastrophe). Did He expect some sort of Paradise on earth to follow on the calamities He foretold? And ought we, on the authority of Jesus, to cherish the hope that one day wars and tyrannies and exploitations will give way to a perfect society which might be called 'the Kingdom of God on earth'?

Our Gospel sources do not encourage such a view. The difficult promise in Mk. x. 29f. does not authorise such a hope; for any blessings promised in this life are to be mixed 'with persecutions,' and 'eternal life' is reserved for 'the world to come.' Nor does the obscure saying about 'twelve thrones,' of which we have variant versions in M (Mt. xix. 28) and L (Lk. xxii. 29f.), justify it: what clues there are point to a better world than this. Our verdict must be that Jesus never taught His disciples to expect a time of unalloyed bliss on this earth when the divine judgements were overpast (cf. Jn. xvi. 33, 'In the world ye shall have tribulation'). Christians must work for the improvement of human society, as they must pray that 'God's will may be done in earth, as it is in heaven'; but they are not committed by their Lord's teaching to any dream of Utopia in this vale of time and tears. For them, the ultimate meaning of history—and the fulfilment of their highest and holiest hopes—lies beyond history, in the supernal world.

2

We turn now to the supra-historical predictions of Jesus, i.e. those which seem to describe not so much coming events in history as events of a supernatural kind: in particular the Day of Judgement and the Day of the Son of Man.

(a) The Day of Judgement

The chief passages from our Gospel sources are:

Mk.: xii. 40.
Q: Lk. vi. 37=Mt. vii. 1; Lk. x. 12–15=Mt. x. 15, xi. 21f.; and Lk. xi. 31f.=Mt. xii. 41f.
M: Mt. v. 22; xii. 36; xxiii. 33; and xxv. 31–46.

Of these we may set aside Mt. xxiii. 33, 'Ye offspring of vipers, how shall ye escape the judgement of hell,' which is an imitation of the Baptist's saying (Lk. iii. 7=Mt. iii. 7, Q).

The fewness of Jesus' sayings on this subject is surprising. Thus, Mark contains the noun 'judgement' but once, the verb never. Moreover, in three of the sayings listed above Jesus, whilst teaching men's liability to divine judgement, does not refer to the Day:

Mk. xii. 40: 'These shall receive greater judgement.'
Lk. vi. 37: 'Judge not, that ye be not judged.'
Mt. v. 22: 'Everyone who is angry with his brother shall be in danger of the judgement.'

There remain four passages for study. According to the first Q passage (Lk. x. 12–15), Jesus in sending out His 'missionaries' declared that 'in that day' it would be more bearable for Sodom than for the Galilean city which rejected them:

'I say unto you, it shall be more tolerable in that day for Sodom than for that city. Woe unto thee, Chorazin! woe unto thee, Bethsaida! for if the mighty works had been done in Tyre and Sidon, which were done in you, they would have repented long ago sitting in sackcloth and ashes. Howbeit it shall be more tolerable for Tyre and Sidon in the judgement, than for you. And thou, Capernaum, shalt thou be exalted unto heaven? thou shalt be brought down unto Hades.'

The judgement in which Sodom figures must lie beyond history; for irretrievable judgement, in a historical sense, had overtaken the Cities of the Plain centuries before. Likewise, when Jesus contrasts the lot of Tyre and Sidon with that of the Galilean cities 'in the judgement,' He cannot be thinking of a historical judgement in terms of war due to a clash with Rome; for no Roman threat overhung Tyre and Sidon.

The same must be said of the second Q saying (Lk. xi. 31f.): 'The queen of the south shall rise up in the judgement with the men of this generation, and shall condemn them: for she came from the ends of the earth to hear the wisdom of Solomon; and behold, something greater than Solomon is here. The men of Nineveh shall stand up in the judgement with the men of this generation, and shall condemn it: for they repented at the preaching of Jonah; and behold, something greater than Jonah is here.'

So far as their mortal bodies were concerned, Sheba and the men of Nineveh were long dust. A judgement in which they figure must lie beyond history.

Of the remaining two passages, both from the M source, one is Mt. xii. 36: 'I say unto you, that every idle word that men shall speak, they shall give account thereof in the day of judgement.' The other passage is the allegory of the Last Judgement (Mt. xxv. 31–46). But since it lies under the suspicion of being a 'Matthaean construction,' based on the Judgement scene in *Enoch* lxii (see note at the end of the chapter) and built round the genuine saying of Jesus in verse 40, we cannot rely on the general picture it provides.

What shall we conclude from this brief survey? It seems clear that Jesus spoke of a divine judgement, but that for Him it lay beyond history. (The traditional picture of an end-of-the-world assize is based on the dubious Matthaean explanations to the parables of the tares and the dragnet and Mt. xxv. 31–46. On the other hand, certain evidence—notably the parable of Dives and Lazarus and our Lord's reply to the penitent thief—indicates that men go to whatever fate awaits them immediately after death.)[1] There is a Q saying (Mt. x. 32f.=Lk. xii. 8f.) which implies that the scene of the judgement will be in heaven, that God will be the judge, and that Jesus as the Son of man will be the chief *witness*[2] for men: 'Everyone therefore who shall confess me before men, him will I also confess before my Father which is in heaven.' (For the last phrase Luke has 'the angels of God.') In all these matters of judgement to come Jesus spoke with reserve, not elaborating the picture (as many of His followers have done) but emphasising men's accountability to God and using the idea of doomsday to persuade men that eternal issues hung upon their response to the Reign of God decisively manifested in His person and mission. This truth finds expression in the words which Jesus speaks through the Fourth Evangelist: 'For judgement came I into this world, that they which see not may see; and that they which see may become blind' (Jn. ix. 39).

(b) The Triumph of the Son of Man

Jesus foresaw His death; but beyond death He foresaw also triumph for the cause of God embodied in His own representative person. The question is, How did He conceive of His coming triumph?

[1] In the Old Testament there are 'intimations' of a similar doctrine in Pss. xlix. 15, lxxiii. 24 and xvi. 10. There is no mention of a resurrection. It is implied that the righteous man is received, after death, into blessed fellowship with God.

[2] Or 'the advocate of the faithful before God.'

When we examine the Synoptic sources, we find two sets of predictions: (1) predictions in which Jesus says that as the Son of man He will rise again 'after three days'; and (2) predictions in which He speaks of the coming, or day, of the Son of man. We must study both in turn.

(handwritten margin note: ①)

(1) According to Mk. viii. 31, ix. 31 and x. 33f., Jesus thrice predicted that as the Son of man He would rise from the dead 'after three days.' What did He mean by 'after three days'? There is abundant evidence[1] that in Biblical times and usage 'after three days' meant 'after a short (indefinite) interval.'[2] So it is in Hos. vi. 2; and it is possible—even probable—that Jesus' phrase contains a reference to that passage: 'After two days will He revive us: on the third day He will raise us up, and we shall live before Him.' (Cf. the LXX: 'On the third day we shall rise (ἀναστησόμεθα) and live before him.') This passage not only comes from a chapter familiar to Jesus (see Mt. ix. 13 and xii. 7) but refers both to 'the third day' and to 'resurrection.' Moreover, in the sayings of Jesus about 'the new sanctuary' preserved in Mk. xiv. 58 and Jn. ii. 19f. (which St, John refers to the Resurrection) we find further reference to 'a three days' interval' and to some sort of 'raising.' Further, the pre-Pauline tradition quoted in 1 Cor. xv. 4 declares that the Resurrection was 'according to the scriptures'; and if we ask which scripture is meant, Hos. vi. 2 seems much the likeliest. Not surprisingly, Burkitt[3] and others have said: 'If there is an Old Testament model which supplied the wording for the Passion and Resurrection prophecies, it is Hos. vi. 2f.' And the most recent writer on the matter, Delling,[4] holds that Jesus found the phrase given Him in the Hosea passage. We may conclude not only that Jesus foretold His victory over death, but that He also probably phrased His prophecy in the words of Hosea.[5]

(handwritten margin note: x predicted that Son of man wd rise "after 3 days")

(handwritten margin note: phrase is from Hos 6².)

(2) In the other set of predictions Jesus foretells the 'coming,' or 'day,' of the Son of man. The passages are:

(handwritten margin note: ②)

Mk.: viii. 38, xiii. 26, and xiv. 62.
Q: Lk. xii. 40 = Mt. xxiv. 44.
L: Lk. xviii. 8*b*.
M: Mt. x. 23 and xxv. 31.
    Cf. also Lk. xvii. 22, 26, 30, probably all Q.

[1] See Cadoux, *The Historic Mission of Jesus*, 287.

[2] Cf. Jn. xvi. 16, '*A little while*, and ye shall see me.'

[3] J. T. S., ii. 112f.   [4] In Kittel's *Theologisches Wörterbuch sub* ἡμέρα.

[5] Mt. and Lk. in the passages parallel to Mk. viii. 31, etc., change 'after three days' into 'on the third day'—probably after the event.

Critical scholarship will not allow us to accept all these passages as good evidence. Thus, in the Q parallel (Lk. xii. 8f.) to Mk. viii. 38, there is no thought of a 'coming' of the Son of man: the scene is laid in heaven. The Q version is commonly regarded as more original. Mk. xiii. 26 we have already excluded. Mt. x. 23, the verse on which Schweitzer built so much, is generally taken to reflect the expectations of the primitive Palestinian Church. And Mt. xxv. 31 looks like a phrase from *Enoch* lxii. 5 (cf. also lxix. 27). Whether all these doubts are justified or not, we shall be wise to use only the sayings above suspicion: Lk. xvii. 22, 26 and 30; Lk. xii. 40 and xviii. 8*b* (though a number of scholars reject this too); and Mk. xiv. 62.

The whole passage, Lk. xvii. 22–37, is puzzling. Verses 22–30 refer to the 'day' (30) or 'days'[1] (22, 30) of the Son of man; whereas most of 31–37, beginning with a *sauve qui peut* and ending with the picture of 'eagles' and a 'corpse,' suggests the Roman attack on Jerusalem. We are told that the Son of man, after His suffering, will be like lightning (24)—one thinks of Paul's experience of the risen Lord—and then that the day of the Son of man's 'revelation' will take men as unawares as did Noah's Flood and the ruin that befell Sodom (26–29). We are not told what rôle the Son of man is to play.

Lk. xii. 40 in its context suggests the unexpectedness of the Son of man's coming, as does Lk. xviii. 8*b*.

Mk. xiv. 62 is much more illuminating. To the high priest's question, 'Are you the Messiah?' Jesus replies, 'I am,' and proceeds: 'And you shall see[2] the Son of man sitting at the right hand of power and coming with the clouds of heaven.' This saying does not predict a Second Advent, as is commonly supposed. It prophesies not a descent, but an ascent. The words come from Dan. vii. 13 with a phrase from Ps. cx. 1. And it is very important to note the context in Daniel. There the verse which begins, 'There came with the clouds of heaven one like unto a son of man' concludes, 'and he came even unto the ancient of days, and they brought him near before him.' Clearly in Daniel the son of man's destination is the immediate presence of God. His guerdon is sovereignty, his coming to 'the highest place

Daniel 7¹³ lies behind refs to "coming"

[1] The 'days' of the Son of man, which are to follow His 'suffering and rejection' (cf. Isa. liii. 3), suggest an echo of 'He shall prolong his days' (Isa. liii. 10), i.e. a reference to the time of the Servant—Son of man's triumph.

[2] 'See' is not to be taken literally any more than in Lk. x. 17f.: 'I saw Satan fall as lightning from heaven.' Though the language is apocalyptic, the meaning is: 'The victory over the Power of evil is virtually won.' See Sanday, *The Life of Christ in Recent Research*, 111. Cp. also the use of ὄψομαι of something not visible to the eye in the LXX version of Pss. xlix. 10 and lxxxix. 48.

that heaven affords.' Jesus must have taken the plain meaning
of the passage. Thus, His declaration, so far from being a predic-
tion of a Second Advent, is an impassioned assertion that despite
the apparent ruin of His cause, He will yet be vindicated by
God and exalted to heaven. This view, whose rightness is
increasingly admitted by scholars (W. Manson, V. Taylor,
Lowther Clarke, T. F. Glasson, M. J. Lagrange and others), may
well supply the clue to what Jesus meant by the Son of man's
'coming.' When He spoke of 'coming,' did He mean it in the
Danielic sense of 'coming to power' or in what we might call
the Jacobite sense of 'coming again'? We are face to face with
the great question (as Schweitzer called it)—the question of the
identity or difference of the Resurrection and the Coming of the
Son of man.

We must, first, consider whether, for Jesus, the Resurrection
'after three days' and the 'coming of the Son of man' were
alternative expressions for the same event—the day of His
triumph over death and His exaltation to the Father.

'Jesus' thought,' writes Vincent Taylor, 'is nearer Daniel
vii. 13 when the Son of man receives "dominion and glory and
a kingdom." The *Parousia* of which he speaks is not a coming for
judgement, the setting up of the kingdom, and the final Restoration of all things; it is rather entrance upon a kingship which is
the Father's gift (cf. Lk. xxii. 29). *It includes all that is meant by
the Resurrection, but is a more ultimate concept.*'[1]

What can be said for this view?

First, not only is it very unlikely that Jesus ever used the
word *Parousia* (the word occurs in the Gospels only in Mt. xxiv.
3, 27, 37 and 39, and all four examples are 'insertions' by
Matthew), but He never speaks in the Synoptic Gospels about
'coming *again*.' Nor is the doctrine of the Messiah's *Parousia* to
be found in the literature of contemporary Judaism, as is often
supposed.[2]

Second, it is significant that though Jesus predicted (*a*) His
Resurrection and (*b*) His coming as the Son of man, we have
no saying in which He predicts *both*. Were the two events, for
Him, one? As a corollary, we may notice that if in Mk. viii. 31
the Passion is to be followed by the Resurrection, in Q, viz.
Lk. xvii. 25, the Passion is to be followed by the coming of the
Son of Man.

Third, the time before the return of the master in parables
like those of the waiting servants and the absent householder is

[1] *Jesus and His Sacrifice*, 31. Italics mine.
[2] See T. F. Glasson, *The Second Advent*, 13-62.

a short, undefined interval. This agrees with the brief indefiniteness of the 'after three days' of the Resurrection-prophecies. As a corollary, we may add that the incredulity of the disciples at the news of the Resurrection (recorded by all evangelists) is intelligible if Jesus' predictions of His triumph over death possessed something of the indefiniteness just mentioned.

Scholars must therefore reckon with the possibility—some would say probability—that Jesus predicted His triumph in two different forms of expression—one, based on Hos. vi. 2, in terms of Resurrection; the other, based on Dan. vii. 13f., in terms of exaltation to God's presence. If it be thought unlikely that Jesus would use two different scriptural phrases, it may be replied that He used yet a third—that of the stone rejected by the builders which God made the head of the corner (Mk. xii. 10f., quoting Ps. cxviii. 22f.). Finally, it may be significant that, save in Acts i, the New Testament writers make no clear distinction between the Resurrection and the Exaltation (see, for example, Phil. ii. 9f.).

If this be the truth, the events of the first Easter Day, the new power that came upon the disciples on the Day of Pentecost, and the victorious expansion of the Church represent the fulfilment of our Lord's predictions.[1]

The common view, however, has been that Jesus predicted two distinct events: (a) His Resurrection and (b) His Return at the end of the world to consummate all things, i.e. the *Parousia*, in which so many early Christians fervently believed.

If, then, the coming of the Son of man is the *Parousia*, when did Jesus expect it? This is not an easy question to answer. Mk. xiii. 30, which speaks of 'all these things' being fulfilled in 'this generation,' is often assumed to refer to the *Parousia*, but may equally well refer to the ruin of Jerusalem. On the one hand,

---

[1] Let Bishop F. R. Barry speak for those who hold this view: 'He [Jesus] spoke of the Coming as immediate. There is nothing in the authentic tradition about a deferred and distant Parousia, such as we describe as "the Second Advent." The New Testament speaks about a Coming, which it expects in the immediate future. And this runs back to the teaching of Jesus. Where the early Church was mistaken was not in expecting the Coming too soon but in failing to see that it had occurred already as the precondition of Christianity and the living source of its own Christian experience. That recognition was not long to be delayed. The probable development of St. Paul's thought finds its climax in the Fourth Gospel. And here, the Coming of the Son of man as the triumphant consequence of the Passion is identified, explicitly and emphatically, with the gift of the Spirit in the hearts of believers. "It is expedient that I go away: if I go not away the Comforter will not come to you . . . I will not leave you orphans: I am coming to you"' (*The Relevance of Christianity*, 96).

the parables of the waiting servants and the absent householder
suggest that the coming of the Son of man will be soon; on the
other, in Mk. xiii. 32—if it refers to the *Parousia*—Jesus declares
that its time is a reserved secret in the breast of God. Those who
think the *Parousia* is meant generally explain the apparent
immediacy of Christ's language in terms of His *certainty* of the
event. But it may be suggested that if the Coming is the *Parousia*
and the end of history, it is something we cannot, strictly speaking,
think (any more than we can think the beginning of history)—it
is something we can only express in parables and pictures; for
it describes symbolically the taking up of time into eternity. If
this is so, we may say two things. First, in a sense the consumma-
tion is always at hand, for the relation of time to eternity is not
one of temporal remoteness, but of continuous immediacy.
Second, the vision of the coming of the Son of man in His glory
is, as Rawlinson well says, 'the perpetual symbol of the ultimate
certitude of the things that are beyond time and history—the
final victory of God and his righteousness . . . the triumph of
Christ and his saints; the utter defeat of all evil; and, for those
who are through Christ redeemed unto God, the wiping away of
all tears, and the endless fruition of life eternal in the final and
perfected kingdom of God.'[1]

Note on Mt. xxv. 31–46

The authenticity of the saying in verse 40 is admitted by most
scholars; but few are prepared to accept the rest as a close
report of what Jesus said, and many call it 'a Matthaean construction.' Here are some of their reasons: (1) The allegory (it is not
a parable) has no parallel elsewhere in the Gospels. Matthew
had a special interest in Doomsday. (2) Burkitt and others have
shown that both its language and ideas are founded on the
Judgement scene in *Enoch* lxii. (3) The allegory contains difficulties. Quite abruptly, the Son of man becomes 'the King.' This
king is evidently Jesus and He is the Judge; whereas in the Q
saying (Mt. x. 32f.=Lk. xii. 8f.) Jesus pictures His rôle at God's
judgement as that of witness. Lecky's view is that the passage
is founded on the *Enoch* Judgement scene and that we cannot
trust the precise terms and images for doctrinal purposes. See
Burkitt, *Jewish and Christian Apocalypses*, 23–25, and Lecky,
The World to Come and Final Destiny, 113.

[1] *Christ in the Gospels*, 51f.

XIV

THE LAST JOURNEY
AND THE PASSION
(Mk. ix. 30-xv)

'It cannot be,' Jesus had said, 'that a prophet perish out of Jerusalem' (Lk. xiii. 33, L). Resolved to finish the work God had given Him to do, Jesus now set His face towards Jerusalem. With His disciples He passed, almost secretly, through Galilee (Mk. ix. 30), halting at Capernaum (ix. 33) before crossing the Jordan into Peraea (x. 1), and recrossing it near Jericho (Mk. x. 46; cf. Lk. xix. 1–10, L). Finally, they reached Bethany and the Mount of Olives (xi. 1).

Of all the glimpses of the last journey none is more wonderful than that in Mk. x. 32: 'And they were in the way, going up to Jerusalem: and they were amazed; and they that followed were afraid.' If anything in the Gospels is authentic, this stark, sombre sentence is. Here, beyond all cavil, is the reminiscence of an eye-witness. We get a picture of two parties—Jesus, a great lonely figure striding on ahead, and the disciples following, awe-stricken, at a distance. What 'amazed' them was the kind of lead Jesus had taken. Never before had He so stepped out ahead of them, as though impatient to reach His goal. He was wholly absorbed in something that passed the wit of His disciples. And if we ask what the thing was, there can be but one answer— the comment of Bengel, *Jesus jam tum habitabat in passione sua*— Jesus was 'dwelling in his passion.'

We cannot stay to comment on the various episodes of the journey; for we must hurry on to the climax in the events of the last week.

From this time on our Lord's actions are best understood in terms of 'prophetic symbolism.' It is well known that the Old Testament prophets often acted out their predictions. Thus, to take one example, Jeremiah once solemnly shattered an earthenware flask before a group of his fellow-countrymen in order to symbolise the 'breaking' of Jerusalem. His action said more eloquently than any word, 'This is what is going to happen to you, O Jerusalem.' (Other examples in Jer. xxvii. 2 and Ezek. iv. 1–3.) Such an action was more than a vivid illustration of the prophet's words. By his action the prophet conceived of himself as entering into the divine purpose and contributing

112

to its fulfilment (see Wheeler Robinson in *Old Testament Essays*, 1–17). His act was an 'earnest' (as Paul would have said) of what would be, 'a little part of the reality as yet unseen as a whole.' To this category belong three of our Lord's actions during His last week in Jerusalem: the Triumphal Entry, the Temple Cleansing and the Breaking of the Loaf at the Last Supper.

The Triumphal Entry (Mk. xi. 1–10; Mt. xxi. 1–9; Lk. xix. 28–38. cf. Jn. xii. 12–19)

In our Lord's mind, the entry was undoubtedly a piece of prophetic or (since He knew Himself to be far more than a prophet) messianic symbolism, carefully and deliberately planned. Borrowing an ass from some staunch friend in the neighbourhood, possibly in Bethphage, 'the village over against you,' He rode the last two miles, via the Mount of Olives, across the Kidron, into the Holy City; while the disciples and pilgrims coming up for the Passover feast strewed their garments and branches in the way and chanted one of the Hallel Psalms: 'Hosanna! Blessed is he that cometh in the name of the Lord! Blessed is the coming kingdom of our father David! Hosanna in the highest!' (Ps. cxviii. 25–26).

Why did Jesus ride on an ass rather than march at the head of His followers into Jerusalem? To suggest (as one modern scholar has done) that it was because 'the road wound uphill all the way' and that He was tired, is to turn pure poetry into flat prose. The clue to the meaning of His action is to be found in Zech. ix. 9. Centuries before a seer had pictured Messiah as 'lowly and riding upon an ass' (the beast of peace), adding that 'he would speak peace unto the nations, and his dominion would be from sea to sea.' This prophecy Jesus now deliberately acted out. By His action He proclaimed in the very home and heart of Israel that He was the Messiah, but a Messiah without arms or an army, a Messiah who was riding 'in lowly pomp' that road of the spirit marked out for the Servant of the Lord, a road on which ever darker fell the shadow of a Cross.

Since the words from Ps. cxviii were the normal welcome given to the pilgrims (by the priests) as they arrived for the feast, some have held that there was nothing messianic about the crowd's ovation. But the second line of the greeting implies that the crowd, like Bartimaeus earlier in the day (Mk. x. 47), saw in Jesus the Davidic Messiah. And it may be that this episode formed part of the charge later laid before Pilate (Mk. xv. 3). At all events, a wave of enthusiasm seized the crowd. So great was the huzzaing as the crowd began the descent from the

H

Mount of Olives, that the Pharisees, fearing trouble from Rome, bade Jesus silence His followers. 'And he answered and said, I tell you, that if these shall hold their peace, the stones will cry out' (Lk. xix. 37–40, L). If men were voiceless, the very stones would cry out that the Kingdom and the Messiah were nigh. As they proceeded, the city broke full on His view, and with tears Jesus declared its coming ruin, and His grief that it should be so, in words, preserved only in Luke, but as authentic as any in the Gospels: 'If thou hadst known in this day, even thou, the things which belong unto peace! but now they are hid from thine eyes. For the days shall come upon thee when thine enemies . . . shall not leave in thee one stone upon another; because thou knewest not the time of thy visitation' (Lk. xix. 41–44, L). The Kingdom of God had drawn near in grace and mercy. But Israel was rejecting that proffered mercy and was walking headlong to ruin. Such was the tragedy over which Jesus wept.[1]

And, with acclamation, they brought Him to the City.

The Temple Cleansing (Mk. xi. 15–19; Mt. xxi. 10–17; Lk. xix. 45–48; cf. Jn. ii. 13–17)

The second symbolic act was the cleansing of the Temple on the following day. St. John places this event early in the ministry, but it seems far more appropriate in the context of the last days. The scene was the court of the Gentiles, the only place in the Temple area assigned to the Gentiles for prayer. This Annas and his Sadducean satellites had turned into a holy market where, at a profit to the priests, pilgrims could buy sacrificial victims, and obtain, at a dear rate of exchange, the prescribed half-shekel of Temple tax. So 'the altar of Mammon had been erected in the Court of the Temple of God.'[2] In a place which Jesus had once called 'My Father's house,' He now found 'all the sweltering of a dirty cattle-market and the haggling of a dirtier exchange of money.' In the sheer strength of His heart's anger He swept it clean of its hucksters in holy things, and stopped the right of way through the Temple courts. And to His action He added stinging words from the old prophets: 'My house shall be called a house of prayer for all nations [Isa. lvi. 7], but you have made it a den of thieves' (Jer. vii. 11).

Do we adequately describe Jesus' action when we call it the indignant gesture of a religious reformer whose soul is shocked at the shameful profanation of holy things? That this is part of

---

[1] T. W. Manson, *The Sayings of Jesus*, 321f.

[2] E. Hoskyns, *The Fourth Gospel*, I, 194.

the explanation we may regard as certain; but there is more to
it. W. R. Maltby has said:

'It is not to be supposed that by one act he expected to alter
the customs that had made the Temple courts a repulsive cattle-
market. He knew that the traders would be back again to-
morrow—a little more wary and the worse because they were
aware. But he was not thinking of what they would do to-morrow.
His act would remain.'[1]

We found the clue to the triumphal entry in the Old Testament,
and it is hard to doubt that some words of Malachi were ringing
in His ears as He cleansed the Temple. 'The Lord whom ye seek
shall suddenly come to his Temple, but who may abide the day
of his coming? . . . And he shall purify the sons of Levi, and purge
them as gold and silver' (Mal. iii. 1ff.). The cleansing was a
symbol of the Lord Messiah coming in His Kingdom—a symbol
proclaiming that the original purpose of God in ordaining
worship in His house was to be honoured, and the people of God
prepared for the advent of His Kingdom and Messiah.

The cleansing was both challenge and threat to the Jewish
authorities. Jesus threw down the gage to the religious leaders;
He threatened both their prestige and their pockets. They had
now to consider how most quickly and quietly they might be
rid of Him.

We shall pass over what is commonly known as the day of
questions (Mk. xi. 27–xii. 44). If Mark's chronology is to be
trusted, we are now at Wednesday of Holy Week, and on this
day there occurred the anointing of Jesus by a woman at Bethany
and the final defection of Judas. (St. John places the anointing
'six days before the Passover' and locates it in the house of
Lazarus.) What was there in the woman's act to evoke such
splendid praise from Jesus? It was a courageous act—that is
obvious. It was a costly act—that we are told. But surely it was
the insight revealed in it which moved Jesus to pronounce it
'a beautiful deed' and to predict that it would go as far in the
world as the Gospel. What was the insight? If we bear two things
in mind—first, that she broke the flask, and second, that it was
an anointing—we may get near the secret. For in anointing the
dead it was customary to break the flask before laying it in the
coffin, and the very name Messiah means 'the anointed one.'
May we then say that the woman had penetrated into the
secret of the suffering and dying Messiah? That her woman's
intuition had brought her into spiritual places where even the
Twelve moved uneasily?

[1] *Christ and His Cross*, 57.

Judas's betrayal is a great riddle. What did he betray, and why did he do it? What Judas betrayed, says Schweitzer, was the Messiahship of Jesus. It was this intelligence, says Bacon—the fact that Jesus had been secretly anointed as the Messiah—which Judas hurried off to divulge to the authorities. It may be so; but is it not far more likely that what Judas told the authorities was where and when Jesus might be quietly arrested? If we ask why Judas betrayed Jesus, we may put aside De Quincey's theory that Judas thought Jesus too unworldly and wished to force Him into a position where He would be compelled to exhibit His divine glory, but with no idea that He would allow Himself to be executed. 'I refuse,' said George Eliot once, speaking of this view, 'to accept a man who has the stomach for such treachery as a hero impatient for the redemption of mankind.' Far likelier it is that Jesus' conception of Messiahship bitterly disappointed Judas (did not even Peter boggle at it?) and that, sensing the peril in which Jesus and His disciples stood, he seized the last chance to extricate himself from it (as well as the chance of making some money) by 'turning king's evidence.'

③

The Last Supper (Mk. xiv. 17–25; Mt. xxvi. 20–29; Lk. xxii. 14–38; 1 Cor. xi. 23–25)

We come now to the third act of Messianic symbolism. On the evening of the day before that on which the Passover lambs were slain, Jesus and His disciples met for supper in an upper room specially lent for the occasion. (Noteworthy is the phrase in Mk. xiv. 14, 'Where is *my* guest-chamber?' The *my* is full of meaning. This was Jesus' guest-chamber, for He was to play the part of host at the banquet. The disciples were His *guests*.)

If St. John's dating be right (see the note at the end of the chapter), the Last Supper can hardly have been a proper Pass-over, unless, of course, Jesus gave it that character, knowing that He would be dead before the actual Passover. The common-est view among scholars is that the Supper was a preparatory meal known as the *Kiddush* ('sanctification'). But whether a Passover, a hurried anticipation of it, or a *Kiddush*, we have to interpret the meaning of Jesus' words and actions at the Last Supper by the light of the Gospel narratives supplemented by 1 Cor. xi. 23–25.

Since Matthew's account follows Mark and Luke's account contains a serious textual problem,[1] we must rely mainly on

[1] Viz. the omission by Codex Bezae and other authorities of Lk. xxii. 19b-20.

St. Mark and St. Paul. When we compare them, we note the following differences:

1. Paul alone records Jesus' command to repeat the rite. (Possibly by Mark's time this was so axiomatic that he does not insert the command.)

2. Paul's version of the word over the loaf is: 'This is my body which is for you.' Mark has: 'This is my body.'

3. Paul's version of the word over the cup is: 'This cup is the new covenant in my blood.' Mark has: 'This is my blood of the covenant which is shed for many.'

Despite these variations, the two accounts agree on the essentials. At the Last Supper, Jesus, after saying a grace over the loaf, broke it and gave it to the disciples with the word: 'This is my body.' Then He gave them the cup with the ruddy wine gleaming in it, saying: 'This [cup] is the [new] covenant in my blood.' Clearly He spoke of a covenant—a new order of relations between God and man—to be established by His blood, i.e. His life freely surrendered to God in death.

In order to understand what He said and did, let us recall three things:[1]

(*a*) Jesus had likened the Kingdom of God to a supper—see the parable of the great feast (Lk. xiv. 15–24; Mt. xxii. 1–10, Q).

(*b*) The Passover commemorated the redemptive act of God by which He had marked out Israel as His special people. But Jesus had declared that the Jews by rejecting their Messiah were no longer God's people and had foretold the creation of a new Israel (Mk. xii. 9, xiv. 58 and Lk. xiii. 34f.=Mt. xxiii. 37f. Q).

(*c*) He had affirmed that He was giving His life to redeem 'the many' (Mk. x. 45; and cf. xiv. 24) and had described His Passion as a 'cup' to be drunk (Mk. x. 38, xiv. 36).

All three ideas—the Kingdom of God as a supper, the new people of God, His death as a cup to be drunk—contribute to our understanding of the Last Supper. In setting apart the bread and the wine, Jesus was offering His disciples (and those who should thereafter believe in Him) a pledge of life in the Kingdom of God soon to come 'with power.' In describing the broken bread as His body and linking the wine with His blood, He was effecting, in splendid symbol, that sacrifice of Himself which He was soon to accomplish in fact. In asking the disciples to partake of the bread and wine (so interpreted), He was giving them a

INTERPRETATION OF SUPPER

---

[1] This interpretation is based on that of C. H. Dodd in *A Companion to the Bible* (ed. T. W. Manson).

share in the virtue of that sacrifice—a share, as Otto puts it,[1]
'in the atoning power of the broken Christ.'

But there is more than simple symbolism here. As the prophetic
act was 'a little bit of the reality as yet unseen,' so the rite in
the Upper Room is an effective sign, a sacrament. Whether they
knew it or not, when the disciples rose from the table, they rose
as men redeemed by the death of their Master. And if anyone
object that they were still frail and sinful men, we may agree,
and say that it is Jesus' final declaration that the gifts of God are
given to undeserving men by Him who 'came not to invite the
righteous but sinners.'

After the Supper Jesus and His disciples left the Upper Room
and made their way through the narrow streets of Jerusalem,
across the Kidron to the Mount of Olives. On the way He
lingered to pray in an olive-grove on the hill-side. Leaving eight
of His disciples on the fringe of the grove, He took with Him
Peter, James and John to share His vigil. A deadly desolation
descended on His spirit. Then advancing a few paces (yet not so
far that they could not hear the main drift of His prayer), He
besought the Father for the removal of the cup. It was the old
temptation—Messiahship without a Cross, salvation without
atonement—that met Him here for the last time with redoubled
force. But He had hardly prayed for the cup's removal when
He was quietly resigning Himself to the Father's sovereign will.
The agony of prayer was scarcely ended when the silence was
broken by the sound of the approaching posse, guided to the
spot by the traitor Judas. After a futile attempt at resistance the
disciples scattered, and Jesus was arrested.

The Trial of Jesus (Mk. xiv. 53–xv. 20; Mt. xxvi. 57–xxvii. 31;
Lk. xxii. 54–xxiii. 25; Jn. xviii. 12–xix. 16)

The trial of Jesus falls into two parts: (i) the Jewish trial before
the Sanhedrin; and (ii) the Roman trial before Pilate. It raises
two sets of problems (*a*) historical, i.e. in what order did the
various events occur, and (*b*) legal, i.e. was Jesus given a fair
trial?

All four Gospels contain accounts. Since Matthew, save for
inserting three M stories (Judas's suicide, Pilate's wife's dream,
and Pilate's hand-washing), reproduces Mark, we may leave
his account out of consideration. If we follow Mark, we must

[1] *The Kingdom of God and the Son of Man*, 304. In Forsyth's words, 'Christ
was giving over to men the Sacrifice He was making once for all to God.
It is Christ's consignment to the Church of the Cross He was offering to
God' (*The Church and the Sacraments*, 214ff.).

remember that Luke had undoubtedly special information at his disposal, and follow him if he seems to have a better tradition than Mark. It is possible too that John may preserve some true tradition not in the Synoptists.

Though the main sequence of events is clear, we cannot harmonise the details from the various Gospels into 'a protocol of the exact proceedings.' But this seems to us the most probable outline of what occurred:

(a) The Jewish Trial: on the Charge of Blasphemy.

(1) After arrest, Jesus is informally examined by the high-priest and suffers mockery from His captors.

(2) At dawn, the Sanhedrin being convened, the high-priest obtains a confession of His Messiahship from Jesus, and the court condemns Him for blasphemy.

But the Sanhedrin had no power to inflict the death-sentence. On the other hand, Pilate would not listen to a charge of blasphemy. So there follows:

(b) The Roman Trial: on the Charge of Majestas (High Treason).

(1) Before Pilate, who, though he obtains a qualified claim to kingship from Jesus, is unwilling to condemn one he knows to be innocent.

(2) He schemes to get Herod to try the prisoner. When that fails,

(3) The trial being resumed, Pilate tries to save Jesus at the expense of Barabbas; finds that the people, instigated by the priests, prefer Barabbas; and finally, yielding to the people's wishes, delivers Jesus for scourging and crucifixion.

There follows, in the barracks, the second mockery.

(*Note:* This summary assumes that Luke rightly places the formal Sanhedrin meeting *at dawn*, nocturnal meetings being illegal; that John may be right in describing a preliminary examination by Annas; that Lk. xxiii. 2 correctly summarises the charge which the Jews laid before Pilate and explains how Pilate (as Mark tells us) came to ask: 'Are you the King of the Jews?'; and lastly that Luke's account of the sending of Jesus to Herod is good history.[1])

On this summary we may add a few comments. In the eyes of Rome, the Jewish trial probably amounted to no more than 'grand jury proceedings' to determine the charge to be brought in the civil court. In itself, the claim to Messiahship was not blasphemy. All turned on the person who made it. Herod's refusal to try Jesus is intelligible. 'The Idumean fox dreaded the lion's paw, while very willing to exchange courtesies with the

[1] See Streeter, *Oxford Studies in the Synoptic Problem*, 229-231.

lion's deputy.' Pilate, though obviously thinking Jesus innocent
of the political charge, knew that it was 'more than his job
was worth' to risk a tumult by refusing the popular demand.
In the last resort, we must hold the Jewish leaders morally
responsible for Jesus' death.

If we ask whether Jesus was fairly tried, it is difficult to answer
the question. The whole affair seems to have been rushed through
with haste and speed. Taylor Innes (himself a lawyer) insists
that the Sanhedrin acted quite illegally. We do not get the
impression of a proper trial at all before Pilate. All we hear are
a few questions asked, the rising temper of the mob, a perplexed
procurator trying in face of their shouted demands to act fairly,
and then his weak surrender to the cry for crucifixion. The sacrifice of yet another provincial was a cheap price to pay for the
preservation of the *Pax Romana*. He had no guess how the verdicts
of history were to be reversed—no presentiment that one day
he would be remembered solely for his association with the
Prisoner whom he sent to the Cross.

The Crucifixion (Mk. xv. 21–47; Mt. xxvii. 32–66; Lk. xxiii. 26–56;
cf. Jn. xix. 17–42)

(To Mark's narrative Matthew adds the historically dubious
stories of the earthquake and resurrection of the Jewish saints and
the sealing of the tomb. Luke adds the saying, 'Daughters of
Jerusalem,' the story of the penitent thief and two other words
from the Cross.)

The story is too familiar to need long rehearsal. Golgotha was
a low, skull-shaped eminence outside the City wall. There at
the third hour, i.e. 9 a.m., Jesus was 'lifted up' on the Cross
between two malefactors. The inscription on the Cross bore
the charge against Him, 'The King of the Jews.' At noon a
strange darkness, perhaps due to 'a black sirocco,' descended on
the scene, and we are told that the curtain in the Temple separat-
ing the Holy of Holies from the Holy Place was rent in two
(cf. Heb. x. 19f.).

'Seven times he spake,' but Mark records only the cry of
dereliction. This, the supreme mystery of the Saviour's Passion,
has been variously interpreted. The suggestion that, because the
words come from Ps. xxii. 1, it is really a cry of triumph, must be
set aside. If we are to take the cry seriously, we must say that so
irrevocably had He betrothed Himself to the cause of sinful men
that, for a brief space, He experienced a sense of that alienation
from God which sin brings with it. The last word from the
Cross according to St. John (xix. 30) was 'It is finished.' Whether

this be history or not, it is true. It is a cry not of despair but of triumphant accomplishment. He had finished the work God had given Him to do. He had drained the cup. He had travelled the road. He had endured the baptism. He had given His life a ransom for many. He died at the ninth hour, i.e. 3 p.m. The last glimpse is of a little group of women 'beholding from afar.' Their loyalty put the disciples to shame.

Jewish law (Deut. xxi. 23) ordained that the bodies of executed criminals should be buried the same day, and the task was the more urgent because in a few hours the Sabbath would begin. So Joseph of Arimathaea, a member of the Sanhedrin and possibly a secret disciple, gaining Pilate's permission to remove Jesus' body from the Cross, shrouded it and laid it in a nearby rock-tomb. The curtain seemed to have fallen on unrelieved tragedy.

Note: The Date of the Crucifixion

The day of the Crucifixion was Friday. Not the day, but the date, is the problem. The Synoptists imply that it was 15 Nisan (March-April); John that it was 14 Nisan.

The Passover was eaten at the beginning of the 15 Nisan. This day began, for the Jew, at sunset on the day counted as 14 Nisan.

Now, the Gospels agree that Jesus and His disciples held the Last Supper on Thursday, and that Jesus was crucified on Friday. But here the agreement ends. For the Synoptists apparently regard the Last Supper as a Passover (e.g. Mk. xiv. 16, 'They made ready the Passover'), i.e. they make Thursday the 14 Nisan, so that the Supper, eaten after sunset, falls on 15 Nisan. John however, equates the Friday with 14 Nisan (see Jn. xiii. 1, xviii. 28, xix. 14). If he is right, the Last Supper was not a Passover proper, and the Crucifixion took place when the Passover lambs were being slain.

Which tradition is to be preferred? John's is clear and consistent; the Synoptists' is not. For, though they assume that the Last Supper was a Passover, they let fall certain comments that point in John's direction. One is Mk. xiv. 2 ('Not during the feast'); another is Mk. xv. 42 (which puts the Crucifixion on 'the day before the Sabbath'); and the third is Lk. xxii. 15 (if it expresses an unfulfilled wish, as most scholars assume).

Moreover, certain facts seem to indicate that the Last Supper was not a Passover:

(i) The description of the meal does not suggest a Passover. (No mention of a lamb, or of unleavened bread; mention of only one cup instead of the normal four at a Passover, etc.)

(ii) The disciples would hardly be carrying arms during Passover.

(iii) Simon the Cyrenian was coming 'from the country.'

For these and other reasons most British scholars think John's dating of the Crucifixion probable. If then the Last Supper was not a Passover, what was it?

(a) Some say a *Kiddush* (whether a Passover or a Sabbath *Kiddush*). The objection to this is that the normal *Kiddush* day was on Friday, not Thursday.

(b) Others, like Otto and Dix, think that the Supper was a *Haburah* meal.

(c) Others think it was a hurried anticipation of the Passover, Jesus knowing that He would be dead before the correct time. Cf. Lk. xxii. 15: 'With desire I have desired to eat this Passover with you before I suffer.'

XV

THE RESURRECTION

Was Jesus the great deceiver and the great deceived? The Cross is really a mighty question-mark against the sky. If the story of Jesus ends there, then it is unmitigated tragedy and—what is more—the supreme proof of the irrationality of the universe in *rationality?* which we live. Let it be established that the life of Jesus went out in darkness, then we might at once conclude that behind the universe is not, as He believed, a supremely wise and good Father, but (in Hardy's phrase) 'a vast Imbecility.' But the story of Jesus does not end there: it has a sequel. For the Gospel story is the story of the Messiah in whom God's saving sovereignty was uniquely manifested, and it must be the story of a victorious conflict, of life achieved through death. Jesus Himself, as we have seen, had predicted such a triumph, and we may add that it could not be otherwise for One who had seen His appointed destiny in that of the suffering Servant of the Lord. For the Servant was to be 'exalted' and to 'prolong his days,' and 'the pleasure [purpose] of the Lord was to prosper in his hand.'

With all this our evidence agrees. Not many days had passed before the disciples were convinced beyond any shadow of doubt that Jesus was alive and had appeared to them; and the whole New Testament literature is radiant with the light of the Resurrection.

THE DOCUMENTARY EVIDENCE

Our earliest documentary evidence for the Resurrection is to be found in 1 Cor. xv. 3ff. There Paul, writing about A.D. 55, reminds the Corinthians of the Church 'tradition' which he had 'received,' presumably after his conversion (A.D. 33?). The passage must therefore date back to the first decade after the Crucifixion, and has been rightly pronounced by Meyer 'the oldest Christian document we possess.' It runs as follows:

'For I delivered unto you first of all that which also I received, how that Christ died for our sins according to the scriptures: and that He was buried, and that He hath been raised[1] on the third day according to the scriptures: and that He appeared to Cephas, then to the Twelve: then He appeared to above five

---

[1] ἐγήγερται. = rose and remains in His risen state.

hundred brethren at once, of whom the greater part remain until now, but some are fallen asleep; then He appeared unto James: then to all the apostles: and, last of all, as unto one born out of due time, He appeared to me also.'

Here we have very early evidence. The four-times repeated 'that' suggests that Paul is quoting a formula—some fixed piece of tradition taught to all converts. What are its limits? Possibly the formula went no further than verse 5 ('then to the Twelve'). Certainly, the final clause is Paul's personal testimony, not a part of the formula. And the parenthesis in verse 6 ('of whom the greater part remain until now,' etc.) seems to have been inserted by St. Paul to make good his attestation. 'Most of the five hundred,' he advises the Corinthians, 'are still alive. If you doubt my word, ask them.'

Observe, next, that though Paul does not mention the empty tomb, he implies it. What otherwise is the point of mentioning the burial? 'Died, buried, raised'—the words are unintelligible unless they mean that what was buried was raised. And we may add that it would have conveyed nothing to St. Paul or to the first Christians to say that it was the *spirit* of Christ which rose into new life. Even sceptics like Schmiedel and Lake agree that Paul's words imply belief in the empty tomb.

Paul goes on to relate six appearances:

> To Cephas. Cf. Lk. xxiv. 34 and note Mk. xvi. 7.
> To the Twelve. Cf. Lk. xxiv. 36ff. and Jn. xx. 19ff.
> To five hundred brethren.
> To James. (The *Gospel to the Hebrews* records a beautiful story of such an appearance.)
> To all the apostles (a wider group than the Twelve).
> To Paul himself (the Damascus Road experience).

It is noteworthy that Paul sets this last appearance to himself on the same level with those to the others: 'he ranks his sight with theirs.'

Here then is our earliest and best documentary evidence. Now let us turn to the Gospels.

Mark (xvi. 1–8) describes how on the first Easter morning the women found the tomb empty, how 'a young man' (John Mark or an angel?) told them of the risen Jesus, and how they fled in terror. The original ending in Mark has probably been lost. Doubtless, in its unmutilated form, Mark's Gospel went on to describe an appearance of the risen Lord in Galilee (cf. Mk. xiv. 28 and xvi. 7); but enough has survived to show what the climax of the Gospel was.

Matthew (xxviii), after describing the empty tomb, records
(*a*) an appearance of the risen Lord to the women fleeing from
the tomb, and (*b*) an appearance to the Eleven on a mountain
in Galilee when, after giving them a missionary charge, He
promised them His continuing presence.

It should be noted that, though Matthew follows Mark in the
story of the empty tomb, he has embroidered it with the story
of the guard and with references to an earthquake and a descending angel—details which we must receive with reserve.

Luke (xxiv) relates how the women, after finding the tomb
empty, brought the news to the incredulous Eleven. He then
records three appearances: (*a*) to Cleopas and another on the
road to Emmaus; (*b*) to Peter (Lk. xxiv. 34); and (*c*) to the
Eleven and others in Jerusalem, before Jesus 'led them out
until they were over against Bethany . . . and parted from them.'

On this account we may make two comments. First, the words
'and was carried up into heaven' are textually doubtful and are
omitted by most modern scholars. Second, in the Jerusalem
appearance to the Eleven, Jesus is said to have eaten 'a piece of
broiled fish.' This detail has troubled many. Is not eating (they
ask) a function of this life which can have no place in the life
of an immortal being? If this difficulty is felt to be real—not all
will find it equally difficult—we may put it down to Luke's
tendency to materialise (compare his 'in bodily form' in the
Baptism story), but we must add that to reject the eating is not
to reject the Resurrection life of Jesus.

John (xx–xxi) relates how Mary Magdalene found the tomb
empty and how Peter and the beloved disciple (John?) visited
the tomb to confirm her news. He then records four appearances:
(*a*) to Mary Magdalene in the garden; (*b*) to ten disciples on
the same Sunday behind closed doors in Jerusalem; (*c*) to ten
disciples and Thomas a week later; and (*d*)—in the appendix—to
seven disciples by the shore of the lake in the grey of a Galilean
dawn.

We may observe that John's stories about the risen Lord,
though at first sight hard to harmonise with the earlier accounts,
in other ways confirm them. Thus, the 'we'[1] in John's story
of Mary Magdalene in the Garden confirms Mark's story of a
group of women. John's account of the appearance to the Eleven
confirms both Luke and Paul. The appendix confirms a Galilean
tradition.

These bald summaries of the various accounts do no sort of
justice to them. Taken as a whole, they must be allowed to

[1] Jn. xx. 2.

be very life-like, vivid and self-authenticating: and it is hard to
escape the conclusion that in Mark's story of the finding of the
empty tomb, Luke's story of the walk to Emmaus, and John's
stories of Mary in the garden and of the Risen Lord by the
Galilean Lake we are dealing with the record of real history.
They do not read like the products of the myth-making faculty,
as we can see by comparing them with the stories which the
apocryphal Gospels tell.

But if the stories are vivid and life-like, we cannot weave them
into one coherent and consistent narrative. Nor is it worth while
to try to do so. There are discrepancies. But, after all, is not this
just what we should expect? Or, rather, should we not be highly
mistrustful if, instead of discrepancies, we found only a neat and
contradiction-free harmony? Nay, the very discrepancies show
that no harmonising instinct was allowed to obliterate them.
Furthermore, discrepancies in different accounts do not prove
that an event did not occur. No one familiar with witnesses and
evidence will maintain that such discrepancies discredit the main
fact attested. Thus, to take but one example, there are startling
discrepancies in the accounts of Waterloo as given by Wellington,
Marshal Ney and Napoleon. Yet no one dreams of denying that
a battle was fought there.

What conclusions may we draw from the documentary evidence? Despite discrepancies, and tendencies (in Matthew) to
embroider and (in Luke) to materialise, there is agreement on
two main points:

(1) The Tomb was empty. (Paul implies this, and three independent sources—Mark, Luke (xxiv. 23), and John (xx. 1–10)—
declare it.)

(2) Jesus made several appearances to His disciples.

But where did Jesus appear? The scene of the Resurrection
appearances is often represented as a capital difficulty. As we
have seen, Matthew and the Appendix to the Fourth Gospel
locate them in Galilee, whereas Luke and Jn. xx locate them in
Jerusalem. So our scholars, apparently assuming that we are
faced with an *entweder-oder*—either Galilee or Jerusalem, but not
both—have argued about locality, Dr. Lake insisting that
Galilee was the place, Dr. Burkitt pleading the case for Jerusalem. But there is no need—for the Christian believer at any
rate—to make the choice between Galilee and Jerusalem. If
we accept the fact that Jesus rose from the dead, it was surely
as easy for Him to appear in Jerusalem and in Galilee, as in
Jerusalem only or Galilee only. We do not have to choose between
localities. It may very well be that, whereas Luke is right in

describing an appearance to the Eleven in Jerusalem on Easter Day, and in taking Jerusalem to be the main centre, there were also appearances in Galilee, as the other evangelists assert.

THE MANNER OF CHRIST'S APPEARING

How then are we to explain the empty tomb and the appearances of Jesus?

We must begin by rejecting the theory of subjective visions, or (as it might better be called) the hallucination-theory (Strauss, Renan, Montefiore.) 'What raised Christ? It was love,' replies Renan.[1] Jesus was raised—but only in the resurgent love of His disciples. This theory asks us to believe that so strongly were the disciples under the influence of Jesus' personality that they imagined they had seen Him again, though in fact their visions had no objective reality. To it there are two decisive objections. To begin with, it caricatures the documentary evidence. In the second place, the psychological conditions necessary for such visions were not present. The Resurrection was not expected. So far from being on the tiptoe of expectation, the disciples were plunged in grief and gloom and received the first tidings of the Resurrection as 'idle tales.'

A second theory is that of 'objective visions' (Keim, Streeter, Cadoux, etc.). On this view, the visions of the Risen Lord were God-given visions granted to the disciples, in order to assure them that the spirit of Jesus survived. In a phrase that became famous, Keim spoke of 'a telegram from heaven.' More recently Cadoux has written of 'real manifestations given to his followers by Jesus himself, not by means of the presence of his physical body but by way of those strange processes sufficiently attested to us by psychical research but as yet very imperfectly understood.'[2]

This view, though less offensive than the previous one, is also unsatisfactory. It consists ill with the evidence of the Gospels; it fails to accord with the view of those who witnessed the resurrection and regarded it not as an illustration of survival, but as an intrusion from the other world; and it cannot account for the empty tomb.

It is there we must begin. Our documentary evidence declares that the body of Jesus had somehow disappeared from the rock-tomb. The theory that the body was stolen or hidden is frankly incredible. Had the Romans or the Jews removed the body from the grave, it would have been an easy matter for them to refute

[1] So Bousset, *Jesus* (Eng. Tr.), 209, speaks of 'Easter in the disciples' hearts.'
[2] *The Life of Jesus*, 165.

the Christians' claim by simply producing the body. We may be sure that they did not, because they could not. On the other hand, to suppose that the disciples themselves hid the body and then went forth to preach a risen Christ whom they knew to be dead, passes belief. This would be to brand them as impostors, and even a Jew like Klausner finds this incredible. 'The nineteen hundred years' faith,' he says, 'is not founded on deception.'[1]

If then we accept the empty tomb, we may choose one of two explanations. First, there is the physical one. On this view, Jesus' physical body was resuscitated, and in that body He manifested Himself to the disciples. With such a view, odd bits of evidence in the Gospels (e.g. Lk. xxiv. 36–43) might consist very well. But if the Resurrection body of Jesus was His actual physical body, it becomes no easy matter to dispose of it. St. Luke, in Acts i. 9, disposes of it by translating it to the sky. Such a view, however acceptable to the ancients with their belief in a three-storied universe, is not acceptable to the modern man. A body of flesh and blood has no proper place in the spiritual world, and translation into the sky is not, for our modern thinking, the equivalent of passing from the mundane to the spiritual sphere.

Therefore it is wisest to follow St. Paul (and a succession of Christian scholars from Origen to Westcott) in believing that the physical body of our Lord was, in some way we cannot understand, *transformed* into a spiritual body, a body which is no impediment to the spirit, a body suited to the conditions of a higher life as our flesh-and-blood body is suited to the conditions of this one. With such a view the evidence of St. John—the undisturbed grave-clothes, the ability of the risen Lord to pass through closed doors, etc.—agrees very well. And it is tolerably certain that this was St. Paul's own view. In 1 Cor. xv. Paul declares that a change from a natural to a spiritual body is the appointed destiny of the Christian believer. Since he speaks of Christ as 'the first fruits of them that sleep,' we infer that he believed the same wonderful change to have occurred in our Lord's body. In his own phrasing, 'the body of humiliation' had become 'the body of glory.' Even Lake admits this: 'An examination of Paul's teaching points to the fact that he believed that at the resurrection the body of Jesus was changed from one of flesh and blood into one that was spiritual, incorruptible and immortal, in such a way that there was no trace left of the corruptible body that had been laid in the grave.'[2]

[1] *Jesus of Nazareth*, 359.   [2] *The Resurrection of Jesus Christ*, 23.

There we may wisely leave the matter. For the chief thing in the Resurrection stories is the disciples' invincible belief that their Master had conquered death. Only on the basis of that belief can we explain the change that came over them: before the Resurrection, like frightened sheep; after it, as bold as lions. There is one adequate cause for such an effect—an experience of the risen Christ. Only on this basis can we explain the converting and saving power of the message they went forth to proclaim. Only so can we explain that conviction of fellowship with a living Lord which has been the nerve of Christianity for nineteen hundred years and the inspiration of a long succession of men from Paul of Tarsus to Samuel Rutherford and David Livingstone.

When we are troubled by discrepancies in the documents, we should remember that there are three great witnesses to the reality of the Resurrection.

First, the existence of the Christian Church. Had the Crucifixion ended the disciples' fellowship with Jesus, it is hard to see how the Church could have come into existence, and harder still to see how it could have continued these nineteen hundred years.

Second, the existence of the New Testament. Who would have troubled to write these documents if Jesus had ended His career as a crucified revolutionary? Every written record made about Him was made by men who believed in a risen Lord. 'It is not this or that in the New Testament,' says Denney, 'it is not the story of the empty tomb, or of the appearing of Jesus in Jerusalem or in Galilee—which is the primary evidence for the Resurrection; it is the New Testament itself. The life that throbs in it from beginning to end, the life that always fills us again with wonder as it beats upon us from its pages, is the life which the risen Saviour has quickened in Christian souls.'[1]

Third, the existence of the Lord's Day. No Christian Jew would have changed the sacred day from Sabbath (Saturday) to 'the first day of the week' (Acts xx. 7; 1 Cor. xvi. 2; Rev. i. 10) except for the reason which the Christian tradition gave—that on this day Jesus was first seen risen.

'When I think of the Resurrection,' H. G. Wells once wrote,[2] 'I am always reminded of the happy endings that editors and actor managers are accustomed to impose on essentially tragic plays and novels.' This is not the New Testament view. For its writers the story of Jesus is not a tragic tale which must at all

---

[1] *Jesus and the Gospel*, 106ff.
[2] *First and Last Things*, 88.

I

costs be converted into a happy one for the benefit of third parties. They do not see the Cross as only a tragic symbol. The Cross, with some sort of theory of atonement attached to it, was part of their Good News from at least the first decade after the Crucifixion (1 Cor. xv. 3). The truth is that for these men the Cross did not stand alone. Cross and Resurrection were two aspects of one great redeeming act of God, the second of which illumined, as with a great shaft of light, the darkness of the first:

'Easter,' wrote R. C. Moberly,[1] 'is the interpretation of Good Friday. The significance of the Cross is revealed in the Resurrection. The Resurrection is not so much a mere sequel to the Cross: or a reversal of the Cross: or a subsequent reward because of the endurance of the Cross. Rather, it is a revealing of what the Cross already was.'

The second thing to be said is that the earliest Christians did not see the Resurrection as simply the supreme illustration of human survival after death. They saw it—witness 1 Pet. i. 3ff.—as a victory uniquely won, and won that men might be enabled to share in its virtue. So far from regarding it as the sensational re-animation of one who had died—another and greater Lazarus recalled to life—they saw the Resurrection as the break-through of the eternal order into this world of suffering and death. It was God's answer to the mighty question-mark against the sky; it was the dynamic declaration that at the heart of the universe there was a living God who would not suffer His Holy One to see corruption, or permit the victory of holiness won on the Cross to be empty, sterile, fruitless. It was the Reign of God made visible.

Moreover, the Resurrection was not an end but a beginning. 'All that Jesus began to do and teach,' says St. Luke, referring to all that led up to Jesus' exaltation. For with the Resurrection the Kingdom came 'with power,' the Holy Spirit was given, and Jesus who during the days of His flesh must needs confine Himself to the little land of Palestine, became the living Lord who by the Spirit incarnated, and still incarnates, Himself in unnumbered men and women so that it may be truly said: 'The Gospels are not four, but ten thousand times ten thousand, and thousands of thousands, and the last word of every one of them is, Lo, I am with you alway, even unto the end of the world.'[2]

Christ our Life, 89.   [2] T. R. Glover, *The Conflict of Religions*, 140.

APPENDICES: THE GOSPEL SOURCES

I. THE TEXT OF Q

The symbol Q designates the sayings-source used by the first and the third evangelists. Existing originally in Aramaic and possibly compiled by the Apostle Matthew, it was put together, probably in Antioch, about A.D. 50, to serve as a moral handbook for catechumens.

Q has often been reconstructed. Though scholars disagree about some items, there is substantial agreement about the main portions of it. Reconstructed, it amounts to roughly 250 verses. It is generally admitted that the order in which Q appears in Luke is superior to that in Matthew; for Matthew likes to group his materials and to conflate his sources. Moreover, in most passages the Lucan wording seems demonstrably more primitive, i.e. nearer the original, than the Matthaean. Therefore it is customary nowadays to reconstruct Q in terms of Luke. When we thus reconstruct it, Q seems to fall into four sections which (following T. W. Manson) we may entitle:

> A. Jesus and John: iii. 7–9, 16–17, 21–22; iv. 1–13; vi. 20–49; vii. 1–10, 18f., 22–35.
> B. Jesus and His Disciples: ix. 57–62; x. 2–16, 21–24; xi. 9–13.
> C. Jesus and His Opponents: xi. 14–52; xii. 2–12, 22–34.
> D. Jesus and the Future: xii. 35–59; xiii. 18–30, 34–35; xiv. 11, 15–27, 34–35; xvi. 13, 16–18; xvii. 1–6, 22–37.

N.B. In the text of Q we have given the Matthaean parallels in footnotes. The sign (=), used to indicate parallels, does not mean that there is exact verbal equivalence: very often is it only approximate.

A. JESUS AND JOHN

The Preaching of John
> iii. 7–9, 16–17=Mt. iii. 7–10, 11–12. Cf. Mk. i. 7–8.

7. He said therefore to the multitudes that went out to be baptised of him, Ye offspring of vipers, who warned you to flee from the wrath to come? 8. Bring forth therefore fruits worthy of repentance, and begin not to say within yourselves, We have Abraham to our father: for I say unto you, that God is able of these stones to raise up children unto Abraham. 9. And even now is the axe also laid unto the root of the trees: every tree therefore that bringeth not forth good fruit is hewn down, and cast into the fire.

16. John answered, saying unto them all, I indeed baptise you with water; but there cometh he that is mightier than I, the latchet of whose shoes I am not worthy to unloose: he shall baptise you with

the Holy Ghost and with fire: 17. whose fan is in his hand, throughly
to cleanse his threshing-floor, and to gather the wheat into his garner;
but the chaff he will burn up with unquenchable fire.

The Baptism of Jesus
21–22=Mt. iii. 16–17. Cf. Mk. i. 9–11

21. Now it came to pass, when all the people were baptised, that,
Jesus also having been baptised, and praying, the heaven was opened,
22. and the Holy Ghost descended in a bodily form, as a dove, upon
him, and a voice came out of heaven, Thou art my beloved Son;
in thee I am well pleased.

The Temptation
iv. 1–13=Mt. iv. 1–11. Cf. Mk. i. 12–13.

1. And Jesus, full of the Holy Spirit, returned from the Jordan,
and was led by the Spirit in the wilderness during forty days, 2. being
tempted of the devil. And he did eat nothing in those days: and
when they were completed, he hungered. 3. And the devil said unto
him, If thou art the Son of God, command this stone that it become
bread. 4. And Jesus answered unto him, It is written, Man shall not
live by bread alone (Deut. viii. 3). 5. And he led him up, and shewed
him all the kingdoms of the world in a moment of time. 6. And the
devil said unto him, To thee will I give all this authority, and the
glory of them: for it hath been delivered unto me; and to whomsoever I will I give it. 7. If thou therefore wilt worship before me, it
shall all be thine. 8. And Jesus answered and said unto him, It is
written, Thou shalt worship the Lord thy God, and him only shalt
thou serve (Deut. vi. 13). 9. And he led him to Jerusalem, and set
him on the pinnacle of the temple, and said unto him, If thou art
the Son of God, cast thyself down from hence: 10. for it is written,
He shall give his angels concerning thee, to guard thee,
and, On their hands they shall bear thee up,
Lest haply thou dash thy foot against a stone (Ps. xci. 11f.).
12. And Jesus answering said unto him, It is said, Thou shalt not
tempt the Lord thy God (Deut. vi. 16).

13. And when the devil had completed every temptation, he
departed from him for a season.

The Sermon
vi. 20–49.

20.[1] And he lifted up his eyes on his disciples, and said, Blessed are
ye poor: for yours is the kingdom of God. 21. Blessed are ye that
hunger now: for ye shall be filled. Blessed are ye that weep now:

[1]=Mt. v. 3, 4, 6, 11f.

for ye shall laugh. 22. Blessed are ye, when men shall hate you, and when they shall separate you from their company, and reproach you, and cast out your name as evil, for the Son of man's sake. 23. Rejoice in that day, and leap for joy: for behold, your reward is great in heaven: for in the same manner did their fathers unto the prophets. 24.[1] But woe unto you that are rich! for ye have received your consolation. 25. Woe unto you, ye that are full now! for ye shall hunger. Woe unto you, ye that laugh now! for ye shall mourn and weep. 26. Woe unto you, when all men shall speak well of you! for in the same manner did their fathers to the false prophets.

27.[2] But I say unto you which hear, Love your enemies, do good to them that hate you, 28. bless them that curse you, pray for them that despitefully use you. 29.[3] To him that smiteth thee on the one cheek offer also the other; and from him that taketh away thy cloke withhold not thy coat also. 30.[4] Give to everyone that asketh thee; and of him that taketh away thy goods ask them not again. 31.[5] And as ye would that men should do to you, do ye also to them likewise. 32.[6] And if ye love them that love you, what thank have ye? for even sinners love those that love them. 33. And if ye do good to them that do good to you, what thank have ye? for even sinners do the same. 34. And if ye lend to them of whom ye hope to receive, what thank have ye? even sinners lend to sinners, to receive again as much. 35.[7] But love your enemies, and do them good, and lend, never despairing; and your reward shall be great, and ye shall be sons of the Most High: for he is kind toward the unthankful and evil. 36.[8] Be ye merciful, even as your Father is merciful. 37.[9] And judge not, and ye shall not be judged: and condemn not, and ye shall not be condemned: release, and ye shall be released: 38. give, and it shall be given unto you; good measure, pressed down, shaken together, running over, shall they give into your bosom. For with what measure ye mete, it shall be measured to you again.

39.[10] And he spake also a parable unto them, Can the blind guide the blind? shall they not both fall into a pit? 40.[11] The disciple is not above his master: but everyone when he is perfected shall be as his master. 41.[12] And why beholdest thou the mote that is in thy brother's eye, but considerest not the beam that is in thine own eye? 42. Or how canst thou say to thy brother, Brother, let me cast out the mote that is in thine eye, when thou thyself beholdest not the beam that

[1] The four 'woes' are not in Mt.   [2] =Mt. v. 44.

[3] =Mt. v. 39f.   [4] =Mt. v. 42.   [5] =Mt. vii. 12.

[6] =Mt. v. 46f.   [7] Cf. Mt. v. 45, M.   [8] Cf. Mt. v. 48, M.

[9] =Mt. vii. 1f.   [10] =Mt. xv. 14.   [11] Cf. Mt. x. 24f., M.

[12] =Mt. vii. 3-5.

is in thine own eye? Thou hypocrite, cast out first the beam out of thine own eye, and then shalt thou see clearly to cast out the mote that is in thy brother's eye. 43.[1] For there is no good tree that bringeth forth corrupt fruit; nor again a corrupt tree that bringeth forth good fruit. 44. For each tree is known by its own fruit. For of thorns men do not gather figs, nor of a bramble bush gather they grapes. 45. The good man out of the good treasure of his heart bringeth forth that which is good; and the evil man out of the evil treasure bringeth forth that which is evil: for out of the abundance of the heart his mouth speaketh.

46.[2] And why call ye me, Lord, Lord, and do not the things which I say? 47.[3] Everyone that cometh unto me, and heareth my words, and doeth them, I will shew you to whom he is like: 48. he is like a man building a house, who digged and went deep, and laid a foundation upon the rock; and when a flood arose, the stream brake against that house, and could not shake it: because it had been well builded. 49. But he that heareth, and doeth not, is like a man that built a house upon the earth without a foundation; against which the stream brake, and straightway it fell in; and the ruin of that house was great.

The Centurion's Servant[4]

vii. 1b–10=Mt. viii. 5–10, 13.

1b. He entered into Capernaum.

2. And a certain centurion's servant, who was dear unto him, was sick and at the point of death. 3. And when he heard concerning Jesus, he sent unto him elders of the Jews, asking him that he would come and save his servant. 4. And they, when they came to Jesus, besought him earnestly, saying, He is worthy that thou shouldest do this for him: 5. for he loveth our nation, and himself built us our synagogue. 6. And Jesus went with them. And when he was now not far from the house, the centurion sent friends to him, saying unto him, Lord, trouble not thyself: for I am not worthy that thou shouldest come under my roof: 7. wherefore neither thought I myself worthy to come unto thee: but say the word, and my servant shall be healed. 8. For I also am a man set under authority, having under myself soldiers: and I say to this one, Go, and he goeth; and to another, Come, and he cometh; and to my servant, Do this, and he doeth it. 9. And when Jesus heard these things, he marvelled at him, and turned and said unto the multitude that followed him, I say unto you, I have not found so great faith, no, not in Israel. 10. And they that were sent, returning to the house, found the servant whole.

---

[1] =Mt. vii. 16-20 and xii. 33-35.   [2] Cf. Mt. vii. 21, M.

[3] =Mt. vii. 24-27.   [4] Some think only the dialogue stood in Q.

John and Jesus
　　vii. 18f., 22–35=Mt. xi. 2–11, 16–19.

18. And the disciples of John told him of all these things. 19. And John calling unto him two of his disciples sent them to the Lord, saying, Art thou he that cometh, or look we for another? 22. And he answered and said unto them, Go your way, and tell John what thing ye have seen and heard; the blind receive their sight, the lame walk, the lepers are cleansed, and the deaf hear, the dead are raised up, the poor have good tidings preached to them. 23. And blessed is he, whosoever shall find none occasion of stumbling in me.

24. And when the messengers of John were departed, he began to say unto the multitudes concerning John, What went ye out into the wilderness to behold? a reed shaken with the wind? 25. But what went ye out to see? a man clothed in soft raiment? Behold, they which are gorgeously apparelled, and live delicately, are in kings' courts. 26. But what went ye out to see? A prophet? Yea, I say unto you, and much more than a prophet. 27. This is he of whom it is written;

　　Behold, I send my messenger before thy face
　　Who shall prepare thy way before thee (Mal. iii. 1).

28. I say unto you, Among them that are born of women there is none greater than John: yet he that is but little in the kingdom of God is greater than he. 29.[1] And all the people when they heard, and the publicans, justified God, being baptised with the baptism of John. 30. But the Pharisees and the lawyers rejected for themselves the counsel of God, being not baptised of him. 31. Whereunto then shall I liken the men of this generation, and to what are they like? 32. They are like unto children that sit in the marketplace, and call one to another; which say, We piped unto you, and ye did not dance; we wailed, and ye did not weep. 33. For John the Baptist is come eating no bread nor drinking wine; and ye say, He hath a devil. 34. The Son of man is come eating and drinking; and ye say, Behold, a gluttonous man, and a winebibber, a friend of publicans and sinners! 35. And wisdom is justified of all her children.

B. JESUS AND HIS DISCIPLES

Prospective Disciples
　　ix. 57–62=Mt. viii. 19–22.

And as they went in the way, a certain man said unto him, I will follow thee whithersoever thou goest. 58. And Jesus said unto him, The foxes have holes, and the birds of the heaven have nests; but the Son of man hath not where to lay his head. 59. And he said unto

[1] 29-30. Not in Mt.

another, Follow me. But he said, Lord, suffer me first to go and bury my father. 60. But he said unto him, Leave the dead to bury their own dead; but go thou and publish abroad the kingdom of God. 61.[1] And another also said, I will follow thee, Lord; but first suffer me to bid farewell to them that are at my house. 62. But Jesus said unto him, No man, having put his hand to the plough, and looking back, is fit for the kingdom of God.

The Mission Charge
x. 2–16.

2.[2] And he said unto them, The harvest is plenteous, but the labourers are few: pray ye therefore the Lord of the harvest, that he send forth labourers into his harvest. 3.[3] Go your ways: behold, I send you forth as lambs in the midst of wolves. 4.[4] Carry no purse, no wallet, no shoes: and salute no man on the way. 5. And into whatsoever house ye shall enter, first say, Peace be to this house. 6. And if a son of peace be there, your peace shall rest upon him: but if not, it shall turn to you again. 7. And in that same house remain, eating and drinking such things as they give: for the labourer is worthy of his hire. Go not from house to house. 8.[5] And into whatsoever city ye enter, and they receive you, eat such things as are set before you: 9. and heal the sick that are therein, and say unto them, The kingdom of God is come nigh unto you. 10.[6] But into whatsoever city ye shall enter, and they receive you not, go out into the streets thereof and say, 11. Even the dust from your city, that cleaveth unto our feet, we do wipe off against you: howbeit know this, that the kingdom of God is come nigh. 12.[7] I say unto you, It shall be more tolerable in that day for Sodom, than for that city. 13.[8] Woe unto thee, Chorazin! woe unto thee, Bethsaida! for if the mighty works had been done in Tyre and Sidon, which were done in you, they would have repented long ago, sitting in sackcloth and ashes. 14. Howbeit it shall be more tolerable for Tyre and Sidon in the judgement, than for you. 15. And thou, Capernaum, shalt thou be exalted unto heaven? thou shalt be brought down unto Hades. 16.[9] He that heareth you heareth me; and he that rejecteth you rejecteth me; and he that rejecteth me rejecteth him that sent me.

The Great Thanksgiving
x. 21–24=Mt. xi. 25–27; xiii. 16–17.

21. In that same hour he rejoiced in the Holy Spirit, and said, I thank thee, O Father, Lord of heaven and earth, that thou didst hide

[1] 61-62 not in Mt.　　[2] =Mt. ix. 37-38.　　[3] =Mt. x. 16.
[4] Cf. Mt. x. 9-13.　　[5] Cf. Mt. x. 7-8, M.　　[6] Cf. Mt. x. 14.
[7] =Mt. x. 15.　　[8] =Mt. xi. 21-23.　　[9] Cf. Mt. x. 40, M, also Mk. ix. 37.

these things from the wise and understanding, and didst reveal them
unto babes: yea, Father; for so it was well-pleasing in thy sight.
22. All things have been delivered unto me of my Father: and no
one knoweth who the Son is, save the Father; and who the Father
is, save the Son, and he to whomsoever the Son willeth to reveal
him. 23. And turning to the disciples, he said privately, Blessed are
the eyes which see the things that ye see: 24. for I say unto you,
that many prophets and kings desired to see the things which ye see,
and saw them not; and to hear the things which ye hear, and heard
them not.

Asking and Receiving
xi. 9–13=Mt. vii. 7–11.
9. And I say unto you, Ask, and it shall be given you; seek, and ye
shall find; knock, and it shall be opened unto you. 10. For everyone
that asketh receiveth; and he that seeketh findeth; and to him that
knocketh it shall be opened. 11. And of which of you that is a father
shall his son ask a loaf, and he give him a stone? or a fish, and he for
a fish give him a serpent? 12. Or if he shall ask an egg, will he give
him a scorpion? 13. If ye then, being evil, know how to give good
gifts unto your children, how much more shall your heavenly Father
give the Holy Spirit[1] to them that ask him?

C. JESUS AND HIS OPPONENTS

The Beelzebub Controversy
xi. 14–26=Mt. xii. 22–30, 43–45. Cf. Mk. iii. 22–27.
14. And he was casting out a devil which was dumb. And it came
to pass, when the devil was gone out, the dumb man spake; and the
multitudes marvelled. 15. But some of them said, By Beelzebub the
prince of the devils casteth he out devils. 16. And others, tempting
him, sought of him a sign from heaven. 17. But he, knowing their
thoughts, said unto them, Every kingdom divided against itself is
brought to desolation; and a house divided against a house falleth.
18. And if Satan also is divided against himself, how shall his kingdom
stand? because ye say that I cast out devils by Beelzebub. 19. And if
I by Beelzebub cast out devils, by whom do your sons cast them out?
therefore shall they be your judges. 20. But if I by the finger of
God[2] cast out devils, then is the kingdom of God come upon you.
21. When the strong man fully armed guardeth his own court his
goods are in peace: 22. but when a stronger than he shall come upon
him, and overcome him, he taketh from him his whole armour
wherein he trusted, and divideth his spoils. 23. He that is not with

[1] Mt. has 'good things.'   [2] Mt. has 'the Spirit of God'.

me is against me; and he that gathereth not with me scattereth. 24. The unclean spirit when he is gone out of the man, passeth through waterless places, seeking rest; and finding none, he saith, I will turn back unto my house whence I came out. 25. And when he is come, he findeth it swept and garnished. 26. Then goeth he, and taketh to him seven other spirits more evil than himself; and they enter in and dwell there: and the last state of that man becometh worse than the first.

The Blessedness of Christ's Mother
xi. 27–28. (No parallel in Mt. Possibly L. Cf. Mk. iii. 31–35.)

27. And it came to pass, as he said these things, a certain woman out of the multitude lifted up her voice, and said unto him, Blessed is the womb that bare thee, and the breasts which thou didst suck. 28. But he said, Yea rather, blessed are they that hear the word of God, and keep it.

Sign of Jonah
xi. 29–32=Mt. xii. 38–42. Cf. Mk. viii. 11f.

29. And when the multitudes were gathering together unto him, he began to say, This generation is an evil generation: it seeketh after a sign; and there shall no sign be given to it but the sign of Jonah. 30. For even as Jonah became a sign unto the Ninevites, so shall also the Son of man be to this generation. 31. The queen of the south shall rise up in the judgement with the men of this generation, and shall condemn them: for she came from the ends of the earth to hear the wisdom of Solomon; and behold, a greater[1] than Solomon is here. 32. The men of Nineveh shall stand up in the judgement with this generation, and shall condemn it: for they repented at the preaching of Jonah; and behold, a greater[1] than Jonah is here.

Lamp and Bushel
xi. 33–36.

33.[2] No man, when he hath lighted a lamp, putteth it in a cellar, neither under the bushel, but on the stand, that they which enter in may see the light. 34.[3] The lamp of thy body is thine eye: when thine eye is single, thy whole body also is full of light; but when it is evil, thy body also is full of darkness. 35. Look therefore whether the light that is in thee be not darkness. 36. If therefore thy whole body be full of light, having no part dark, it shall be wholly full of light, as when the lamp with its bright shining doth give thee light.

[1] Lit. 'something greater,' i.e. the kingdom of God.

[2] Cf. Mt. v. 15 and Mk. iv. 21.   [3] =Mt. vi. 22f.

Against Pharisees and Scribes
   xi. 37–52.

37. Now as he spake, a Pharisee asketh him to dine with him: and he went in, and sat down to meat. 38. And when the Pharisee saw it, he marvelled that he had not first washed before dinner. 39.[1] And the Lord said unto him, Now do ye Pharisees cleanse the outside of the cup and of the platter; but your inward part is full of extortion and wickedness. 40. Ye foolish ones, did not he that made the outside make the inside also? 41. Howbeit give for alms[2] those things which are within; and behold, all things are clean unto you.

42.[3] But woe unto you Pharisees! for ye tithe mint and rue and every herb, and pass over judgement and the love of God: but these ought ye to have done, and not to leave the other undone. 43.[4] Woe unto you Pharisees! for ye love the chief seats in the synagogues, and the salutations in the marketplaces. 44.[5] Woe unto you! for ye are as the tombs which appear not, and the men that walk over them know it not.

45. And one of the lawyers answering saith unto him, Master, in saying this thou reproachest us also. 46.[6] And he said, Woe unto you lawyers also! for ye lade men with burdens grievous to be borne, and ye yourselves touch not the burdens with one of your fingers. 47.[7] Woe unto you! for ye build the tombs of the prophets, and your fathers killed them. 48. So ye are witnesses and consent unto the works of your fathers: for they killed them, and ye build their tombs. 49.[8] Therefore also said the wisdom of God,[9] I will send unto them prophets and apostles; and some of them they shall kill and persecute; 50. that the blood of all the prophets which was shed from the foundation of the world, may be required of this generation; 51. from the blood of Abel unto the blood of Zachariah,[10] who perished between the altar and the sanctuary: yea, I say unto you, it shall be required of this generation. 52.[11] Woe unto you lawyers! for ye took away the key of knowledge: ye entered not in yourselves, and them that were entering in ye hindered.

[1] Cf. Mt. xxiii. 25f., M.

[2] 'Give for alms' probably renders the Aramaic *zakki*. Probably Luke has confused *zakki* with *dakki*='cleanse,' which is Matthew's version (xxiii. 26).

[3] Cf. Mt. xxiii. 23.   [4] Cf. Mt. xxiii. 6f., M.   [5] Cf. Mt. xxiii. 27, M.

[6] Cf. Mt. xxiii. 4, M.   [7] Cf. Mt. xxiii. 29ff., M.   [8] =Mt. xxiii. 34ff.

[9] I.e. God in His wisdom.

[10] 2 Chron. xxiv. 20f. 2 Chron., the last book in the Hebrew Bible, records the death of Zacharias, as Genesis, the first book, records the death of Abel.

[11] Cf. Mt. xxiii. 13, M.

Disciples in Persecution
   xii. 2–12.

2.[1] But there is nothing covered up, that shall not be revealed: and hid, that shall not be known. 3. Wherefore whatsoever ye have said in the darkness shall be heard in the light; and what ye have spoken in the ear in the inner chambers shall be proclaimed upon the housetops. 4.[2] And I say unto you my friends, Be not afraid of them which kill the body, and after that have no more that they can do. 5. But I will warn you whom ye shall fear: Fear him, which after he hath killed hath power to cast into hell; yea, I say unto you, Fear him. 6. Are not five sparrows sold for two farthings? and not one of them is forgotten in the sight of God. 7. But the very hairs of your head are all numbered. Fear not: ye are of more value than many sparrows. 8.[3] And I say unto you, Every one who shall confess me before men, him shall the Son of man also confess before the angels of God: 9. but he that denieth me in the presence of men shall be denied in the presence of the angels of God. 10.[4] And everyone who shall speak a word against the Son of man, it shall be forgiven him: but unto him that blasphemeth against the Holy Spirit it shall not be forgiven. 11.[5] And when they bring you before the synagogues, and the rulers, and the authorities, be not anxious how or what ye shall answer, or what ye shall say: 12. for the Holy Spirit shall teach you in that very hour what ye ought to say.

Trust in God
   xii. 22–34

22.[6] And he said unto his disciples, Therefore I say unto you, Be not anxious for your life, what ye shall eat; nor yet for your body, what ye shall put on. 23. For the life is more than the food, and the body than the raiment. 24. Consider the ravens, that they sow not, neither reap; which have no store-chamber nor barn; and God feedeth them: of how much more value are ye than the birds! 25. And which of you by being anxious can add a cubit unto his stature? 26. If ye then are not able to do even that which is least, why are ye anxious concerning the rest? 27. Consider the lilies, how they grow: they toil not, neither do they spin; yet I say unto you, Even Solomon in all his glory was not arrayed like one of these. 28. But if God doth so clothe the grass in the field, which to-day is, and to-morrow is cast into the oven; how much more shall he clothe you, O ye of little faith? 29. And seek not ye what ye shall eat, and what ye shall drink,

[1] =Mt. x. 26f.; cf. Mk. iv. 22.   [2] =Mt. x. 28-33.
[3] Cf. Mk. viii. 38.   [4] =Mt. xii. 32; cf. Mk. iii. 28f.
[5] =Mt. x. 19f.; cf. Mk. xiii. 11 and Lk. xxi. 14f.   [6] =Mt. vi. 25-33.

neither be ye of doubtful mind. 30. For all these things do the nations of the world seek after: but your Father knoweth that ye have need of these things. 31. Howbeit seek ye his kingdom, and these things shall be added unto you. 32.[1] Fear not, little flock; for it is your Father's good pleasure to give you the kingdom. 33.[2] Sell that ye have, and give alms; make for yourselves purses which wax not old, a treasure in the heavens that faileth not, where no thief draweth near, neither moth destroyeth. 34.[3] For where your treasure is, there will your heart be also.

D. JESUS AND THE FUTURE

Watchfulness and Faithfulness
  xii. 35-48.

35.[4] Let your loins be girded about, and your lamps burning; 36. and be ye yourselves like unto men looking for their lord, when he shall return from the marriage feast; that, when he cometh and knocketh, they may straightway open unto him. 37. Blessed are those servants, whom the lord when he cometh shall find watching: verily I say unto you, that he shall gird himself, and make them sit down to meat, and shall come and serve them. 38. And if he shall come in the second watch, and if in the third, and find them so, blessed are those servants. 39.[5] But know this, that if the master of the house had known in what hour the thief was coming, he would have watched, and not have left his house to be broken through. 40. Be ye also ready; for in an hour that ye think not the Son of man cometh.

41. And Peter said, Lord, speaketh thou this parable unto us, or even unto all? 42. And the Lord said, Who then is the faithful and wise steward, whom his lord shall set over his household, to give them their portion of food in due season? 43. Blessed is that servant, whom his lord when he cometh shall find so doing. 44. Of a truth I say unto you, that he will set him over all that he hath. 45. But if that servant shall say in his heart, My lord delayeth his coming; and shall begin to beat the menservants and the maid-servants, and to eat and drink, and to be drunken; 46. the lord of that servant shall come in a day when he expecteth not, and in an hour when he knoweth not, and shall cut him asunder,[6] and appoint his portion with the unfaithful. 47.[7] And that servant, which knew his lord's will, and made not ready, nor did according to his will, shall be beaten with many stripes; 48. but he that knew not, and did things worthy of stripes, shall be beaten with few stripes. And to

[1] No parallel in Mt.   [2] Cf. Mt. vi. 19-20, M.   [3] =Mt. vi. 21.
[4] Cf. Mt. xxv. 1-13, M.   [5] =Mt. xxiv. 43-51; cf. Mk. xiii. 35f.
[6] The Aramaic possibly meant 'shall separate him' (from the rest).
[7] 47-48 not in Mt.

whomsoever much is given, of him shall much be required: and to whom they commit much, of him will they ask the more.

Fire upon the Earth—Weather Signs—The Parable of the Defendant
    xii. 49–59.

49.[1] I came to cast fire upon the earth; and what will I, if it is already kindled?[2] 50. But I have a baptism to be baptised with; and how am I straitened till it be accomplished! 51.[3] Think ye that I am come to give peace in the earth? I tell you, Nay; but rather division: 52. for there shall be from henceforth five in one house divided, three against two, and two against three. 53. They shall be divided, father against son, and son against father; mother against daughter, and daughter against her mother; mother in law against her daughter in law, and daughter in law against her mother in law.

54.[4] And he said to the multitudes also, When ye see a cloud rising in the west, straightway ye say, There cometh a shower; and so it cometh to pass. 55. And when ye see a south wind blowing, ye say, There will be a scorching heat; and it cometh to pass. 56. Ye hypocrites, ye know how to interpret the face of the earth and the heaven; but how is it that ye know not how to interpret this time? 57. And why even of yourselves judge ye not what is right?

58.[5] For as thou art going with thine adversary before the magistrate, on the way give diligence to be quit of him; lest haply he hale thee unto the judge, and the judge shall deliver thee to the officer, and the officer shall cast thee into prison. 59. I say unto thee, Thou shalt by no means come out thence, till thou have paid the very last mite.

The Mustard Seed and the Leaven
    xiii. 18–21: Mt. xiii. 31–33. Cf. Mk. iv. 30–32.

18. He said therefore, Unto what is the kingdom of God like? and whereunto shall I liken it? 19. It is like unto a grain of mustard seed, which a man took, and cast into his own garden; and it grew, and became a tree; and the birds of the heaven lodged in the branches thereof. 20. And again he said, Whereunto shall I liken the kingdom of God? 21. It is like unto leaven, which a woman took and hid in three measures of meal, till it was all leavened.

The Narrow Door
    xiii. 22–30.

22. And he went on his way through cities and villages, teaching,

---

[1] 49-50 not in Mt.

[2] The probable meaning is: 'How I wish that it were already kindled!'

[3] =Mt. x. 34-36.   [4] 54-57 have no parallel in Mt.   [5] =Mt. v. 25-26.

and journeying on unto Jerusalem. 23. And one said unto him,
Lord, are they few that be saved? And he said unto them, 24.[1] Strive
to enter in by the narrow door: for many, I say unto you, shall seek
to enter in, and shall not be able. 25.[2] When once the master of the
house is risen up, and hath shut to the door, and ye begin to stand
without, and to knock at the door, saying, Lord, open to us; and
he shall answer and say to you, I know you not whence ye are;
26.[3] then shall ye begin to say, We did eat and drink in thy presence,
and thou didst teach in our streets; 27. and he shall say, I tell you,
I know not whence ye are; depart from me, all ye workers of iniquity.
28.[4] There shall be the weeping and gnashing of teeth, when ye shall
see Abraham, and Isaac, and Jacob, and all the prophets, in the
kingdom of God, and yourselves cast forth without. 29. And they
shall come from the east and west, and from the north and south,
and shall sit down in the kingdom of God. 30.[5] And behold, there
are last which shall be first, and there are first which shall be last.

Lament over Jerusalem
xiii. 34–35=Mt. xxiii. 37–39.

34. O Jerusalem, Jerusalem, which killeth the prophets, and stoneth
them that are sent unto her! how often would I have gathered thy
children together, even as a hen gathereth her own brood under her
wings, and ye would not! 35. Behold, your house is left unto you
desolate: and I say unto you, Ye shall not see me, until ye shall say,
Blessed is he that cometh in the name of the Lord.

xiv. 11=Mt. xxiii. 12. Everyone that exalteth himself shall be
humbled; and he that humbleth himself shall be exalted.

The Great Supper
xiv. 15–24. Cf. Mt. xxii. 1–10 (the M version of the parable).

15. And when one of them that sat at meat with him heard these
things, he said unto him, Blessed is he that shall eat bread in the
kingdom of God. 16. But he said unto him, A certain man made a
great supper; and he bade many: 17. and he sent forth his servant
at supper time to say to them that were bidden, Come; for all things
are now ready. 18. And they all with one consent began to make
excuse. The first said unto him, I have bought a field, and I must
needs go out and see it: I pray thee have me excused. 19. And another
said, I have bought five yoke of oxen, and I go to prove them: I pray
thee have me excused. 20. And another said, I have married a wife,
and therefore I cannot come. 21. And the servant came, and told

[1] Cf. Mt. vii. 13f., M.　[2] Cf. Mt. xxv. 10-12, M.　[3] Cf. Mt. vii. 22f., M.
[4] =Mt. viii. 11f.　[5] Cf. Mt. xix. 30 and Mk. x. 31.

his lord these things. Then the master of the house being angry said
to his servant, Go out quickly into the streets and lanes of the city,
and bring in hither the poor and maimed and blind and lame.
22. And the servant said, Lord, what thou didst command is done,
and yet there is room. 23. And the lord said unto the servant, Go out
into the highways and hedges, and constrain them to come in, that
my house may be filled. 24. For I say unto you, that none of those
men which were bidden shall taste of my supper.

Cross-bearing
    xiv. 25–27=Mt. x. 37–38.

25. Now there went with him great multitudes: and he turned, and
said unto them, 26. If any man cometh unto me, and hateth[1] not
his own father, and mother, and wife, and children, and brethren,
and sisters, yea, and his own life also, he cannot be my disciple.
27.[2] Whosoever doth not bear his own cross, and come after me,
cannot be my disciple.

The Parable of the Salt
    xiv. 34–35 = Mt. v. 13. Cf. Mk. ix. 50.

34. Salt therefore is good: but if even the salt have lost its savour,
wherewith shall it be seasoned? 35. It is fit neither for the land nor
for the dunghill: men cast it out. He that hath ears to hear, let him
hear.

God and Mammon
    xvi. 13=Mt. vi. 24.

13. No servant can serve two masters: for either he will hate the
one, and love the other; or else he will hold to one, and despise the
other. Ye cannot serve God and mammon.

Old and New
    xvi. 16–18.

16.[3] The law and the prophets were until John: from that time the
gospel of the kingdom of God is preached, and every man entereth
violently into it.
    17.[4] But it is easier for heaven and earth to pass away, than for
one tittle of the law to fall.[5]
    18.[6] Everyone that putteth away his wife, and marrieth another,
committeth adultery: and he that marrieth one that is put away
from a husband committeth adultery.

[1] 'hate'=love less.   [2] Cf. Mk. viii. 34.
[3] =Mt. xi. 12f.   [4] Cf. Mt. v. 18, M.
[5] Probably an ironic comment on the rigid conservatism of the scribes.
[6] Cf. Mt. v. 32, M; also Mk. x. 11f.

Stumbling-blocks, etc.
   xvii. 1–6.

1.[1] And he said unto his disciples, It is impossible but that occasions of stumbling should come: but woe unto him, through whom they come! 2. It were well for him if a millstone were hanged about his neck, and he were thrown into the sea, rather than that he should cause one of these little ones to stumble. 3.[2] Take heed to yourselves: if thy brother sin, rebuke him; and if he repent, forgive him. 4. And if he sin against thee seven times in the day, and seven times turn again to thee, saying, I repent; thou shalt forgive him.

   5.[3] And the apostles said unto the Lord, Increase our faith. 6. And the Lord said, If ye have faith as a grain of mustard seed, ye would say unto this sycamine tree, Be thou rooted up, and be thou planted in the sea; and it would have obeyed you.

The Day of the Son of Man
   xvii. 22–37.

22. And he said unto the disciples, The days will come, when ye shall desire to see one of the days of the Son of man, and ye shall not see it. 23.[4] And they shall say to you, Lo, there! Lo, here! go not away, nor follow after them: 24. for as the lightning, when it lighteneth out of the one part under the heaven, shineth unto the other part under heaven: so shall the Son of man be in his day. 25. But first must he suffer many things and be rejected of this generation. 26.[5] And as it came to pass in the days of Noah, even so shall it be also in the days of the Son of man. 27. They ate, they drank, they married, they were given in marriage, until the day that Noah entered into the ark, and the flood came, and destroyed them all. 28. Likewise even as it came to pass in the days of Lot; they ate, they drank, they bought, they sold, they planted, they builded; 29. but in the day that Lot went out from Sodom it rained fire and brimstone from heaven, and destroyed them all: 30. after the same manner shall it be in the day that the Son of man is revealed. 31.[6] In that day, he which shall be on the housetop, and his goods in the house, let him not go down to take them away: and let him that is in the field likewise not return back. 32. Remember Lot's wife. 33.[7] Whosoever shall seek to gain his life shall lose it: but whosoever shall lose his life shall preserve it. 34.[8] I say unto you, In that night there shall be two men on one bed; the one shall be taken, and the other shall

---

[1] =Mt. xviii. 6-7; cf. Mk. ix. 42.   [2] Cf. Mt. xviii. 15, 21, 22, M.
[3] Cf. Mt. xvii. 20, M; also Mk. xi. 23 and 1 Cor. xiii. 2.   [4] =Mt. xxiv. 26ff.
[5] =Mt. xxiv. 37-41.   [6] Cf. Mk. xiii. 15f.
[7] =Mt. x. 39; cf. Mk. viii. 35.   [8] =Mt. xxiv. 40f.
K

be left. 35. There shall be two women grinding together; the one shall be taken, and the other shall be left.[1] 37.[2] And they answering say unto him, Where, Lord? And he said unto them, Where the body is, thither will the eagles also be gathered together.

[1] 36 of the A.V. is not found in our best MSS.   [2] =Mt. xxiv. 28.

II. THE TEXT OF M

We use the symbol M to denote the Gospel tradition peculiar to Matthew—'Special Matthew.'

Apart from editorial insertions, it consists of (*a*) about a dozen O.T. proof-texts, which we shall not print; (*b*) some dozen narratives: The Nativity Narrative (i–ii), Peter's Walking on the Water, the Coin in the Fish's Mouth, and stories connected with the Passion and Resurrection (the death of Judas, Pilate's Wife's Dream, the Handwashing, the resurrection of the Jewish Saints, the Watch at the Tomb, the Earthquake, the Appearance to the Women, the Bribing of the Guard, and the Final Commission); and (*c*) many sayings and parables in chap. v–xxv, of which the chief are:

> three-fifths of the Sermon on the Mount (v–vii),
> more than twelve verses of the Mission Charge (x),
> five parables of the Kingdom (xiii),
> most of xviii,
> almost all the speech against the Pharisees (xxiii),
> the three eschatological parables of xxv,

plus such sayings as 'Come unto me,' the two 'ecclesiastical' sayings (xvi. 17–19 and xviii. 15–20) and such parables as the Labourers in the Vineyard, the Two Sons, the Marriage Feast and the Wedding Garment.

Many of the narratives in (*b*) sound like Jerusalem gossip and 'rarely rise above the level of edifying stories to that of historicity' (Moffatt). This is the least valuable bit of the Synoptic tradition.

It is to (*c*) the teaching peculiar to Matthew that Streeter and others apply the symbol M. Some portions of it are 'divergent versions' of sayings in Q. Did it all reach 'Matthew' orally, or did he derive it from some hypothetical document M? Scholars are divided between these two views. What is certain is that it represents a distinct cycle of tradition with a clear Jewish tincture. Its respect for the law, coupled with its hatred of the lawyers, its Palestinian Jewish atmosphere, sayings like x. 6 and its strong Church interest suggest that it emanated from the Churches of Judaea, which were centred in the Jerusalem Mother Church; and that it belongs to the years just before the Fall of Jerusalem.

M undoubtedly contains much genuine teaching of Jesus; but since it has suffered adulteration from the Jewish side, we must use it with considerable caution.

The Birth Stories
    i–ii.

John the Baptist's Hesitation
    iii. 14–15.

14. But John would have hindered him, saying, I have need to be

baptised of thee, and comest thou to me? 15. But Jesus answering said unto him, Suffer it now: for thus it becometh us to fulfil all righteousness. Then he suffereth him.

The Sermon on the Mount
v–vii. (Verses probably derived from Q are bracketed.)

1. And seeing the multitudes, Jesus went up into the mountain: and when he had sat down, his disciples came unto him: 2. and he opened his mouth and taught them, saying,

[3. Blessed are the poor in spirit: for theirs is the kingdom of heaven.]

[4. Blessed are they that mourn: for they shall be comforted.]

5. Blessed are the meek: for they shall inherit the earth.

[6. Blessed are they that hunger and thirst after righteousness: for they shall be filled.]

7. Blessed are the merciful: for they shall obtain mercy.

8. Blessed are the pure in heart: for they shall see God.

9. Blessed are the peacemakers: for they shall be called sons of God.

10. Blessed are they that have been persecuted for righteousness' sake: for theirs in the kingdom of heaven.

[11. Blessed are ye when men shall reproach you, and persecute you, and say all manner of evil against you falsely, for my sake.]

[12. Rejoice, and be exceeding glad: for great is your reward in heaven: for so persecuted they the prophets which were before you.]

Salt and Light
13–16.

13. Ye are the salt of the earth: [but if the salt have lost its savour, wherewith shall it be salted? it is thenceforth good for nothing, but to be cast out and trodden under foot of men.] 14. Ye are the light of the world. A city set on a hill cannot be hid. [15. Neither do men light a lamp, and put it under the bushel, but on the stand; and it shineth unto all that are in the house.] 16. Even so let your light shine before men, that they may see your good works, and glorify your Father which is in heaven.

Jesus and the Law
17–20.

17. Think not that I came to destroy the law or the prophets: I came not to destroy, but to fulfil. 18. For verily I say unto you, Till heaven or earth pass away, one jot or one tittle shall in no wise pass away from the law, till all things be accomplished. 19. Whosoever therefore shall break one of these least commandments, and shall

teach men so, shall be called least in the kingdom of heaven: but
whosoever shall do and teach them, he shall be called great in the
kingdom of heaven. 20. For I say unto you, that except your righteousness shall exceed the righteousness of the scribes and Pharisees,
ye shall in no wise enter into the kingdom of heaven.

On Murder
   21–26.

21. Ye have heard that it was said to them of old time, Thou shalt
not kill; and whosoever shall kill shall be in danger of the judgement:
22. but I say unto you, that every one who is angry with his brother
shall be in danger of the judgement; and whosoever shall say to his
brother, Raca, shall be in danger of the council; and whosoever
shall say, Thou fool, shall be in danger of the hell of fire. 23. If
therefore thou art offering thy gift at the altar, and there rememberest
that thy brother hath aught against thee, 24. leave there thy gift
before the altar, and go thy way, first be reconciled to thy brother,
and then come and offer thy gift. [25. Agree with thine adversary
quickly, whiles thou art with him in the way; lest haply the adversary
deliver thee to the judge, and the judge deliver thee to the officer,
and thou be cast into prison. 26. Verily, I say unto thee, Thou shalt
by no means come out thence, till thou have paid the last farthing.]

On Adultery
   27–30.

27. Ye have heard that it was said, Thou shalt not commit adultery:
28. but I say unto you, that everyone that looketh on a woman to
lust after her hath committed adultery with her already in his heart.
29.[1] And if thy right eye causeth thee to stumble, pluck it out, and
cast it from thee: for it is profitable for thee that one of thy members
should perish, and not thy whole body be cast into hell. 30. And if
thy right hand causeth thee to stumble, cut it off, and cast it from
thee: for it is profitable for thee that one of thy members should
perish, and not thy whole body go into hell.

On Divorce
   31–32. Cf. Lk. xvi. 18 and Mk. x. 11–12.

31. It was said also, Whosoever shall put away his wife, let him give
her a writing of divorcement: 32. but I say unto you, that every one
that putteth away his wife, saving for the cause of fornication, maketh
her an adulteress: and whosoever shall marry her when she is put
away committeth adultery.

[1] Cf. Mk. ix. 43-48.

On Vows and Oaths
33-37.

33. Again, ye have heard that it was said to them of old time, Thou shalt not forswear thyself, but shalt perform unto the Lord thine oaths: 34. but I say unto you, Swear not at all; neither by the heaven, for it is the throne of God; 35. nor by the earth, for it is the footstool of his feet; nor by Jerusalem, for it is the city of the great King. 36. Neither shalt thou swear by thy head, for thou canst not make one hair white or black. 37. But let your speech be, Yea, yea; Nay, nay: and whatsoever is more than these is of the evil one.

On Retribution
38-42.

38. Ye have heard that it was said, An eye for an eye, and a tooth for a tooth: 39. but I say unto you, Resist not him that is evil: [but whosoever smiteth thee on thy right cheek, turn to him the other also.] [40. And if any man would go to law with thee, and take away thy coat, let him have thy cloke also.] 41. And whosoever shall compel thee to go one mile, go with him twain. [42. Give to him that asketh thee, and from him that would borrow of thee, turn not thou away.]

On Love of Neighbour
43-48.

43. Ye have heard that it was said, Thou shalt love thy neighbour, and hate thine enemy: [44. but I say unto you, Love your enemies, and pray for them that persecute you] 45. that ye may be sons of your Father which is in heaven: for he maketh his sun to rise on the evil and the good, and sendeth rain on the just and the unjust. [46. For if ye love them that love you, what reward have ye? do not even the publicans the same?] 47. And if ye salute your brethren only, what do ye more than others? do not even the Gentiles the same? 48. Ye therefore shall be perfect, as your heavenly Father is perfect.

On Almsgiving
vi. 1-4.

1. Take heed that ye do not your righteousness before men, to be seen of them: else ye have no reward with your Father which is in heaven.

2. When therefore thou doest alms, sound not a trumpet before thee, as the hypocrites do in the synagogues and in the streets, that they may have glory of men. Verily I say unto you, They have received their reward. 3. But when thou doest alms, let not thy left hand know what thy right hand doeth: 4. that thine alms may be

in secret: and thy Father which seeth in secret shall recompense thee.

On Prayer
5-15. Cf. Lk. xi. 2-4.

5. And when ye pray, ye shall not be as the hypocrites: for they love to stand and pray in the synagogues and in the corners of the streets, that they may be seen of men. Verily I say unto you, They have received their reward. 6. But thou, when thou prayest, enter into thine inner chamber, and having shut thy door, pray to thy Father which is in secret, and thy Father which seeth in secret shall recompense thee. 7. And in praying use not vain repetitions, as the Gentiles do: for they think that they shall be heard for their much speaking. 8. Be not therefore like unto them: for your Father knoweth what things ye have need of, before ye ask him. 9. After this manner therefore pray ye: Our Father which art in heaven, Hallowed be thy name. 10. Thy kingdom come. Thy will be done, as in heaven, so on earth. 11. Give us this day our daily bread. 12. And forgive us our debts, as we also have forgiven our debtors. 13. And bring us not into temptation, but deliver us from the evil one. 14. For if ye forgive men their trespasses, your heavenly Father will also forgive you. 15. But if ye forgive not men their trespasses, neither will your Father forgive your trespasses.

On Fasting
16-18.

16. Moreover, when ye fast, be not, as the hypocrites, of a sad countenance: for they disfigure their faces, that they may be seen of men to fast. Verily I say unto you, They have received their reward. 17. But thou, when thou fastest, anoint thy head, and wash thy face; 18. that thou be not seen of men to fast, but of thy Father which is in secret: and thy Father, which seeth in secret, shall recompense thee.

Treasures
19-21. Cf. Lk. xii. 33.

19. Lay not up for yourselves treasures upon the earth, where moth and rust doth consume, and where thieves break through and steal: 20. but lay up for yourselves treasures in heaven, where neither moth nor rust doth consume, and where thieves do not break through nor steal: [21. for where thy treasure is, there will thy heart be also.]

Light
22-23.

[22. The lamp of the body is the eye: if therefore thine eye be single, thy whole body shall be full of light. But if thine eye be evil, thy whole body shall be full of darkness. 23. If therefore the light that is in thee be darkness, how great is the darkness!]

Loyalty
24.

[No man can serve two masters: for either he will hate the one, and love the other; or else he will hold to one, and despise the other. Ye cannot serve God and mammon.]

Freedom from Worry
25–34.

[25. Therefore I say unto you, Be not anxious for your life, what ye shall eat, or what ye shall drink; nor yet for your body, what ye shall put on. Is not the life more than the food, and the body than the raiment? 26. Behold the birds of the heaven, that they sow not, neither do they reap, nor gather into barns; and your heavenly Father feedeth them. Are not ye of much more value than they? 27. And which of you by being anxious can add one cubit unto his stature? 28. And why are ye anxious concerning raiment? Consider the lilies of the field, how they grow; they toil not, neither do they spin: 29. yet I say unto you, that even Solomon in all his glory was not arrayed like one of these. 30. But if God so clothe the grass of the field, which to-day is, and to-morrow is cast into the oven, shall he not much more clothe you, O ye of little faith? 31. Be not therefore anxious, saying, What shall we eat? or, What shall we drink? or, Wherewithal shall we be clothed? 32. For after all these things do the Gentiles seek; for your heavenly Father knoweth that ye have need of all these things. 33. But seek ye first his kingdom, and his righteousness; and all these things shall be added unto you.] 34. Be not therefore anxious for the morrow: for the morrow will be anxious for itself. Sufficient unto the day is the evil thereof.

Against Judging
vii. 1–5.

[1. Judge not, that ye be not judged. 2. For with what judgement ye judge, ye shall be judged: and with what measure ye mete, it shall be measured unto you. 3. And why beholdest thou the mote that is in thy brother's eye, but considerest not the beam that is in thine own eye? 4. Or how wilt thou say to thy brother, Let me cast out the mote out of thine eye; and lo, the beam is in thine own eye? 5. Thou hypocrite, cast out first the beam out of thine own eye; and then shalt thou see clearly to cast out the mote out of thy brother's eye.]

On Discrimination
    6.

Give not that which is holy unto the dogs, neither cast your pearls before the swine, lest haply they trample them under their feet, and turn and rend you.

On asking God
    7–11.

[7. Ask, and it shall be given you; seek, and ye shall find; knock, and it shall be opened unto you: 8. for every one that asketh receiveth; and he that seeketh findeth; and to him that knocketh it shall be opened. 9. Or what man is there of you, who, if his son shall ask him for a loaf, will give him a stone; 10. or if he shall ask for a fish, will give him a serpent? 11. If ye then, being evil, know how to give good gifts unto your children, how much more shall your Father which is in heaven give good things to them that ask him?]

The Golden Rule
    12.

[All things therefore whatsoever ye would that men should do unto you, even so do ye also unto them]: for this is the law and the prophets.

The Two Ways
    13–14. Cf. Lk. xiii. 23–24.

13. Enter ye in by the narrow gate: for wide is the gate, and broad is the way, that leadeth to destruction, and many be they that enter in thereby. 14. For narrow is the gate, and straitened the way, that leadeth unto life, and few be they that find it.

False Prophets
    15–20.

15. Beware of false prophets, which come to you in sheep's clothing, but inwardly are ravening wolves. 16. By their fruits ye shall know them. [Do men gather grapes of thorns, or figs of thistles? 17. Even so every good tree bringeth forth good fruit; but the corrupt tree bringeth forth evil fruit. 18. A good tree cannot bring forth evil fruit, neither can a corrupt tree bring forth good fruit. 19. Every tree that bringeth not forth good fruit is hewn down, and cast into the fire.[1]] 20. Therefore by their fruits ye shall know them.

Exorcists
    21–23. Cf. Lk. vi. 46 and xiii. 26–27.

21. Not every one that saith unto me, Lord, Lord, shall enter into

[1] This verse belongs to the Q report of the Baptist's teaching. See Lk. iii. 9.

the kingdom of heaven; but he that doeth the will of my Father which is in heaven. 22. Many will say to me in that day, Lord, Lord, did we not prophesy by thy name, and by thy name cast out devils, and by thy name do many mighty works? 23. And then will I profess unto them, I never knew you: depart from me, ye that work iniquity.

Parable of the Two Houses
    24–27.

24. [Every one therefore which heareth these words of mine, and doeth them, shall be likened unto a wise man, which built his house upon the rock: 25. and the rain descended, and the floods came, and the winds blew, and beat upon that house; and it fell not; for it was founded upon the rock. 26. And every one that heareth these words of mine, and doeth them not, shall be likened unto a foolish man, which built his house upon the sand: 27. and the rain descended, and the floods came, and the winds blew, and smote upon that house; and it fell: and great was the fall thereof.]

    ix. 13*a*.

But go ye and learn what this meaneth, I desire mercy, and not sacrifice.

The Mission Charge
    x. 5–8.

5. Go not into any way of the Gentiles, and enter not into any city of the Samaritans: 6. but go rather to the lost sheep of the house of Israel. 7. And as ye go, preach, saying, The kingdom of heaven is at hand. 8. Heal the sick, raise the dead, cleanse the lepers, cast out devils: freely ye received, freely give.

    9–13,[1] 16*b*.

9. Get you no gold, nor silver, nor brass in your purses; no wallet for your journey, neither two coats, nor shoes, nor staff: for the labourer is worthy of his food. 11. And into whatsoever city or village ye shall enter, search out who in it is worthy; and there abide till ye go forth. 12. And as ye enter into the house, salute it. 13. And if the house be worthy, let your peace come upon it: but if it be not worthy, let your peace return to you . . . be ye therefore wise as serpents, and harmless as doves.

    23.

But when they persecute you in this city, flee into the next: for verily I say unto you, Ye shall not have gone through the cities of Israel, till the Son of man be come.

---

[1] 9–13 are a mixture of Mk. and M.

24–25.

24. A disciple is not above his master, nor a servant above his lord. 25. It is enough for the disciple that he be as his master, and the servant as his lord. If they have called the master of the house Beelzebub, how much more shall they call them of his household!

40–42.

40. He that receiveth you receiveth me, and he that receiveth me receiveth him that sent me. 41. He that receiveth a prophet in the name of a prophet shall receive a prophet's reward; and he that receiveth a righteous man in the name of a righteous man shall receive a righteous man's reward. 42. And whosoever shall give to drink unto one of these little ones a cup of cold water only, in the name of a disciple, verily I say unto you, he shall in no wise lose his reward.

xi. 14f.

14. And if ye are willing to receive it, this is Elijah which is to come. 15. He that hath ears to hear, let him hear.

The Great Invitation
28–30

28. Come unto me, all ye that labour and are heavy laden, and I will give you rest. 29. Take my yoke upon you, and learn of me; for I am meek and lowly in heart: and ye shall find rest unto your souls. 30. For my yoke is easy, and my burden is light.

On the Sabbath
xii. 5–7.

5. Or have ye not read in the law, how that on the sabbath day the priests in the temple profane the sabbath, and are guiltless? 6. But I say unto you, that one greater than the temple is here. 7. But if ye had known what this meaneth, I desire mercy, and not sacrifice, ye would not have condemned the guiltless.

11–12a.

11. And he said unto them, What man shall there be of you, that shall have one sheep, and if this fall into a pit on the sabbath day, will he not lay hold of it, and lift it out? 12. How much then is a man of more value than a sheep!

Idle Words
36–37.

36. And I say unto you, that every idle word that men shall speak,

they shall give account thereof in the day of judgement. 37. For by thy words thou shalt be justified, and by thy words thou shalt be condemned.

Parable of the Tares
xiii. 24–30, 36–43.

24. Another parable set he before them, saying, The kingdom of heaven is likened unto a man that sowed good seed in his field: 25. but while men slept, his enemy came and sowed tares also among the wheat, and went away. 26. But when the blade sprang up, and brought forth fruit, then appeared the tares also. 27. And the servants of the householder came and said unto him, Sir, didst thou not sow good seed in thy field? whence then hath it tares? 28. And he said unto them, An enemy hath done this. And the servants say unto him, Wilt thou then that we go and gather them up? 29. But he saith, Nay: lest haply while ye gather up the tares, ye root up the wheat with them. 30. Let both grow together until the harvest: and in the time of the harvest I will say to the reapers, Gather up first the tares, and bind them in bundles to burn them: but gather the wheat into my barn.

36. Then he left the multitudes, and went into the house: and his disciples came unto him, saying, Explain unto us the parable of the tares of the field. 37. And he answered and said, He that soweth the good seed is the Son of man, 38. and the field is the world; and the good seed, these are the sons of the kingdom; and the tares are the sons of the evil one; 39. and the enemy that sowed them is the devil: and the harvest is the end of the world; and the reapers are angels. 40. As therefore the tares are gathered up and burned with fire; so shall it be in the end of the world. 41. The Son of man shall send forth his angels, and they shall gather out of his kingdom all things that cause stumbling, and them that do iniquity, 42. and shall cast them into the furnace of fire: there shall be the weeping and gnashing of teeth. 43. Then shall the righteous shine forth as the sun in the kingdom of their Father. He that hath ears, let him hear.

Parables of Hid Treasure and Costly Pearl
44–46.

44. The kingdom of heaven is like unto a treasure hidden in the field; which a man found, and hid; and in his joy he goeth and selleth all that he hath, and buyeth that field.

45. Again, the kingdom of heaven is like unto a man that is a merchant seeking goodly pearls: 46. and having found one pearl of great price, he went and sold all that he had, and bought it.

Parable of the Drag-net, etc.
   47–52.

47. Again, the kingdom of heaven is like unto a net, that was cast into the sea, and gathered of every kind: 48. which, when it was filled, they drew up on the beach; and they sat down, and gathered the good into vessels, but the bad they cast away. 49. So shall it be in the end of the world: the angels shall come forth, and sever the wicked from among the righteous, 50. and shall cast them into the furnace of fire: there shall be the weeping and gnashing of teeth.

   51. Have ye understood all these things? They say unto him, Yea. 52. And he said unto them, Therefore every scribe who hath been made a disciple to the kingdom of heaven, is like unto a man that is a householder, which bringeth forth out of his treasure things new and old.

Peter's Walking on the Water
   xiv. 28–33.

28. And Peter answered him and said, Lord, if it be thou, bid me come unto thee upon the waters. And he said, Come. 29. And Peter went down from the boat, and walked upon the waters, to come to Jesus. 30. But when he saw the wind, he was afraid; and beginning to sink, he cried out, saying, Lord, save me. 31. And immediately Jesus stretched forth his hand, and took hold of him, and saith unto him, O thou of little faith, wherefore didst thou doubt? 32. And when they were gone up into the boat, the wind ceased. 33. And they that were in the boat worshipped him, saying, Of a truth thou art the Son of God.

   xv. 12–13.

12. Then came the disciples, and said unto him, Knowest thou that the Pharisees were offended, when they heard this saying? 13. But he answered and said, Every plant which my heavenly Father planted not, shall be rooted up.

The Canaanitish Woman
   22–25

22. And behold, a Canaanitish woman came out from those borders, and cried, saying, Have mercy on me, O Lord, thou son of David; my daughter is grievously vexed with a devil. 23. But he answered her not a word. And his disciples came and besought him, saying, Send her away; for she crieth after us. 24. But he answered and said, I was not sent but unto the lost sheep of the house of Israel. 25. But she came and worshipped him, saying, Lord, help me.

The Promise to Peter
    xvi. 17–19.

17. And Jesus answered and said unto him, Blessed art thou, Simon Bar-Jonah: for flesh and blood hath not revealed it unto thee, but my Father which is in heaven. 18. And I also say unto thee, that thou art Peter, and upon this rock I will build my church; and the gates of Hades shall not prevail against it. 19. I will give unto thee the keys of the kingdom of heaven: and whatsoever thou shalt bind on earth shall be bound in heaven: and whatsoever thou shalt loose on earth shall be loosed in heaven.

A Saying about Faith
    xvii. 20. Cf. Lk. xvii. 6, Q; Mk. xi. 23; 1 Cor. xiii. 2.

20. And he saith unto them, Because of your little faith: for verily I say unto you, If ye have faith as a grain of mustard seed, ye shall say unto this mountain, Remove hence to yonder place; and it shall remove; and nothing shall be impossible unto you.

Coin in the Fish's Mouth
    24–27.

24. And when they were come to Capernaum, they that received the half-shekel came to Peter, and said, Doth not your master pay the half-shekel? 25. He saith, Yea. And when he came into the house, Jesus spake first to him, saying, What thinkest thou, Simon? the kings of the earth, from whom do they receive toll or tribute? from their sons, or from strangers? 26. And when he said, From strangers, Jesus said unto him, Therefore the sons are free. 27. But, lest we cause them to stumble, go thou to the sea, and cast a hook, and take up the fish that first cometh up; and when thou hast opened his mouth, thou shalt find a shekel: that take, and give unto them for me and thee.

Parable of the Lost Sheep
    xviii. 10, 12–14. Cf. Lk. xv. 3–7, L.

10. See that ye despise not one of these little ones; for I say unto you, that in heaven their angels do always behold the face of my Father which is in heaven.
12. How think ye? if any man have a hundred sheep, and one of them be gone astray, doth he not leave the ninety and nine, and go unto the mountains, and seek that which goeth astray? 13. And if so be that he find it, verily I say unto you, he rejoiceth over it more than over the ninety and nine which have not gone astray. 14. Even so it is not the will of your Father which is in heaven, that one of these little ones should perish.

Life within the Church
15–20.

15. And if thy brother sin against thee, go shew him his fault between thee and him alone; if he hear thee, thou hast gained thy brother. 16. But if he hear thee not, take with thee one or two more, that at the mouth of two witnesses or three every word may be established. 17. And if he refuse to hear them, tell it unto the church: and if he refuse to hear the church also, let him be unto thee as the Gentile and the publican. 18. Verily I say unto you, What things soever ye shall bind on earth shall be bound in heaven: and what things soever ye shall loose on earth shall be loosed in heaven. 19. Again I say unto you, that if two of you shall agree on earth as touching anything that they shall ask, it shall be done for them of my Father which is in heaven. 20. For where two or three are gathered together in my name, there am I in the midst of them.

On Forgiveness: the Unmerciful Servant
21–35.

21. Then came Peter, and said to him, Lord, how oft shall my brother sin against me, and I forgive him? until seven times? 22. Jesus saith unto him, I say not unto thee, Until seven times; but, Until seventy times seven.

23. Therefore is the kingdom of heaven likened unto a certain king, which would make a reckoning with his servants. 24. And when he had begun to reckon, one was brought unto him, which owed him ten thousand talents. 25. But forasmuch as he had not wherewith to pay, his lord commanded him to be sold, and his wife, and children, and all that he had, and payment to be made. 26. The servant therefore fell down and worshipped him, saying, Lord, have patience with me, and I will pay thee all. 27. And the lord of that servant, being moved with compassion, released him, and forgave him the debt. 28. But that servant went out, and found one of his fellow-servants, which owed him a hundred pence: and he laid hold on him, and took him by the throat, saying, Pay what thou owest. 29. So his fellow-servant fell down and besought him, saying, Have patience with me, and I will pay thee. 30. And he would not: but went and cast him into prison, till he should pay that which was due. 31. So when his fellow-servants saw what was done, they were exceeding sorry, and came and told unto their lord all that was done. 32. Then his lord called him unto him, and saith to him, Thou wicked servant, I forgave thee all that debt, because thou besoughtest me: 33. shouldest not thou also have had mercy on thy fellow-servant, even as I had mercy on thee? 34. And his lord was wroth, and delivered him to the tormentors, till he should pay all that was due.

35. So shall also my heavenly Father do unto you, if ye forgive not every one his brother from your hearts.

Celibacy and the Kingdom
xix. 10–12.

10. The disciples say unto him, If the case of the man is so with his wife, it is not expedient to marry. 11. But he said unto them, All men cannot receive this saying, but they to whom it is given. 12. For there are eunuchs, which were so born from their mother's womb: and there are eunuchs, which were made eunuchs by men: and there are eunuchs, which made themselves eunuchs[1] for the kingdom of heaven's sake. He that is able to receive it, let him receive it.

The Twelve Thrones
28. Cf. Lk. xxii. 28–30, L.

28. And Jesus said unto them, Verily I say unto you, that ye which have followed me, in the regeneration when the Son of man shall sit on the throne of his glory, ye also shall sit upon twelve thrones, judging the twelve tribes of Israel.

Parable of the Labourers in the Vineyard
xx. 1–16.

1. For the kingdom of heaven is like unto a man that is a householder, which went out early in the morning to hire labourers into his vineyard. 2. And when he had agreed with the labourers for a penny a day, he sent them into his vineyard. 3. And he went out about the third hour, and saw others standing in the marketplace idle; 4. and to them he said, Go ye also into the vineyard, and whatsoever is right I will give you. And they went their way. 5. Again he went out about the sixth and ninth hour, and did likewise. 6. And about the eleventh hour he went out, and found others standing; and he saith unto them, Why stand ye here all the day idle? 7. They say unto him, Because no man hath hired us. He saith unto them, Go ye also into the vineyard. 8. And when even was come, the lord of the vineyard saith unto his steward, Call the labourers, and pay them their hire, beginning from the last unto the first. 9. And when they came that were hired about the eleventh hour, they received every man a penny. 10. And when the first came, they supposed that they would receive more; and they likewise received every man a penny. 11. And when they received it, they murmured against the householder, saying, 12. These last have spent but one hour, and thou hast made them equal unto us, which have borne the burden of the day and the scorching heat. 13. But he answered and said to

---

[1] I.e. remained celibate.

one of them, Friend, I do thee no wrong: didst not thou agree with me for a penny? 14. Take up that which is thine, and go thy way; it is my will to give unto this last, even as unto thee. 15. Is it not lawful for me to do what I will with mine own? or is thine eye evil, because I am good? 16. So the last shall be first, and the first last.

Who is this?
xxi. 10–11.

10. And when he was come into Jerusalem, all the city was stirred, saying, Who is this? 11. And the multitude said, This is the prophet, Jesus, from Nazareth of Galilee.

The Children's Hosannas
14–16.

14. And the blind and the lame came to him in the temple: and he healed them. 15. But when the chief priests and the scribes saw the wonderful things that he did, and the children that were crying in the temple and saying, Hosanna to the son of David; 16. they were moved with indignation, and said unto him, Hearest thou what these are saying? And Jesus saith unto them, Yea: did ye never read, Out of the mouth of babes and sucklings thou hast perfected praise?

The Parable of the Two Sons
28–32.

28. But what think ye? A man had two sons; and he came to the first, and said, 29. Son, go work to-day in the vineyard. And he answered and said, I will not: but afterward he repented himself, and went. 30. And he came to the second, and said likewise. And he answered and said, I go, sir: and went not. 31. Whether of the twain did the will of his father? They say, The first. Jesus saith unto them, Verily I say unto you, that the publicans and the harlots go into the kingdom of God before you. 32.[1] For John came unto you in the way of righteousness, and ye believed him not: but the publicans and the harlots believed him: and ye, when ye saw it, did not even repent yourselves afterward, that ye might believe him.

The Parables of the Marriage Feast and the Wedding Garment
xxii. 1–14.

1. And Jesus answered and spake again in parables unto them, saying, 2. The kingdom of heaven is likened unto a certain king, which made a marriage feast for his son, 3. and sent forth his servants to call them that were bidden to the marriage feast: and they would not come. 4. Again he sent forth other servants, saying, Tell them

---

[1] Cf. Lk. vii. 29.

L

that are bidden, Behold, I have made ready my dinner: my oxen and my fatlings are killed, and all things are ready: come to the marriage feast. 5. But they made light of it, and went their ways, one to his own farm, another to his merchandise: 6. and the rest laid hold on his servants, and entreated them shamefully, and killed them. 7. But the king was wroth; and he sent his armies, and destroyed those murderers, and burned their city. 8. Then saith he to his servants, The wedding is ready, but they that were bidden were not worthy. 9. Go ye therefore unto the partings of the highways, and as many as ye shall find, bid to the marriage feast. 10. And those servants went out into the highways, and gathered together all as many as they found, both bad and good: and the wedding was filled with guests. 11. But when the king came in to behold the guests, he saw there a man which had not on a wedding-garment: 12. and he saith unto him, Friend, how camest thou in hither not having a wedding-garment? 13. And he was speechless. Then the king said to the servants, Bind him hand and foot, and cast him out into the outer darkness; there shall be the weeping and gnashing of teeth. 14. For many are called, but few chosen.

Woes on Scribes and Pharisees[1]
xxiii. 1–39.

1. Then spake Jesus to the multitudes and to his disciples, 2. saying, The scribes and the Pharisees sit on Moses' seat: 3. all things therefore whatsoever they bid you, these do and observe: but do not ye after their works; for they say, and do not. 4. Yea, they bind heavy burdens and grievous to be borne, and lay them on men's shoulders; but they themselves will not move them with their finger. 5.[2] But all their works they do for to be seen of men: for they make broad their phylacteries, and enlarge the borders of their garments, 6. and love the chief place at feasts, and chief seats in the synagogues, 7. and the salutations in the marketplaces, and to be called of men, Rabbi. 8. But be not ye called Rabbi: for one is your teacher, and all ye are brethren. 9. And call no man your father on the earth: for one is your Father, which is in heaven. 10. Neither be ye called masters: for one is your master, even the Christ. 11. But he that is greatest among you shall be your servant. [12. And whosoever shall exalt himself shall be humbled; and whosoever shall humble himself shall be exalted.]

13. But woe unto you, scribes and Pharisees, hypocrites! because ye shut the kingdom of heaven against men: for ye enter not in yourselves, neither suffer ye them that are entering in to enter.

[1] Verses assignable to Q are bracketed. But most of the chapter is M.
[2] With 5-7 cf. Mk. xii. 38-40.

15. Woe unto you, scribes and Pharisees, hypocrites! for ye compass sea and land to make one proselyte; and when he is become so, ye make him twofold more a son of hell than yourselves.

16. Woe unto you, ye blind guides, which say, Whosoever shall swear by the temple, it is nothing; but whosoever shall swear by the gold of the temple, he is a debtor. 17. Ye fools and blind; for whether is greater, the gold, or the temple that hath sanctified the gold? 18. And, whosoever shall swear by the altar, it is nothing; but whosoever shall swear by the gift that is upon it, he is a debtor. 19. Ye blind: for whether is greater, the gift, or the altar that sanctifieth the gift? 20. He therefore that sweareth by the altar, sweareth by it, and by all things thereon. 21. And he that sweareth by the temple, sweareth by it, and by him that dwelleth therein. 22. And he that sweareth by the heaven, sweareth by the throne of God, and by him that sitteth thereon.

[23. Woe unto you, scribes and Pharisees, hypocrites! for ye tithe mint and anise and cummin, and have left undone the weightier matters of the law, judgement, and mercy, and faith: but these ye ought to have done, and not to have left the other undone.] 24. Ye blind guides, which strain out the gnat, and swallow the camel!

25. Woe unto you, scribes and Pharisees, hypocrites! for ye cleanse the outside of the cup and of the platter, but within they are full from extortion and excess. 26. Thou blind Pharisee, cleanse first the inside of the cup and of the platter, that the outside thereof may become clean also.

27. Woe unto you, scribes and Pharisees, hypocrites! for ye are like unto whited sepulchres, which outwardly appear beautiful, but inwardly are full of dead men's bones, and of all uncleanness. 28. Even so ye also outwardly appear righteous unto men, but inwardly ye are full of hypocrisy and iniquity.

29. Woe unto you, scribes and Pharisees, hypocrites! for ye build the sepulchres of the prophets, and garnish the tombs of the righteous, 30. and say, If we had been in the days of our fathers, we should not have been partakers with them in the blood of the prophets. 31. Wherefore ye witness to yourselves, that ye are sons of them that slew the prophets. 32. Fill ye up then the measure of your fathers. 33. Ye serpents, ye offspring of vipers, how shall ye escape the judgement of hell?[1]

[34.[2] Therefore, behold, I send unto you prophets, and wise men, and scribes: some of them shall ye kill and crucify; and some of them shall ye scourge in your synagogues, and persecute from city to city: 35. that upon you may come all the righteous blood shed on the earth, from the blood of Abel the righteous unto the blood of

[1] Probably a saying of the Baptist; cf. Lk. iii. 7, Q.   [2] Cf. Lk. xi. 49-51.

Zachariah son of Barachiah, whom ye slew between the sanctuary and the altar. 36. Verily I say unto you, All these things shall come upon this generation.]

[37. O Jerusalem, Jerusalem, which killeth the prophets, and stoneth them that are sent unto her! how often would I have gathered thy children together, even as a hen gathereth her chickens under her wings, and ye would not! 38. Behold, your house is left unto you desolate. 39. For I say unto you, Ye shall not see me henceforth, till ye shall say, Blessed is he that cometh in the name of the Lord.]

Apocalyptic Sayings
    xxiv. 10–12, 30.

10. And then shall many stumble, and shall deliver up one another, and shall hate one another. 11. And many false prophets shall arise, and shall lead many astray. 12. And because iniquity shall be multiplied, the love of the many shall wax cold. 30. And then shall appear the sign of the Son of man in heaven: and then shall all the tribes of the earth mourn.

Parable of the Ten Virgins
    xxv. 1–13.

1. Then shall the kingdom of heaven be likened unto ten virgins, which took their lamps, and went forth to meet the bridegroom. 2. And five of them were foolish, and five were wise. 3. For the foolish, when they took their lamps, took no oil with them: 4. but the wise took oil in their vessels with their lamps. 5. Now while the bridegroom tarried, they all slumbered and slept. 6. But at midnight there is a cry, Behold, the bridegroom! Come ye forth to meet him. 7. Then all those virgins arose, and trimmed their lamps. 8. And the foolish said unto the wise, Give us of your oil; for our lamps are going out. 9. But the wise answered, saying, Peradventure there will not be enough for us and you: go ye rather to them that sell, and buy for yourselves. 10. And while they went away to buy, the bridegroom came; and they that were ready went in with him to the marriage feast: and the door was shut. 11. Afterward come also the other virgins, saying, Lord, Lord, open to us. 12. But he answered and said, Verily I say unto you, I know you not. 13. Watch therefore, for ye know not the day nor the hour.

Parable of the Talents
    14–30. Cf. Lk. xix. 11–27, L.

14. For it is as when a man, going into another country, called his own servants, and delivered unto them his goods. 15. And unto one he gave five talents, to another two, to another one; to each according

to his several ability; and he went on his journey. 16. Straightway he that received the five talents went and traded with them, and made other five talents. 17. In like manner he also that received the two gained other two. 18. But he that received the one went away and digged in the earth, and hid his lord's money. 19. Now after a long time the lord of those servants cometh, and maketh a reckoning with them. 20. And he that received the five talents came and brought other five talents, saying, Lord, thou deliveredst unto me five talents: lo, I have gained other five talents. 21. His lord said unto him, Well done, good and faithful servant: thou hast been faithful over a few things, I will set thee over many things: enter thou into the joy of thy lord. 22. And he also that received the two talents came and said, Lord, thou deliveredst unto me two talents: lo, I have gained other two talents. 23. His lord said unto him, Well done, good and faithful servant; thou hast been faithful over a few things, I will set thee over many things: enter thou into the joy of thy lord. 24. And he also that had received the one talent came and said, Lord, I knew thee that thou art a hard man, reaping where thou didst not sow, and gathering where thou didst not scatter: 25. and I was afraid, and went away and hid thy talent in the earth: lo, thou hast thine own. 26. But his lord answered and said unto him, Thou wicked and slothful servant, thou knewest that I reap where I sowed not, and gather where I did not scatter; 27. thou oughtest therefore to have put my money to the bankers, and at my coming I should have received back mine own with interest. 28. Take ye away therefore the talent from him, and give it unto him that hath the ten talents. 29. For unto every one that hath shall be given, and he shall have abundance: but from him that hath not, even that which he hath shall be taken away. 30. And cast ye out the unprofitable servant into the outer darkness: there shall be the weeping and gnashing of teeth.

Parable of the Sheep and the Goats
    31–46.

31. But when the Son of man shall come in his glory, and all the angels with him, then shall he sit on the throne of his glory: 32. and before him shall be gathered all the nations: and he shall separate them one from another, as the shepherd separateth the sheep from the goats: 33. and he shall set the sheep on his right hand, but the goats on the left. 34. Then shall the King say unto them on his right hand, Come, ye blessed of my Father, inherit the kingdom prepared for you from the foundation of the world: 35. for I was an hungred, and ye gave me meat: I was thirsty, and ye gave me drink: I was a stranger, and ye took me in; 36. naked, and ye clothed me: I was sick, and

ye visited me: I was in prison, and ye came unto me. 37. Then shall the righteous answer him, saying, Lord, when saw we thee an hungred, and fed thee? or athirst, and gave thee drink? 38. And when saw we thee a stranger, and took thee in? or naked, and clothed thee? 39. And when saw we thee sick, or in prison, and came unto thee? 40. And the King shall answer and say unto them, Verily I say unto you, Inasmuch as ye did it unto one of these my brethren, even these least, ye did it unto me. 41. Then shall he say also unto them on the left hand, Depart from me, ye cursed, into the eternal fire which is prepared for the devil and his angels: 42. for I was an hungred, and ye gave me no meat: I was thirsty, and ye gave me no drink: 43. I was a stranger, and ye took me not in; naked, and ye clothed me not; sick, and in prison, and ye visited me not. 44. Then shall they also answer, saying, Lord, when saw we thee an hungred, or athirst, or a stranger, or naked, or sick, or in prison, and did not minister unto thee? 45. Then shall he answer them, saying, Verily I say unto you, Inasmuch as ye did it not unto one of these least, ye did it not unto me. 46. And these shall go away into eternal punishment: but the righteous into eternal life.

Sayings to the Traitor
xxvi. 25, 50a.

25. And Judas, which betrayed him, answered and said, Is it I, Rabbi? He saith unto him, Thou hast said. 50a. And Jesus said unto him, Friend, do that for which thou art come.

Twelve Legions of Angels
52-54.

52. Then Jesus saith unto him, Put up again thy sword into its place: for all they that take the sword shall perish with the sword. 53. Or thinkest thou that I cannot beseech my Father, and he shall even now send me more than twelve legions of angels? 54. How then should the scriptures be fulfilled, that thus it must be?

The Death of Judas
xxvii. 3-8.

3. Then Judas, which betrayed him, when he saw that he was condemned, repented himself, and brought back the thirty pieces of silver to the chief priests and elders, 4. saying, I have sinned in that I betrayed innocent blood. But they said, What is that to us? see thou to it. 5. And he cast down the pieces of silver into the sanctuary, and departed; and he went away and hanged himself. 6. And the chief priests took the pieces of silver, and said, It is not lawful to put them into the treasury, since it is the price of blood.

7. And they took counsel, and bought with them the potter's field, to bury strangers in. 8. Wherefore that field was called, The field of blood, unto this day.

Pilate's Wife
19.

19. And while he was sitting on the judgement-seat, his wife sent unto him, saying, Have thou nothing to do with that righteous man: for I have suffered many things this day in a dream because of him.

Pilate's Hand-washing
24–25.

24. So when Pilate saw that he prevailed nothing, but rather that a tumult was arising, he took water, and washed his hands before the multitude, saying, I am innocent of the blood of this righteous man: see ye to it. 25. And all the people answered and said, His blood be on us, and on our children.

The Resurrection of the Jewish Saints
51b–53.

51b. And the earth did quake; and the rocks were rent; 52. and the tombs were opened; and many bodies of the saints that had fallen asleep were raised; 53. and coming forth out of the tombs after his resurrection they entered into the holy city and appeared unto many.

The Watch at the Tomb
62–66.

62. Now on the morrow, which is the day after the Preparation, the chief priests and the Pharisees were gathered together unto Pilate, 63. saying, Sir, we remember that that deceiver said, while he was yet alive, After three days I rise again. 64. Command therefore that the sepulchre be made sure until the third day, lest haply his disciples come and steal him away, and say unto the people, He is risen from the dead: and the last error will be worse than the first. 65. Pilate said unto them, Ye have a guard: go your way, make it as sure as ye can. 66. So they went, and made the sepulchre sure, sealing the stone, the guard being with them.

The Earthquake
xxviii. 2–4.

2. And behold, there was a great earthquake; for an angel of the Lord descended from heaven, and came and rolled away the stone, and sat upon it. 3. His appearance was as lightning, and his raiment

white as snow: 4. and for fear of him the watchers did quake, and became as dead men.

Appearance to the Women
9–10.

9. And behold, Jesus met them, saying, All hail. And they came and took hold of his feet, and worshipped him. 10. Then saith Jesus unto them, Fear not: go tell my brethren that they depart into Galilee, and there shall they see me.

The Bribing of the Guard
11–15.

11. Now while they were going, behold, some of the guard came into the city, and told unto the chief priests all the things that were come to pass. 12. And when they were assembled with the elders, and had taken counsel, they gave large money unto the soldiers, 13. saying, Say ye, His disciples came by night, and stole him away while we slept. 14. And if this come to the governor's ears, we will persuade him, and rid you of care. 15. So they took the money, and did as they were taught: and this saying was spread abroad among the Jews, and continueth until this day.

The Final Commission
16–20.

16. But the eleven disciples went into Galilee, unto the mountain where Jesus had appointed them. 17. And when they saw him, they worshipped him: but some doubted. 18. And Jesus came to them and spake unto them, saying, All authority hath been given unto me in heaven and on earth. 19. Go ye therefore, and make disciples of all the nations, baptising them into the name of the Father and of the Son and of the Holy Ghost: 20. teaching them to observe all things whatsoever I commanded you: and lo, I am with you alway, even unto the end of the world.

THE TEXT OF L

The symbol L denotes the Gospel tradition peculiar to St. Luke's Gospel. It comprises narrative and teaching matter, and adds much to our knowledge of the Passion Story. L probably represents the oral tradition about Jesus which Luke gathered at Caesarea when staying there during Paul's imprisonment, A.D. 57–59. As a source, it is much superior in historical value to M. In the list of contents which follows we do not include the Birth Stories (i–ii) which stand apart and possibly depend on Hebrew or Aramaic sources.

I. John and Jesus:
   (a) The Mission of John: iii. 1–6, 10–14, 18–20.
   (b) The Genealogy of Jesus: iii. 23–38.

II. The Rejection at Nazareth: iv. 16–30.

III. Mighty Works:
   (a) The Wonderful Draught: v. 1–11.
   (b) The Widow of Nain's Son: vii. 11–17.
   (c) The Woman who was a Sinner: vii. 36–viii. 3.

IV. Lessons:
   (a) To the Disciples in Samaria: ix. 51–56.
   (b) To the Seventy: x. 1, 17–20.
   (c) To a Rabbi—the Good Samaritan: x. 25–37.
   (d) To Martha—the Good Part: x. 38–42.
   (e) How to Pray—the Friend at Midnight: xi. 1–8, 53f.; xii. 1.

V. Warnings:
   (a) Against Greed—the Rich Fool: xii. 13–21.
   (b) On Repentance—the Barren Fig Tree: xiii. 1–9.
   (c) Sabbath Observance—(1) the Hunch-backed Woman: xiii. 10–17.
   (d) To Herod Antipas: xiii. 31–33.
   (e) Sabbath Observance—(2) the Man with Dropsy: xiv. 1–6.
   (f) On Precedence and Hospitality: xiv. 7–14.
   (g) On Counting the Cost: xiv. 28–33.

VI. Parables of the Lost (Lost Sheep, Lost Coin, Lost Son): xv.

VII. Parables, etc., of Responsibility:
   (a) Foresight—the Unjust Steward: xvi. 1–12.
   (b) Money—Dives and Lazarus: xvi. 14–15, 19–31.
   (c) On Serving God—Master and Servant: xvii. 7–10.
   (d) On Gratitude—the Ten Lepers: xvii. 11–21.
   (e) On Perseverance—the Importunate Widow: xviii. 1–8.
   (f) On Prayer—the Pharisee and the Publican: xviii. 9–14.

(g) On Opportunities—Zaccheus: the Parable of the Pounds: xix. 1–27.

VIII. Jerusalem:

(a) Approach to the City: xix. 37–44.
(b) Apocalyptic Sayings: xxi. 11b, 18, 25b, 26a, 28, 34–36.
(c) The Passion and the Resurrection: xxii. 14–xxiv (less Marcan passages).

I. JOHN AND JESUS

(a) *The Mission of John*
   iii. 1–6, 10–14, 18–20.

1. Now in the fifteenth year of the reign of Tiberius Caesar, Pontius Pilate being governor of Judaea, and Herod being tetrarch of Galilee, and his brother Philip tetrarch of the region of Ituraea and Trachonitis, and Lysanias tetrarch of Abilene, 2. in the high-priesthood of Annas and Caiaphas, the word of God came unto John the son of Zacharias in the wilderness. 3. And he came into all the region round about Jordan, preaching the baptism of repentance unto remission of sins; 4. as it is written in the book of the words of Isaiah the prophet,

> The voice of one crying in the wilderness,
> Make ye ready the way of the Lord,
> Make his paths straight.
> 5. Every valley shall be filled,
> And every mountain and hill shall be brought low;
> And the crooked shall become straight,
> And the rough ways smooth;
> 6. And all flesh shall see the salvation of God (Isa. xl. 3ff.).

10. And the multitudes asked him, saying, What then must we do? 11. And he answered and said unto them, He that hath two coats, let him impart to him that hath none; and he that hath food, let him do likewise. 12. And there came also publicans to be baptised, and they said unto him, Master, what must we do? 13. And he said unto them, Extort no more than that which is appointed you. 14. And soldiers also asked him, saying, And we, what must we do? And he said unto them, Do violence to no man, neither exact anything wrongfully; and be content with your wages.

18. With many other exhortations therefore preached he good tidings unto the people; 19. but Herod the tetrarch, being reproved by him for Herodias his brother's wife, and for all the evil things which Herod had done, 20. added yet this above all, that he shut up John in prison.

(b) *The Genealogy of Jesus*
  iii. 23–28. Cf. Mt. i. 1–17.

23. And Jesus himself, when he began to teach, was about thirty years of age, being the son (as was supposed) of Joseph, the son of Heli. (Here follows the genealogy.)

II. THE REJECTION AT NAZARETH
(iv. 16–30)

16. And he came to Nazareth, where he had been brought up: and he entered, as his custom was, into the synagogue on the sabbath day, and stood up to read. 17. And there was delivered unto him the book of the prophet Isaiah. And he opened the book, and found the place where it was written,

> 18. The Spirit of the Lord is upon me,
>   Because he anointed me to preach good tidings to the poor:
>   He hath sent me to proclaim release to the captives,
>   And recovering of sight to the blind,
>   To set at liberty them that are bruised,
> 19. To proclaim the acceptable year of the Lord (Isa. lxi. 1f.).

20. And he closed the book, and gave it back to the attendant, and sat down: and the eyes of all in the synagogue were fastened on him. 21. And he began to say unto them, To-day hath this scripture been fulfilled in your ears. 22. And all bare him witness, and wondered at the words of grace which proceeded out of his mouth: and they said, Is not this Joseph's son? 23. And he said unto them, Doubtless ye will say unto me this parable, Physician, heal thyself: whatsoever we have heard done at Capernaum, do also here in thine own country. 24. And he said, Verily I say unto you, No prophet is acceptable in his own country. 25. But of a truth I say unto you, There were many widows in Israel in the days of Elijah, when the heaven was shut up three years and six months, when there came a great famine over all the land; 26. and unto none of them was Elijah sent, but only to Zarephath, in the land of Sidon, unto a woman that was a widow. 27. And there were many lepers in Israel in the time of Elisha the prophet; and none of them was cleansed, but only Naaman the Syrian. 28. And they were all filled with wrath in the synagogue, as they heard these things; 29. and they rose up, and cast him forth out of the city, and led him unto the brow of the hill whereon their city was built, that they might throw him down headlong. 30. But he passing through the midst of them went his way.

III. MIGHTY WORKS

(a) The Wonderful Draught
v. 1–11. Cf. Mk. i. 16–20 and Jn. xxi. 1–14.

1. Now it came to pass, while the multitude pressed upon him and heard the word of God, that he was standing by the lake of Gennesaret; 2. and he saw two boats standing by the lake: but the fishermen had gone out of them, and were washing their nets. 3. And he entered into one of the boats, which was Simon's, and asked him to put out a little from the land. And he sat down and taught the multitudes out of the boat. 4. And when he had left speaking, he said unto Simon, Put out into the deep, and let down your nets for a draught. 5. And Simon answered and said, Master, we toiled all night, and took nothing: but at thy word I will let down the nets. 6. And when they had this done, they inclosed a great multitude of fishes; and their nets were breaking; 7. and they beckoned unto their partners in the other boat, that they should come and help them. And they came, and filled both the boats, so that they began to sink. 8. But Simon Peter, when he saw it, fell down at Jesus' knees, saying, Depart from me; for I am a sinful man, O Lord. 9. For he was amazed, and all that were with him, at the draught of the fishes which they had taken; 10. and so were also James and John, sons of Zebedee, which were partners with Simon. And Jesus said unto Simon, Fear not; from henceforth thou shalt catch men. 11. And when they had brought their boats to land, they left all, and followed him.

(b) The Widow of Nain's Son
vii. 11–17.

11. And it came to pass soon afterwards, that he went to a city called Nain; and his disciples went with him, and a great multitude. 12. Now when he drew near to the gate of the city, behold, there was carried out one that was dead, the only son of his mother, and she was a widow: and much people of the city was with her. 13. And when the Lord saw her, he had compassion on her, and said unto her, Weep not. 14. And he came nigh and touched the bier: and the bearers stood still. And he said, Young man, I say unto thee, Arise. 15. And he that was dead sat up, and began to speak. And he gave him to his mother. 16. And fear took hold on all: and they glorified God, saying, A great prophet is arisen among us: and, God hath visited his people. 17. And this report went forth concerning him in the whole of Judaea, and all the region round about.

(c) The Woman who was a Sinner
vii. 36–viii. 3. Cf. Mk. xiv. 3f.

36. And one of the Pharisees desired him that he would eat with

him. And he entered into the Pharisee's house, and sat down to meat. 37. And behold, a woman which was in the city, a sinner; and when she knew that he was sitting at meat in the Pharisee's house, she brought an alabaster cruse of ointment, 38. and standing behind at his feet, weeping, she began to wet his feet with her tears, and wiped them with the hair of her head, and kissed his feet, and anointed them with the ointment. 39. Now when the Pharisee which had bidden him saw it, he spake within himself, saying, This man, if he were a prophet, would have perceived who and what manner of woman this is which toucheth him, that she is a sinner. 40. And Jesus answering said unto him, Simon, I have somewhat to say unto thee. And he saith, Master, say on. 41. A certain lender had two debtors: the one owed five hundred pence, and the other fifty. 42. When they had not wherewith to pay, he forgave them both. Which of them therefore will love him most? 43. Simon answered and said, He, I suppose, to whom he forgave the most. And he said unto him, Thou hast rightly judged. 44. And turning to the woman, he said unto Simon, Seest thou this woman? I entered into thine house, thou gavest me no water for my feet: but she hath wetted my feet with her tears, and wiped them with her hair. 45. Thou gavest me no kiss: but she, since the time I came in, hath not ceased to kiss my feet. 46. My head with oil thou didst not anoint: but she hath anointed my feet with ointment. 47. Wherefore I say unto thee, Her sins, which are many, are forgiven; for she loved much: but to whom little is forgiven, the same loveth little. 48. And he said unto her, Thy sins are forgiven. 49. And they that sat at meat with him began to say within themselves, Who is this that even forgiveth sins? 50. And he said unto the woman, Thy faith hath saved thee; go in peace.

viii. 1. And it came to pass soon afterwards, that he went about through cities and villages, preaching and bringing the good tidings of the kingdom of God, and with him the twelve, 2. and certain women which had been healed of evil spirits and infirmities, Mary that was called Magdalene, from whom seven devils had gone out, 3. and Joanna the wife of Chuza Herod's steward, and Susanna, and many others, which ministered unto them of their substance.

IV. LESSONS

(a) *To the Disciples in Samaria*
    ix. 51–56.

51. And it came to pass, when the days were well-nigh come that he should be received up, he stedfastly set his face to go to Jerusalem, 52. and sent messengers before his face: and they went, and entered

thee. 36. Which of these three, thinkest thou, proved neighbour unto him that fell among the robbers? 37. And he said, He that shewed mercy on him. And Jesus said unto him, Go, and do thou likewise.

(d) *To Martha—the Good Part*
     x. 38–42.

38. Now as they went on their way, he entered into a certain village: and a certain woman named Martha received him into her house. 39. And she had a sister called Mary, which also sat at the Lord's feet, and heard his word. 40. But Martha was cumbered about much serving; and she came up to him, and said, Lord, dost thou not care that my sister did leave me to serve alone? bid her therefore that she help me. 41. But the Lord answered and said unto her, Martha, Martha, thou art anxious and troubled about many things: 42. but one thing is needful: for Mary hath chosen the good part, which shall not be taken away from her.

(e) *How to Pray—the Friend at Midnight*
     xi. 1–8, 53f., xii. 1.

1. And it came to pass, as he was praying in a certain place, that when he ceased, one of his disciples said unto him, Lord, teach us to pray, even as John also taught his disciples. 2. And he said unto them, When ye pray, say, Father, Hallowed be thy name. Thy kingdom come. 3. Give us day by day our daily bread. 4. And forgive us our sins; for we ourselves also forgive every one that is indebted to us. And bring us not into temptation.

5. And he said unto them, Which of you shall have a friend, and shall go unto him at midnight, and say to him, Friend, lend me three loaves; 6. for a friend of mine is come to me from a journey, and I have nothing to set before him; 7. and he from within shall answer and say, Trouble me not: the door is now shut, and my children are with me in bed; I cannot rise and give thee? 8. I say unto you, Though he will not rise and give him, because he is his friend, yet because of his importunity he will arise and give him as many as he needeth.

53. And when he was come out from thence, the scribes and the Pharisees began to press upon him vehemently, and to provoke him to speak of many things; 54. laying wait for him, to catch something out of his mouth.

xii. 1. In the mean time, when the many thousands of the multitude were gathered together, insomuch that they trode one upon another, he began to say unto his disciples first of all, Beware ye of the leaven of the Pharisees, which is hypocrisy.

V. WARNINGS

(a) Against Greed—the Rich Fool
xii. 13–21.

13. And one out of the multitude said unto him, Master, bid my brother divide the inheritance with me. 14. But he said unto him, Man, who made me a judge or a divider over you? 15. And he said unto them, Take heed, and keep yourselves from all covetousness: for a man's life consisteth not in the abundance of the things which he possesseth. 16. And he spake a parable unto them, saying, The ground of a certain rich man brought forth plentifully: 17. and he reasoned within himself, saying, What shall I do, because I have not where to bestow my fruits? 18. And he said, This will I do: I will pull down my barns, and build greater; and there will I bestow all my corn and my goods. 19. And I will say to my soul, Soul, thou hast much goods laid up for many years; take thine ease, eat, drink, be merry. 20. But God said unto him, Thou foolish one, this night is thy soul required of thee; and the things which thou hast prepared, whose shall they be? 21. So is he that layeth up treasure for himself, and is not rich toward God.

(b) On Repentance—the Barren Fig Tree
xiii. 1–9.

1. Now there were some present at that very season which told him of the Galilaeans, whose blood Pilate had mingled with their sacrifices. 2. And he answered and said unto them, Think ye that these Galilaeans were sinners above all the Galilaeans, because they have suffered these things? 3. I tell you, Nay: but, except ye repent, ye shall all in like manner perish. 4. Or those eighteen, upon whom the tower in Siloam fell, and killed them, think ye that they were offenders above all the men that dwell in Jerusalem? 5. I tell you, Nay: but, except ye repent, ye shall all likewise perish.

6. And he spake this parable; A certain man had a fig tree planted in his vineyard; and he came seeking fruit thereon, and found none. 7. And he said unto the vine-dresser, Behold, these three years I come seeking fruit on this fig tree, and find none: cut it down; why doth it also cumber the ground? 8. And he answering saith unto him, Lord, let it alone this year also, till I shall dig about it, and dung it: 9. and if it bear fruit thenceforth, well; but if not, thou shalt cut it down.

(c) Sabbath Observance—(1) The Hunch-backed Woman
xiii. 10–17.

10. And he was teaching in one of the synagogues on the sabbath day. 11. And behold, a woman which had a spirit of infirmity eighteen

years; and she was bowed together, and could in no wise lift herself up. 12. And when Jesus saw her, he called her, and said to her, Woman, thou art loosed from thine infirmity. 13. And he laid his hands upon her: and immediately she was made straight, and glorified God. 14. And the ruler of the synagogue, being moved with indignation because Jesus had healed on the sabbath, answered and said to the multitude, There are six days in which men ought to work: in them therefore come and be healed, and not on the day of the sabbath. 15. But the Lord answered him, and said, Ye hypocrites, doth not each one of you on the sabbath loose his ox or his ass from the stall, and lead him away to watering? 16. And ought not this woman, being a daughter of Abraham, whom Satan had bound, lo, these eighteen years, to have been loosed from this bond on the day of the sabbath? 17. And as he said these things, all his adversaries were put to shame: and all the multitude rejoiced for all the glorious things that were done by him.

(d) To Herod Antipas
  xiii. 31–33.

31. In that very hour there came certain Pharisees, saying to him, Get thee out, and go hence: for Herod would fain kill thee. 32. And he said unto them, Go and say to that fox, Behold, I cast out devils and perform cures to-day and to-morrow, and the third day I am perfected. 33. Howbeit I must go on my way to-day and to-morrow and the day following: for it cannot be that a prophet perish out of Jerusalem.

(e) Sabbath Observance—(2) the Man with Dropsy
  xiv. 1–6.

1. And it came to pass, when he went into the house of one of the rulers of the Pharisees on a sabbath to eat bread, that they were watching him. 2. And behold, there was before him a certain man which had the dropsy. 3. And Jesus answering spake unto the lawyers and the Pharisees, saying, Is it lawful to heal on the sabbath, or not? 4. But they held their peace. And he took him, and healed him, and let him go. 5. And he said unto them, Which of you shall have an ass or an ox fallen into a well, and will not straightway draw him up on a sabbath day? 6. And they could not answer again unto these things.

(f) On Precedence and Hospitality
  xiv. 7–10, 12–14.

7. And he spake a parable unto those which were bidden, when he marked how they chose out the chief seats; saying unto them, 8. When

M

thou art bidden of any man to a marriage feast, sit not down in the chief seat; lest haply a more honourable man than thou be bidden of him, 9. and he that bade thee and him shall come and say to thee, Give this man place; and then thou shalt begin with shame to take the lowest place. 10. But when thou art bidden, go and sit down in the lowest place; that when he that hath bidden thee cometh, he may say to thee, Friend, go up higher: then shalt thou have glory in the presence of all that sit at meat with thee.

12. And he said to him also that had bidden him, When thou makest a dinner or a supper, call not thy friends, nor thy brethren, nor thy kinsmen, nor rich neighbours; lest haply they also bid thee again, and a recompense be made thee. 13. But when thou makest a feast, bid the poor, the maimed, the lame, the blind: 14. and thou shalt be blessed; because they have not wherewith to recompense thee: for thou shalt be recompensed in the resurrection of the just.

(g) *On Counting the Cost*
    xiv. 28–33.

28. For which of you, desiring to build a tower, doth not first sit down and count the cost, whether he have wherewith to complete it? 29. Lest haply, when he hath laid a foundation, and is not able to finish, all that behold begin to mock him, 30. saying, This man began to build, and was not able to finish. 31. Or what king, as he goeth to encounter another king in war, will not sit down first and take counsel whether he is able with ten thousand to meet him that cometh against him with twenty thousand? 32. Or else, while the other is yet a great way off, he sendeth an ambassage, and asketh conditions of peace. 33. So therefore whosoever he be of you that renounceth not all that he hath, he cannot be my disciple.

VI. PARABLES OF THE LOST

(a) *The Lost Sheep*
    xv. 1–7. Cf. Mt. xviii. 12–14, M.

1. Now all the publicans and sinners were drawing near unto him for to hear him. 2. And both the Pharisees and the scribes murmured, saying, This man receiveth sinners, and eateth with them.

3. And he spake unto them this parable, saying, 4. What man of you, having a hundred sheep, and having lost one of them, doth not leave the ninety and nine in the wilderness, and go after that which is lost, until he find it? 5. And when he hath found it, he layeth it on his shoulders, rejoicing. 6. And when he cometh home, he calleth together his friends and his neighbours, saying unto them, Rejoice with me, for I have found my sheep which was lost. 7. I say unto

you, that even so there shall be joy in heaven over one sinner that repenteth, more than over ninety and nine righteous persons, which need no repentance.

(b) The Lost Coin
    xv. 8–10.

8. Or what woman having ten pieces of silver, if she lose one piece, doth not light a lamp, and sweep the house, and seek diligently until she find it? 9. And when she hath found it, she calleth together her friends and neighbours, saying, Rejoice with me, for I have found the piece which I had lost. 10. Even so, I say unto you, there is joy in the presence of the angels of God over one sinner that repenteth.

(c) The Lost Son
    xv. 11–32.

11. And he said, A certain man had two sons: 12. and the younger of them said to his father, Father, give me the portion of thy substance that falleth to me. And he divided unto them his living. 13. And not many days after the younger son gathered all together, and took his journey into a far country; and there he wasted his substance with riotous living. 14. And when he had spent all, there arose a mighty famine in that country; and he began to be in want. 15. And he went and joined himself to one of the citizens of that country; and he sent him into his fields to feed swine. 16. And he would fain have been filled with the husks that the swine did eat: and no man gave unto him. 17. But when he came to himself he said, How many hired servants of my father's have bread enough and to spare, and I perish here with hunger! 18. I will arise and go to my father, and will say unto him, Father, I have sinned against heaven, and in thy sight: 19. I am no more worthy to be called thy son: make me as one of thy hired servants. 20. And he arose, and came to his father. But while he was yet afar off, his father saw him, and was moved with compassion, and ran, and fell on his neck, and kissed him. 21. And the son said unto him, Father, I have sinned against heaven, and in thy sight: I am no more worthy to be called thy son. 22. But the father said to his servants, Bring forth quickly the best robe, and put it on him; and put a ring on his hand, and shoes on his feet: 23. and bring the fatted calf, and kill it, and let us eat, and make merry: 24. for this my son was dead, and is alive again; he was lost, and is found. And they began to be merry. 25. Now his elder son was in the field: and as he came and drew nigh to the house, he heard music and dancing. 26. And he called to him one of the servants, and inquired what these things might be. 27. And he said unto him, Thy brother is come; and thy father hath killed the fatted calf, because

he hath received him safe and sound. 28. But he was angry, and would not go in: and his father came out, and intreated him. 29. But he answered and said to his father, Lo, these many years do I serve thee, and I never transgressed a commandment of thine: and yet thou never gavest me a kid, that I might make merry with my friends: 30. but when this thy son came, which hath devoured thy living with harlots, thou killedst for him the fatted calf. 31. And he said unto him, Son, thou art ever with me, and all that is mine is thine. 32. But it was meet to make merry and be glad: for this thy brother was dead, and is alive again; and was lost, and is found.

VII. PARABLES, ETC., OF RESPONSIBILITY

(a) *Foresight—the Unjust Steward*
    xvi. 1–12.

1. And he said also unto the disciples, There was a certain rich man, which had a steward; and the same was accused unto him that he was wasting his goods. 2. And he called him, and said unto him, What is this that I hear of thee? render the account of thy stewardship; for thou canst be no longer steward. 3. And the steward said within himself, What shall I do, seeing that my lord taketh away the stewardship from me? I have not strength to dig; to beg I am ashamed. 4. I am resolved what to do, that, when I am put out of the stewardship, they may receive me into their houses. 5. And calling to him each one of his lord's debtors, he said to the first, How much owest thou unto my lord? 6. And he said, A hundred measures of oil. And he said unto him, Take thy bond, and sit down quickly and write fifty. 7. Then said he to another, And how much owest thou? And he said, A hundred measures of wheat. He saith unto him, Take thy bond, and write fourscore. 8. And his lord commended the unrighteous steward because he had done wisely: for the sons of this world are for their own generation wiser than the sons of the light. 9. And I say unto you, Make to yourselves friends by means of the mammon of unrighteousness; that, when it shall fail, they may receive you in the eternal tabernacles. 10. He that is faithful in a very little is faithful also in much: and he that is unrighteous in a very little is unrighteous also in much. 11. If therefore ye have not been faithful in the unrighteous mammon, who will commit to your trust the true riches? 12. And if ye have not been faithful in that which is another's, who will give you that which is your own?

(b) *Money—Dives and Lazarus*
    xvi. 14–15, 19–31.

14. And the Pharisees, who were lovers of money, heard all these

things; and they scoffed at him. 15. And he said unto them, Ye are
they that justify yourselves in the sight of men; but God knoweth
your hearts: for that which is exalted among men is an abomination
in the sight of God. 19. Now there was a certain rich man, and he
was clothed in purple and fine linen, faring sumptuously every day:
20. and a certain beggar named Lazarus was laid at his gate, full of
sores, 21. and desiring to be fed with the crumbs that fell from the
rich man's table; yea, even the dogs came and licked his sores. 22. And
it came to pass, that the beggar died, and that he was carried away
by the angels into Abraham's bosom: and the rich man also died,
and was buried. 23. And in Hades he lifted up his eyes, being in
torments, and seeth Abraham afar off, and Lazarus in his bosom.
24. And he cried and said, Father Abraham, have mercy on me, and
send Lazarus, that he may dip the tip of his finger in water, and
cool my tongue; for I am in anguish in this flame. 25. But Abraham
said, Son, remember that thou in thy lifetime receivedst thy good
things, and Lazarus in like manner evil things: but now here he is
comforted, and thou art in anguish. 26. And beside all this, between
us and you there is a great gulf fixed, that they which would pass
from hence to you may not be able, and that none may cross over
from thence to us. 27. And he said, I pray thee therefore, father,
that thou wouldest send him to my father's house; 28. for I have five
brethren; that he may testify unto them, lest they also come into this
place of torment. 29. But Abraham saith, They have Moses and
the prophets; let them hear them. 30. And he said, Nay, father
Abraham: but if one go to them from the dead, they will repent.
31. And he said unto him, If they hear not Moses and the prophets,
neither will they be persuaded, if one rise from the dead.

(c) *On Serving God—Master and Servant*
    xvii. 7–10.

7. But who is there of you, having a servant plowing or keeping
sheep, that will say unto him, when he is come in from the field,
Come straightway and sit down to meat: 8. and will not rather say
unto him, Make ready wherewith I may sup, and gird thyself, and
serve me, till I have eaten and drunken; and afterward thou shalt
eat and drink? 9. Doth he thank the servant because he did the things
that were commanded? 10. Even so ye also, when ye shall have done
all the things that are commanded you, say, We are unprofitable
servants; we have done that which it was our duty to do.

(d) *On Gratitude—the Ten Lepers*
    xvii. 11–21.

11. And it came to pass, as they were on the way to Jerusalem, that

he was passing through the midst of Samaria and Galilee. 12. And as he entered into a certain village, there met him ten men that were lepers, which stood afar off: 13. and they lifted up their voices, saying, Jesus, Master, have mercy on us. 14. And when he saw them, he said unto them, Go and shew yourselves unto the priests. And it came to pass, as they went, they were cleansed. 15. And one of them, when he saw that he was healed, turned back, with a loud voice glorifying God; 16. and he fell upon his face at his feet, giving him thanks: and he was a Samaritan. 17. And Jesus answering said, Were not the ten cleansed? but where are the nine? 18. Were there none found that returned to give glory to God, save this stranger? 19. And he said unto him, Arise, and go thy way: thy faith hath made thee whole.

20. And being asked by the Pharisees, when the kingdom of God cometh, he answered them and said, The kingdom of God cometh not with observation: 21. neither shall they say, Lo, here! or, There! for lo, the kingdom of God is within you.

(e) *On Perseverance—the Importunate Widow*
    xviii. 1–8.

1. And he spake a parable unto them to the end that they ought always to pray, and not to faint; 2. saying, There was in a city a judge, which feared not God, and regarded not man: 3. and there was a widow in that city; and she came oft unto him, saying, Avenge me of mine adversary. 4. And he would not for a while: but afterward he said within himself, Though I fear not God, nor regard man; 5. yet because this widow troubleth me, I will avenge her, lest she wear me out by her continual coming. 6. And the Lord said, Hear what the unrighteous judge saith. 7. And shall not God avenge his elect, which cry to him day and night, and he is longsuffering over them? 8. I say unto you, that he will avenge them speedily. Howbeit when the Son of man cometh, shall he find faith on the earth?

(f) *On Prayer—the Pharisee and the Publican*
    xviii. 9–14.

9. And he spake also this parable unto certain which trusted in themselves that they were righteous, and set all others at nought: 10. Two men went up into the temple to pray; the one a Pharisee, and the other a publican. 11. The Pharisee stood and prayed thus with himself, God, I thank thee, that I am not as the rest of men, extortioners, unjust, adulterers, or even as this publican. 12. I fast twice in the week; I give tithes of all that I get. 13. But the publican, standing afar off, would not lift up so much as his eyes unto heaven, but smote his breast, saying, God, be merciful to me a sinner. 14. I say

unto you, This man went down to his house justified rather than the other: for every one that exalteth himself shall be humbled; but he that humbleth himself shall be exalted.

(g) On Opportunities—Zaccheus: the Parable of the Pounds
   xix. 1–27.

1. And he entered and was passing through Jericho. 2. And behold, a man called by name Zacchaeus; and he was a chief publican, and he was rich. 3. And he sought to see Jesus who he was; and could not for the crowd, because he was little of stature. 4. And he ran on before, and climbed up into a sycomore tree to see him: for he was to pass that way. 5. And when Jesus came to the place, he looked up, and said unto him, Zacchaeus, make haste, and come down; for to-day I must abide at thy house. 6. And he made haste, and came down, and received him joyfully. 7. And when they saw it, they all murmured, saying, He is gone in to lodge with a man that is a sinner. 8. And Zacchaeus stood, and said unto the Lord, Behold, Lord, the half of my goods I give to the poor; and if I have wrongfully exacted aught of any man, I restore fourfold. 9. And Jesus said unto him, To-day is salvation come to this house, forasmuch as he also is a son of Abraham. 10. For the Son of man came to seek and to save that which was lost.

Parable of the Pounds
   11–27. Cf. Mt. xxv. 14–30, M.

11. And as they heard these things, he added and spake a parable, because he was nigh to Jerusalem, and because they supposed that the kingdom of God was immediately to appear. 12. He said therefore, A certain nobleman went into a far country, to receive for himself a kingdom, and to return. 13. And he called ten servants of his, and gave them ten pounds, and said unto them, Trade ye herewith till I come. 14. But his citizens hated him, and sent an ambassage after him, saying, We will not that this man reign over us. 15. And it came to pass, when he was come back again, having received the kingdom, that he commanded these servants, unto whom he had given the money, to be called to him, that he might know what they had gained by trading. 16. And the first came before him, saying, Lord, thy pound hath made ten pounds more. 17. And he said unto him, Well done, thou good servant: because thou wast found faithful in a very little, have thou authority over ten cities. 18. And the second came, saying, Thy pound, Lord, hath made five pounds. 19. And he said unto him also, Be thou also over five cities. 20. And another came, saying, Lord, behold, here is thy pound, which I kept laid up in a napkin: 21. for I feared thee, because thou art an

austere man: thou takest up that thou layedst not down, and reapest that thou didst not sow. 22. He saith unto him, Out of thine own mouth will I judge thee, thou wicked servant. Thou knewest that I am an austere man, taking up that I laid not down, and reaping that I did not sow; 23. then wherefore gavest thou not my money into the bank, and I at my coming should have required it with interest? 24. And he said unto them that stood by, Take away from him the pound, and give it unto him that hath the ten pounds. 25. And they said unto him, Lord, he hath ten pounds. 26. I say unto you, that unto every one that hath shall be given; but from him that hath not, even that which he hath shall be taken away from him. 27. Howbeit these mine enemies, which would not that I should reign over them, bring hither, and slay them before me.

VIII. JERUSALEM

(a) *Approach to the City*
   xix. 37–44.

37. And as he was now drawing nigh, even at the descent of the mount of Olives, the whole multitude of the disciples began to rejoice and praise God with a loud voice for all the mighty works which they had seen; 38. saying, Blessed is the King that cometh in the name of the Lord: peace in heaven, and glory in the highest. 39. And some of the Pharisees from the multitude said unto him, Master, rebuke thy disciples. 40. And he answered and said, I tell you that, if these shall hold their peace, the stones will cry out.

41. And when he drew nigh, he saw the city and wept over it, 42. saying, If thou hadst known in this day, even thou, the things which belong unto peace! but now they are hid from thine eyes. 43. For the days shall come upon thee, when thine enemies shall cast up a bank about thee, and compass thee round, and keep thee in on every side, and shall dash thee to the ground, and thy children within thee; 44. and they shall not leave in thee one stone upon another; because thou knewest not the time of thy visitation.

   xx. 18.

Every one that falleth on that stone shall be broken to pieces; but on whomsoever it shall fall, it will scatter him as dust.

(b) *Apocalyptic Sayings*
   xxi. 11b, 18, 25b, 26a, 28, 34–36.

(N.B. The basis of Lk. xxi seems to be Mk. xiii which Luke has revised and, in parts, re-written in the light of A.D. 70, and to which he has added the following sayings.)

11*b*. And there shall be terrors and great signs from heaven.

18. And not a hair of your head shall perish.

25*b*–26*a*. And there shall be . . . upon the earth distress of nations, in perplexity for the roaring of the sea and the billows; men fainting for fear, and for expectation of the things which are coming on the world.

28. But when these things begin to come to pass, look up, and lift up your heads; because your redemption draweth nigh.

34–36. But take heed to yourselves, lest haply your hearts be overcharged with surfeiting, and drunkenness, and cares of this life, and that day come on you suddenly as a snare: 35. for so shall it come upon all them that dwell on the face of all the earth. 36. But watch ye at every season, making supplication, that ye may prevail to escape all these things that shall come to pass, and to stand before the Son of man.

(c) The Passion and the Resurrection
       xxii. 14–xxiv.

(Narratives which seem to be based on Mark are bracketed.)

xxii. 14. And when the hour was come, he sat down, and the apostles with him. 15. And he said unto them, With desire I have desired to eat this passover with you before I suffer: 16. for I say unto you, I will not eat it, until it be fulfilled in the kingdom of God. 17. And he received a cup, and when he had given thanks, he said, Take this and divide it among yourselves: [18. for I say unto you, I will not drink from henceforth of the fruit of the vine, until the kingdom of God shall come. 19. And he took bread, and when he had given thanks, he brake it, and gave to them, saying, This is my body][1] which is given for you: this do in remembrance of me. 20. And the cup in like manner after supper, saying, This cup is the new covenant in my blood, even that which is poured out for you [21. But behold, the hand of him that betrayeth me is with me on the table. 22. For the Son of man indeed goeth, as it hath been determined: but woe unto that man through whom he is betrayed! 23. And they began to question among themselves, which of them it was that should do this thing.]

24. And there arose also a contention among them, which of them is accounted to be the greatest. 25. And he said unto them, The kings of the Gentiles have lordship over them; and they that have authority over them are called Benefactors. 26. But ye shall not be so: but he that is the greater among you, let him become as the younger; and he that is chief, as he that doth serve. 27. For whether

[1] 19*b*-20 textually doubtful.

is greater, he that sitteth at meat, or he that serveth? is not he that sitteth at meat? but I am in the midst of you as he that serveth. 28. But ye are they which have continued with me in my temptations; 29. and I appoint unto you a kingdom, even as my Father appointed unto me, 30. that ye may eat and drink at my table in my kingdom; and ye shall sit on thrones judging the twelve tribes of Israel. 31. Simon, Simon, behold, Satan asked to have you, that he might sift you as wheat: 32. but I have made supplication for thee, that thy faith fail not; and do thou, when once thou hast turned again, stablish thy brethren. 33. And he said unto him, Lord, with thee I am ready to go both to prison and to death. [34. And he said, I tell thee, Peter, the cock shall not crow this day, until thou shalt thrice deny that thou knowest me.]

35. And he said unto them, When I sent you forth without purse, and wallet, and shoes, lacked ye anything? And they said, Nothing. 36. And he said unto them, But now, he that hath a purse, let him take it, and likewise a wallet: and he that hath none, let him sell his cloke, and buy a sword. 37. For I say unto you, that this which is written must be fulfilled in me, And he was reckoned with transgressors: for that which concerneth me hath fulfilment. 38. And they said, Lord, behold, here are two swords. And he said unto them, It is enough.

[39. And he came out, and went, as his custom was, unto the mount of Olives; and the disciples also followed him. 40. And when he was at the place, he said unto them, Pray that ye enter not into temptation. 41. And he was parted from them about a stone's cast; and he kneeled down and prayed, 42. saying, Father, if thou be willing, remove this cup from me: nevertheless not my will, but thine, be done.] 43.[1] And there appeared unto him an angel from heaven, strengthening him. 44. And being in an agony he prayed more earnestly: and his sweat became as it were great drops of blood falling down upon the ground. [45. And when he rose up from his prayer, he came unto the disciples, and found them sleeping for sorrow, 46. and said unto them, Why sleep ye? rise and pray, that ye enter not into temptation.]

[47. While he yet spake, behold, a multitude, and he that was called Judas, one of the twelve, went before them; and he drew near unto Jesus to kiss him.] 48. But Jesus said unto him, Judas, betrayest thou the Son of man with a kiss? 49. And when they that were about him saw what would follow, they said, Lord, shall we smite with the sword? [50. And a certain one of them smote the servant of the high priest, and struck off his right ear.] 51. But Jesus answered and said, Suffer ye thus far. And he touched his ear, and healed him. [52. And

---

[1] 43-44 textually doubtful.

Jesus said unto the chief priests, and captains of the temple, and elders, which were come against him, Are ye come out, as against a robber, with swords and staves? 53. When I was daily with you in the temple, ye stretched not forth your hands against me:] but this is your hour, and the power of darkness.

[54. And they seized him, and led him away, and brought him into the high priest's house. But Peter followed afar off. 55. And when they had kindled a fire in the midst of the court, and had sat down together, Peter sat in the midst of them. 56. And a certain maid seeing him as he sat in the light of the fire, and looking stedfastly upon him, said, This man also was with him. 57. But he denied, saying, Woman, I know him not. 58. And after a little while another saw him, and said, Thou also art one of them. But Peter said, Man, I am not. 59. And after the space of about one hour another confidently affirmed, saying, Of a truth this man also was with him: for he is a Galilaean. 60. But Peter said, Man, I know not what thou sayest. And immediately, while he yet spake, the cock crew. 61. And the Lord turned, and looked upon Peter. And Peter remembered the word of the Lord, how that he said unto him, Before the cock crow this day, thou shalt deny me thrice. 62. And he went out, and wept bitterly.]

63. And the men that held Jesus mocked him, and beat him. [64. And they blindfolded him, and asked him, saying, Prophesy: who is he that struck thee?] 65. And many other things spake they against him, reviling him.

[66. And as soon as it was day, the assembly of the elders of the people was gathered together, both chief priests and scribes; and they led him away into their council, saying, 67. If thou art the Christ, tell us. But he said unto them, If I tell you, ye will not believe: 68. and if I ask you, ye will not answer. 69. But from henceforth shall the Son of man be seated at the right hand of the power of God. 70. And they all said, Art thou then the Son of God? And he said unto them, Ye say that I am. 71. And they said, What further need have we of witness? for we ourselves have heard from his own mouth.]

xxiii. 1. And the whole company of them rose up, and brought him before Pilate. 2. And they began to accuse him, saying, We found this man perverting our nation, and forbidding to give tribute to Caesar, and saying that he himself is Christ a king. [3. And Pilate asked him, saying, Art thou the King of the Jews? And he answered him and said, Thou sayest.] 4. And Pilate said unto the chief priests and the multitudes, I find no fault in this man. 5. But they were the more urgent, saying, He stirreth up the people, teaching throughout all Judaea, and beginning from Galilee even unto this place. 6. But when Pilate heard it, he asked whether the man were a Galilaean.

7. And when he knew that he was of Herod's jurisdiction, he sent him unto Herod, who himself also was at Jerusalem in these days. 8. Now when Herod saw Jesus, he was exceeding glad: for he was of a long time desirous to see him, because he had heard concerning him; and he hoped to see some miracle done by him. 9. And he questioned him in many words; but he answered him nothing. 10. And the chief priests and the scribes stood, vehemently accusing him. 11. And Herod with his soldiers set him at nought, and mocked him, and arraying him in gorgeous apparel sent him back to Pilate. 12. And Herod and Pilate became friends with each other that very day: for before they were at enmity between themselves.

13. And Pilate called together the chief priests and the rulers and the people, 14, and said unto them, Ye brought unto me this man, as one that perverteth the people: and behold, I, having examined him before you, found no fault in this man touching those things whereof ye accuse him: 15. no, nor yet Herod: for he sent him back unto us; and behold, nothing worthy of death hath been done by him. 16. I will therefore chastise him, and release him. [18. But they cried out all together, saying, Away with this man, and release unto us Barabbas: 19. one who for a certain insurrection made in the city, and for murder, was cast into prison. 20. And Pilate spake unto them again, desiring to release Jesus; 21. but they shouted, saying, Crucify, crucify him. 22. And he said unto them the third time, Why, what evil hath this man done? I have found no cause of death in him: I will therefore chastise him and release him. 23. But they were instant with loud voices, asking that he might be crucified. And their voices prevailed. 24. And Pilate gave sentence that what they asked for should be done. 25. And he released him that for insurrection and murder had been cast into prison, whom they asked for; but Jesus he delivered up to their will.]

[26. And when they led him away, they laid hold upon one Simon of Cyrene, coming from the country, and laid on him the cross, to bear it after Jesus.]

27. And there followed him a great multitude of the people, and of women who bewailed and lamented him. 28. But Jesus turning unto them said, Daughters of Jerusalem, weep not for me, but weep for yourselves, and for your children. 29. For behold, the days are coming, in which they shall say, Blessed are the barren, and the wombs that never bare, and the breasts that never gave suck. 30. Then shall they begin to say to the mountains, Fall on us; and to the hills, Cover us. 31. For if they do these things in the green tree, what shall be done in the dry?

[32. And there were also two others, malefactors, led with him to be put to death.]

[33. And when they came unto the place which is called The skull, there they crucified him, and the malefactors, one on the right hand and the other on the left.] 34.[1] And Jesus said, Father, forgive them; for they know not what they do. [And parting his garments among them, they cast lots. 35. And the people stood beholding. And the rulers also scoffed at him, saying, He saved others; let him save himself, if this is the Christ of God, his chosen. 36. And the soldiers also mocked him, coming to him, offering him vinegar, 37. and saying, If thou art the King of the Jews, save thyself. 38. And there was also a superscription over him, THIS IS THE KING OF THE JEWS.]

39. And one of the malefactors which were hanged railed on him, saying, Art not thou the Christ? save thyself and us. 40. But the other answered, and rebuking him said, Dost thou not even fear God, seeing thou art in the same condemnation? 41. And we indeed justly; for we receive the due rewards of our deeds: but this man hath done nothing amiss. 42. And he said, Jesus, remember me when thou comest in thy kingdom. 43. And he said unto him, Verily I say unto thee, To-day shalt thou be with me in Paradise. [44. And it was now about the sixth hour, and a darkness came over the whole land until the ninth hour, 45. the sun's light failing: and the veil of the temple was rent in the midst. 46. And when Jesus had cried with a loud voice] he said, Father, into thy hands I commend my spirit: and having said this, [he gave up the ghost. 47. And when the centurion saw what was done, he glorified God, saying, Certainly this was a righteous man.] 48. And all the multitudes that came together to this sight, when they beheld the things that were done, returned smiting their breasts. [49. And all his acquaintance, and the women that followed with him from Galilee, stood afar off, seeing these things.]

[50. And behold, a man named Joseph, who was a councillor, a good man and a righteous (51. he had not consented to their counsel and deed), a man of Arimathaea, a city of the Jews, who was looking for the kingdom of God: 52. this man went to Pilate, and asked for the body of Jesus. 53. And he took it down, and wrapped it in a linen cloth, and laid him in a tomb, that was hewn in stone, where never man had yet lain. 54. And it was the day of the Preparation, and the sabbath drew on]. 55. And the women, which had come with him out of Galilee, followed after, and beheld the tomb, and how his body was laid. 56. And they returned, and prepared spices and ointments.

56b. And on the sabbath they rested according to the commandment. xxiv. [1. But on the first day of the week, at early dawn, they

[1] 34a textually doubtful.

came unto the tomb, bringing the spices which they had prepared.
2. And they found the stone rolled away from the tomb. 3. And they
entered in, and found not the body of the Lord Jesus. 4. And it came
to pass, while they were perplexed thereabout, behold, two men
stood by them in dazzling apparel: 5. and as they were affrighted,
and bowed down their faces to the earth, they said unto them, Why
seek ye the living among the dead? 6.[1] He is not here, but is risen:
remember how he spake unto you when he was yet in Galilee, 7. saying
that the Son of man must be delivered up into the hands of sinful
men, and be crucified, and the third day rise again.] 8. And they
remembered his words, 9. and returned from the tomb, and told all
these things to the eleven, and to all the rest. 10. Now they were
Mary Magdalene, and Joanna, and Mary the mother of James: and
the other women with them told these things unto the apostles. 11.
And these words appeared in their sight as idle talk; and they dis-
believed them. 12.[2] But Peter arose, and ran unto the tomb; and
stooping and looking in, he seeth the linen cloths by themselves; and
he departed to his home, wondering at that which was come to
pass.

   13. And behold, two of them were going that very day to a village
named Emmaus, which was threescore furlongs from Jerusalem.
14. And they communed with each other of all these things which
had happened. 15. And it came to pass, while they communed and
questioned together, that Jesus himself drew near, and went with
them. 16. But their eyes were holden that they should not know him.
17. And he said unto them, What communications are these that ye
have one with another, as ye walk? And they stood still, looking sad.
18. And one of them, named Cleopas, answering said unto him, Dost
thou alone sojourn in Jerusalem and not know the things which are
come to pass there in these days? 19. And he said unto them, What
things? And they said unto him, The things concerning Jesus of
Nazareth, which was a prophet mighty in deed and word before
God and all the people: 20. and how the chief priests and our rulers
delivered him up to be condemned to death, and crucified him.
21. But we hoped that it was he which should redeem Israel. Yea
and beside all this, it is now the third day since these things came
to pass. 22. Moreover certain women of our company amazed us,
having been early at the tomb; 23. and when they found not his
body, they came, saying, that they had also seen a vision of angels,
which said that he was alive. 24. And certain of them that were
with us went to the tomb, and found it even so as the women had
said: but him they saw not. 25. And he said unto them, O foolish

---

[1] 6a textually doubtful.

[2] 12 textually doubtful.

men, and slow of heart to believe in all that the prophets have spoken!
26. Behoved it not the Christ to suffer these things, and to enter into
his glory? 27. And beginning from Moses and from all the prophets,
he interpreted to them in all the scriptures the things concerning
himself. 28. And they drew nigh unto the village, whither they were
going: and he made as though he would go further. 29. And they
constrained him, saying, Abide with us: for it is toward evening, and
the day is now far spent. And he went in to abide with them. 30. And
it came to pass, when he had sat down with them to meat, he took
the bread, and blessed it, and brake, and gave to them. 31. And
their eyes were opened, and they knew him; and he vanished out of
their sight. 32. And they said one to another, Was not our heart
burning within us, while he spake to us in the way, while he opened
to us the scriptures? 33. And they rose up that very hour, and returned
to Jerusalem, and found the eleven gathered together, and them
that were with them, 34. saying, The Lord is risen indeed, and hath
appeared to Simon. 35. And they rehearsed the things that happened
in the way, and how he was known of them in the breaking of the
bread.

36. And as they spake these things, he himself stood in the midst
of them, [1] and saith unto them, Peace be unto you. 37. But they
were terrified and affrighted, and supposed that they beheld a spirit.
38. And he said unto them, Why are ye troubled? and wherefore do
reasonings arise in your heart? 39. See my hands and my feet, that
it is I myself: handle me, and see; for a spirit hath not flesh and
bones, as ye behold me having. 40.[2] And when he had said this, he
shewed them his hands and his feet. 41. And while they still dis-
believed for joy, and wondered, he said unto them, Have ye here
anything to eat? 42. And they gave him a piece of a broiled fish.
43. And he took it, and did eat before them.

44. And he said unto them, These are my words which I spake
unto you, while I was yet with you, how that all things must needs
be fulfilled, which are written in the law of Moses, and the prophets,
and the psalms, concerning me. 45. Then opened he their mind,
that they might understand the scriptures; 46. and he said unto them,
Thus it is written, that the Christ should suffer, and rise again from
the dead the third day; 47. and that repentance and remission of
sins should be preached in his name unto all the nations, beginning
from Jerusalem. 48. Ye are witnesses of these things. 49. And behold,
I send forth the promise of my Father upon you: but tarry ye in the
city, until ye be clothed with power from on high.

50. And he led them out until they were over against Bethany:

[1] 36b textually doubtful.
[2] 40 textually doubtful.

and he lifted up his hands, and blessed them. 51. And it came to pass, while he blessed them, he parted from them, [1]and was carried up into heaven. 52. And they worshipped him, and returned to Jerusalem with great joy: 53. and were continually in the temple, blessing God.

[1] 51-52 the words 'and . . . into heaven' and 'worshipped him, and' are textually doubtful.

INDEX OF SUBJECTS

INDEX OF AUTHORS

195

into a village of the Samaritans, to make ready for him. 53. And they did not receive him, because his face was as though he were going to Jerusalem. 54. And when his disciples James and John saw this, they said, Lord, wilt thou that we bid fire to come down from heaven, and consume them? 55. But he turned, and rebuked them. 56. And they went to another village.

(b) To the Seventy
x. 1, 17–20.

1. Now after these things the Lord appointed seventy others, and sent them two and two before his face into every city and place, whither he himself was about to come.

17. And the seventy returned with joy, saying, Lord, even the devils are subject unto us in thy name. 18. And he said unto them, I beheld Satan fallen as lightning from heaven. 19. Behold, I have given you authority to tread upon serpents and scorpions, and over all the power of the enemy: and nothing shall in any wise hurt you, 20. Howbeit in this rejoice not, that the spirits are subject unto you; but rejoice that your names are written in heaven.

(c) To a Rabbi—the Good Samaritan
x. 25–37.

25. And behold, a certain lawyer stood up and tempted him, saying, Master, what shall I do to inherit eternal life? 26. And he said unto him, What is written in the law? how readest thou? 27. And he answering said, Thou shalt love the Lord thy God with all thy heart, and with all thy soul, and with all thy strength, and with all thy mind; and thy neighbour as thyself. 28. And he said unto him, Thou hast answered right: this do, and thou shalt live. 29. But he, desiring to justify himself, said unto Jesus, And who is my neighbour? 30. Jesus made answer and said, A certain man was going down from Jerusalem to Jericho; and he fell among robbers, which both stripped him and beat him, and departed, leaving him half dead. 31. And by chance a certain priest was going down that way: and when he saw him, he passed by on the other side. 32. And in like manner a Levite also, when he came to the place, and saw him, passed by on the other side. 33. But a certain Samaritan, as he journeyed, came where he was: and when he saw him, he was moved with compassion, 34. and came to him, and bound up his wounds, pouring on them oil and wine; and he set him on his own beast, and brought him to an inn, and took care of him. 35. And on the morrow he took out two pence, and gave them to the host, and said, Take care of him; and whatsoever thou spendest more, I, when I come back again, will repay